PTL CLUB
DEVOTIONAL
GUIDE

PTL CLUB DEVOTIONAL GUIDE

BY: JIM BAKKER, THE PTL FAMILY AND FRIENDS

Edited By: Anton Marco

PTL TELEVISION NETWORK
CHARLOTTE, NC 28279

Henceforth I call you not servants; for the servant knoweth not what his lord doeth: but I have called you friends; for all things that I have heard of my Father I have made known unto you.

JOHN 15:15

Dear PTL Friends,

In this day when perhaps Satan's greatest attack is upon the family and home, it is very important that Christian families share together in God's Word and devotions on a regular basis. That is why we have especially prepared this PTL Club Devotional Guide for you, our supporters.

The great variety of guests on the PTL Club program has been a daily blessing to me and I'm sure to you, too. So in this devotional guide, we have compiled the favorite scriptures and insights of all our recent PTL guests and members of the PTL family. As you enjoy this daily inspiration, I hope you will get to know each guest better and pray for the ministries each represent.

In warmest Christian love,

Jim Bakker

Jim Bakker

"But the Word of the Lord came to me, saying..." *1 CHRONICLES 22:8*

I wish to express my thanks to God for the privilege of sharing His Word and His love with the precious people who have given of their hearts and souls to bring this Devotional Guide to you, our friends. You are sure to enjoy with me the rich and sweet fellowship, the laughter and tears, the wonder and joy that came from delighting in Jesus with the many friends you're about to meet.

You will find here an intense variety of human experiences from all walks of life that will help bring to you the multi-colored light of God's Word. Remember that in the perfect creation of the Bible itself, God used many human beings, each with unique personality and style, over ages of time, that we might be brought His Word. What a miracle of variety that was! The poetry of David's Psalms differs so from that of Jeremiah's Lamentations. The rapier-like intelligence of Paul contrasts so vividly with the radiant, simple message of God's love in John's letters. And yet, through each distinct voice, we are able to discern the Voice of God!

Some day perhaps we will know just how God uses men to speak for Him, yet lets us remain completely ourselves. But until we see Him face to face, and know as we are known, we can expect confidently that His Word will keep coming to us, through the scriptures, through the voices of others, and through the Holy Spirit as He speaks to our spirits within.

As His Word has come to those who share with you from these pages, let it speak to you. Let it strengthen your faith, help make you whole, and lift you into praise for the great Savior who has made all of us one, as His Body and Bride.

Freedom From Fear

*"But the fearful, and un-
believing, and the abomina-
ble, and murderers, and
whoremongers, and sorcerers,
and idolaters, and all liars,
shall have their part in . . .
the second death."*

Revelation 21:8

Tammy Faye Bakker
Singer/PTL Club Co-Host

When I was thumbing through my Bible one day and came across this scripture, it almost scared me to death! Especially when I saw what was at the top of that list: the fearful. Right there, above all those sins we think are so horrible, was fear! If we're fearful, we can't get to heaven—that's what the Bible was saying.

God used this verse to free me from fear. I was desperately afraid to fly in an airplane. I would be physically ill for days before I flew. And when I did have to fly, I'd spend the whole time in the bathroom because I was so terribly sick. But now, I can get on an airplane and cuddle up and go to sleep. God completely freed me!

God did it by showing me that fear is the opposite of faith. Fear dishonors God. Faith honors God. Without faith, says Hebrews 11:6, it's impossible to please God. And if we're filled with fear, we don't have that faith, and we just can't please God. That's why He put fear so high on the list! I realized how important it was to ask God to take that fear out of my life and replace it with faith.

But it wasn't enough just to ask Him to do it. I had to honor God by facing that fear. I found out that there are 365 scriptures God's given us that say "fear not." God showed me all the wonderful people of faith in the Bible who honored God by running in faith straight towards their fears. And He told me that if I would do the same, He would honor me. So from then on, whenever I got on an airplane, I just walked straight toward it, really wanting to honor Him. And He freed me! Remember: every time you do God's will in spite of fear, you're honoring Him. So today, start to face your fears boldly. Honor God in this way, and He won't fail to free you from your fear and honor you!

God Will Keep You

"He that dwelleth in the secret place of the Most High shall abide under the shadow of the Almighty." Psalm 91:1

Rev. Thomas F. Zimmerman, II
General Superintendent,
Assemblies of God

If you totally commit your life to the Lord, and want more than anything else in the world for the will of God to be done in your life, you can be very confident that God will keep you in any and all circumstances. Man is not a victim of circumstances. God allows, I believe, certain things to occur in our lives, not to destroy us, but to build us.

A difficulty is not necessarily bad in and of itself. What makes it a loss or a gain is our attitude. Often a person may feel that a certain situation is a stumbling block, while in the providence of God, it may well be a stepping stone, to bring him to a higher plane of spiritual realization, for which he may see the outworking of God's will in his life.

The life of faith has to be equally a life of trust. I believe that when we have exercised faith, to accept that God has heard and will answer our prayers, we need the discipline of trust. Faith is the element that appropriates to us the things of God's provision. Trust is the tranquillity of soul that patiently waits in hope for the fulfillment of God's purpose.

In the center of this God-committed life, He will sustain you by His grace, cover you with His protection, and continue working, in all the experiences through which you pass. He is at work right now, and there is nothing that can prevent Him from bringing to pass all that He has promised.

Sold On Being Bold

". . . the righteous are as bold as a lion." Proverbs 28:1

Don Gossett
Author/Evangelist

Boldness was one of the chief characteristics of believers at the time of the early church. Over 20 references to boldness can be found in scripture, most referring to the activities and attitude of that small band of newly Spirit-filled followers of Jesus who turned the world upside down.

The boldness spoken of here is not the arrogance, egotism, and forwardness we've known in certain worldly individuals who are always pushing their way past others. The boldness the early believers had was a quality which they had learned from observing the Master himself. Throughout His ministry, He was confident, courageous, fearless, and daring in whatever situation, difficulty or challenge He faced. It was said of Jesus when He walked on the earth, "Lo, He speaketh boldly." Thus He Himself showed us the boldness we should have in God.

Yes, you too, can experience boldness in your Christian walk because Jesus was bold, and "as He is, *so are we* in *this* world" (I John 4:17). If you know the Lord Jesus as your Saviour, you have been made righteous in God's eyes, and you have the bold nature of the Lion of Judah Himself within you! You may think, "but I'm not a forceful person." No, not in yourself, but you have boldness from "Jesus Christ our Lord: in whom we have boldness." (Ephesians 3:11-12)

When I was a young man, I was told that I was too timid and shy ever to be of much use to God. But I began to accept by faith what God said about me rather than letting these feelings hold me back. I soon discovered that His boldness was indeed in me, to walk and speak in confidence as He did. Ask God today to reveal to you also, the holy boldness of the Lion of Judah in *your* heart.

Rest In God

"And we know that all things work together for good to them that love God, to them who are the called according to His purpose."Romans 8:28

Karen Linderman
Missionary

I've especially been thankful for this verse when things have happened that I've found hard to accept, like the illnesses of my children. In the face of difficult circumstances, it is just natural to ask, "Well, why, Lord? Why is this happening?" But when you know He's there working everything out, you can take heart, and rest in His hands.

Our baby, who is now two, was born with an enlarged heart. Here I was in the hospital thanking God that she had all her fingers and toes. The delivery had gone perfectly; and when the nurse walked in and told me that I wouldn't be able to see my baby—that she was very ill—the bottom dropped out. My mouth fell open. "Lord, I was just thanking you! Why has this happened?"

We had dedicated her to the Lord before she was born, but I just had to give her up to Him again. I said, "Lord, I don't know why you'd give us a baby just to take her away, but I just trust you; she's your child—even to the point that, if you take her life, you know what's best."

She was healed and is completely well and full of energy today. Looking back, I can thank God for this trial because it gave me a chance to say, yes, this child is very important to me, but I have to have my priorities straight. God must come first.

You may have no idea of all the things God is doing through circumstances you're in. But give Him praise, even when you can't see how things will work out, because He's promised that they *will* work out—and for good!

Working And Sharing Together

*"Behold, how good and
how pleasant it is for brethren
to dwell together in unity!"*
Psalm 133:1

Mr. Roosevelt Johnson
Father of 19 children

There is great strength in unity. This world's philosophy today is so often "I've got mine—you go out and get yours if you can!" But the Lord has proved through us as a family that His way of giving to one another and building one another up in love is far better than the world's selfish way.

We were just a sharecropping family, not wealthy in the world's goods, but rich towards God. He enabled us, as we all shared what we had with one another, to put 13 young ones through college and buy the farm on which we'd been tenants.

Here's how we did it: whatever we had to do as a family, we all did together. A lot of the children liked music, but we had no musical instruments. So the children went out to work picking fruit for a few cents an hour. And instead of just keeping the money to themselves, they put it all together and kept saving it until they had enough to buy a piano.

When the first child got old enough for college, everybody pooled together what little they made and helped contribute to the expenses. And when she got out of college and got a job, she started sending money back to put the next one through. And as each child got through, they just kept on giving. When they all got through college, they gave to me and Momma so we could buy the farm.

You see, if everyone had just kept for him or herself, probably nobody would have gotten much of anything. Think today about what we did. It's simple, really, just doing what God says, putting the needs of others before your own. If you want your needs met, try meeting others' first. And build together, so all will be built up.

Imitate The Ants

"Go to the ant, thou sluggard; consider her ways, and be wise." Proverbs 6:6

Mrs. Clara Johnson
Farmer's Wife
Mother of 19 Children

Ants are always busy, scurrying here and there in search of food, and storing up for their young against hard times. The Lord wants us to keep busy, too, and not just so we can keep out of trouble.

As a large family, we used to do a considerable lot of gardening. The children would, of course, help with the hoeing and weeding. They had to help out if they hoped to eat! When the garden came up, we would go out and pick the vegetables and fruit, each at just the right time. When it was time for the canning, we would put quite a lot of the crop up for winter use.

At each stage of the food's growth, I would talk to the children while they were working and bring a little lesson about the things of the Lord. I used to tell them, "We're doing just what God says; we're working hard putting in the seed, tending the crops, harvesting them, and putting them up for later. That's what the ants do, isn't it?

"Now, God has told us to do these things so our earthly needs might be met. But He also wants us to sow and tend and harvest and store up good deeds and love and faith in His big storehouse in Heaven."

It's important that we work hard and make use of every little bit of time God has gifted us with here on earth. But the greatest treasures we can work for and store up are those that are laid up in Heaven. I thank God today that my whole family is "stored up" already for Jesus; that was what I worked for all my life.

So work hard while there's time, but not just for food that perishes. Life is so short, and there's so much good to do. What sense does it make to sit around looking at it all? "Go to the ant . . . and be wise!"

To Live Is Christ

"I beseech you therefore, brethren, by the mercies of God, that ye present your bodies a living sacrifice . . ."
Romans 12:1

Gary McSpadden
Teacher/Singer

Dying is a one-time thing: Living has to be done over and over again every day. In some ways, it's easier to die than it is to live for Christ. I think Paul realized this when he wrote to the Philippians: "For me to live is Christ, and to die is gain." To live in this world with Christ in your hearts brings problems, temptation, and tribulation, for as we walk with Him, we are open to all these things, just as He was.

To have been a martyr in the early Church was glorious, but God demands that we be *living* sacrifices first. We often forget that Jesus Himself lived thirty years of ordinary life here on earth before His ministry began. He had no reputation or celebrity, no pulpit to shield Him from everyday problems. He lived sinlessly in a little village in Nazareth, so quietly that when His ministry began some who knew Him commented "isn't that Joseph the carpenter's son?" Jesus proved Himself in the trials of ordinary life.

When I counsel married couples, I often ask the husband, "If an intruder were to break into your house with a gun and you had to choose whether you or your wife would be killed, who would it be?" When he answers, as usual, "Myself," I ask, "If you would choose to die for her why won't you choose to live for her?"

God wants us to offer up our lives daily to Him, to meet, in His strength and love, all of the responsibilities He's given us—for each other, for our jobs, for our church fellowships.

Right now, offer yourself to the Lord, as a *living* sacrifice, devoted to fulfilling His perfect will and walk in you today.

Blessed, Broken, Given

"And He commanded the multitude to sit down on the grass, and took the five loaves, and the two fishes, and looking up to heaven, He blessed, and brake, and gave the loaves to His disciples, and the disciples to the multitude." Matthew 14:19

Dr. F. Kefa Sempangi
Pastor

This, of course, is the story of Jesus' feeding of the 5,000. I'd like you to notice especially three verbs that describe what Jesus did to this small supply of food on that occasion: Jesus took the bread and fish and He *blessed* it, and He *broke* it, and then He *gave* it. There is meaning here for your life as a Christian.

The word "blessed" means "spoken well of." This is what you are because you belong to Jesus Christ. You are spoken well of before God because you are found in Jesus. Just as the bread was, you are lifted up before the Father, interceded for, and advocated by Jesus Himself.

And as Jesus has lifted you up, He has also broken you. The word "broken" in my Ugandan language means "devoid of pride." When you are willing to go to someone and admit when you have done wrong and ask for forgiveness, you are broken. That first breaking took place when you asked God to forgive your sins.

God broke you so He could share you with others. This points ahead to Jesus' sufferings. Remember, the same night Jesus was *betrayed*, He also took bread and did the same thing: blessed, broke, and gave it, saying, "This is My body broken for you; take and eat." Jesus was being blessed and broken and given to those who were against Him.

Do you see that you, too, have been blessed, broken, and given for those not just your friends, but also your enemies? Yes, you are in the hand of God today, ready to be released to those most in need: sinners, enemies, God's betrayers. As you have partaken of Christ, though undeserving, and then been blessed in Him, will you today be broken and passed on to others hungry for eternal life?

Willing To Obey

"And we know that all things work together for good to them that love God, to them who are the called according to His purpose."Romans 8:28

Jeannie C. Riley
Christian Entertainer

There was a time in my life when I was very afraid of what God's will would mean for me. I was afraid there would be no joy in doing what He was asking me to do. That was going back to my ex-husband, from whom I'd been divorced for five years. And though I was a Christian, I was miserable, because I was arguing wills with God.

I told God, "But my divorce came before I met you." I wanted an easy way out. I'd already met someone else. The funny thing was that, though we'd set wedding date after wedding date, I never had the peace to go through with it. I kept thinking that it was too much of a sacrifice to give this man up and too much to go back to my husband, too. But the Lord said, "You just bail out on faith. Don't wait for the answer first. You keep expecting to be in love with your husband before you'll say, 'Yes, I'll go back.' I want to hear you say that you'll go back to him even if you think it will make you miserable! Will you be willing to do that for me? I was willing to die for you!"

So I said, "I'll do it." A month later, the other man had been removed from my life. My husband and I were reunited in the Lord's Chapel in Nashville, with our own daughter as flower girl! I never shed a tear for the other fellow. The weight of the world was gone from my shoulders. God had answered our little daughter's prayer of five years that Mommy and Daddy would get back together!

You may be living in shadows right now, but God may be weaving a tapestry on the other side. All you may see are the tangles underneath. But I can assure you that God's making something beautiful of your life right now, for His honor and glory. Wait, and you'll see!

No Barriers

"For I am persuaded that neither death, nor life . . . nor any other creature, shall be able to separate us from the love of God, which is in Christ Jesus." Romans 8:35

Tami Cheré
Singer

At prisons where I sing, there are a lot of people who are down and hurting. When Paul wrote the words above, he was speaking as a man who'd known the horrors and discouragements of prison life. He went on to write some of his greatest epistles from prisons before he was executed as a supposed criminal himself in Rome. It just thrills me to know that there is no place or thing that can keep God's love from reaching us.

In reality, the only prison that can keep out God's love is the prison of self. If a prisoner were given a pardon, but refused to leave his cell, the offer of freedom wouldn't do him any good. Jesus' offer of salvation can't do any man any good either, unless he accepts it.

Is there any barrier in your life that you've placed between yourself and God? Have you placed yourself behind any bars of self or sin and not accepted Jesus' pardon completely? Nothing, not your past sin or your present weaknesses, whatever they may be, can separate you from Him, if you will only put your hand in His, rise up, and walk out into the freedom He has waiting for you.

You Are Special

"For we are His work-manship, created in Christ Jesus unto good works, which God hath before ordained that we should walk in them."
Ephesians 2:10

Austin Miles
Circus Ringmaster

All of us are special, and you are created especially for a certain something God wants you to do. And in God's eyes there is no one who has any limitation. The only limitations we have are ones we put on ourselves. In other words, nothing is impossible with God, and that goes for all of His people.

One thing we must remember is that the bodies we've been given are only temporary. I have known midgets and giants. It doesn't really matter if your bed is a couple of feet shorter or taller than someone else's—it's how much of Jesus Christ flows through you. If a midget gives himself fully to Christ, God will do far more with him than a giant without Jesus could ever do.

The important thing is that you recognize yourself as a work of God, formed just as you are for just what He wants to do in you.

So take a look in the mirror, and examine yourself constructively. Stop finding so much fault with yourself. Build up your best points, take them, and you'll find you have something beautiful for God to use. Stir up that gift that's in you. Everyone has one, at least, and you surely haven't been left out.

Now, whether you're young or old, a midget or a giant, stout or lean, an athlete or bedfast, I'd like you to pray this prayer with me: "Lord, thank You for the vessel you've given me. Thank You that I'm me and not someone else. I don't care what this vessel looks like or feels like to me, to You it's an absolute work of art. Help me today to use it to the fullest for Your glory. Amen and amen."

Agreeing For Things

". . . if two of you shall agree on earth as touching any thing that they shall ask, it shall be done of My Father which is in heaven."
Matthew 18:19

Bob Bonner
Professional Baseball Player

One beautiful thing about being married in the Lord Jesus: you always have someone close by you to agree with. The Lord has provided my wife Becky and me with all kinds of miracles. Let me share just a couple with you.

When I was leaving my home in Texas to play ball in North Carolina I found myself with only $80 to pay for the whole long car trip for Becky and me and our two little girls. I tried to borrow money from relatives, but they were all out of work just then and broke. Becky and I decided to lift the problem up to the Lord. We agreed that God would supply the need, and then went to Church that night.

While sitting there listening to the message, I made up my mind to leave on faith the next morning, whether the money was in my hand or not. I felt complete confidence come over me right then. When we were dismissed a while later, a man from my Sunday school class walked straight up to me and gave me $50 saying, "The Lord told me to." Praise God!

Well, on the road the next day, we sprang a bad leak in our car's water pump. We didn't have the money or time to fix it, so we agreed again that the Lord would take control. The Lord fixed the leak so well that when I took it to a garage after we got all the way to Charlotte, the mechanic couldn't even find it.

Remember that this verse says you can agree about any *thing* you shall ask. The Lord wants you to trust Him with all the *things* in your life, too. You've given Him your soul: now give Him your house, car, furniture, dishes, clothes, tools, makeup, and purse or wallet, too.

The Greatest Miracle

"He, therefore, that ministereth to you the Spirit, and worketh miracles among you, doeth He it by works of the law, or by the hearing of faith?"   Galatians 3:5

Becky Bonner
Housewife

Every day of knowing Jesus should be full of miracles. Oh, I don't mean that you have to go around parting seas and withering fig trees. But life with Christ in the Holy Spirit ought to be filled with the wonder of God's presence and joy in seeing Him act in all the little things as well as in the big things in your day.

The Lord has taught me in the short time I've known Him that I need to recognize every good thing that happens to me as a miracle from Him. After all, my life in Jesus began with a miracle when my spirit which was dead was made alive as I was reborn in Christ. So everything I've done since, really originated in that miracle, and is part of it: the great miracle of new birth, split into all the tiny pieces of my life!

Why should you believe in a life of miracles? Because if you're anything like me, you'll be tempted to take credit personally for many good things in your life—unless you're sure in your heart that God really did them. But if you ask God to fill your life with wonderful events and happenings, better than you could expect on your own, then when they happen, *you'll know* that God in His love *gave* you those things, not because of how great you were, but just because He loves you. And that's where your deepest joy will be found—in what God in His love has done.

Rejoice in the Lord today for your family, for your home, for your job, for yourself and all that you are through the Miracles of God. But above all, especially for Jesus, the greatest Miracle of all: *God* made human and living in your heart!

Power Of The Indwelling Spirit

"And the ark of the Lord continued in the house of Obededom the Gittite three months; and the Lord blessed Obededom, and all his household." 2 Samuel 6:11

Demos Shakarian
*Pres., Full Gospel Business
Men's International*

Here's something I'm excited about: that wooden box, the ark of the covenant. The story here is that David was bringing the ark up to Jerusalem, where he'd established his capitol. In those days, the presence of God's Holy Spirit was thought to dwell in that box. When David was walking beside the cart the ark was riding on, he was surrounded by great fanfare and celebration. During one stretch, the road got rough, the ark began to shake, and a priest tried to steady it and was struck dead right there. It had displeased God because he touched it.

David was afraid, so he left the ark at a nearby farm. After a while, David came back for the ark, this time with greater care! And he found that farm, and its owner, and everyone in the household, prospering greatly, just because the ark had been there.

Now, this box is just a symbol of what you and I are since Jesus ascended into heaven. We're just "earthen vessels," but before Jesus left, He said, "I'm going to send another Comforter, and I'm going to dwell with you." So the Holy Spirit that was in that box—now dwells in us! Wow! Think of this: if God can take a box and put His Spirit within it, and make everything around it prosper, then how much more should we have health and prosperity and the blessings of God!

So everywhere we're walking or staying, or talking or playing, we should be a blessing to God, and a blessing to everyone and everything around us! No wonder Jesus called us "the salt of the earth." We're what's making this old world tasty! Expect God to bless the people and the places you're in today. Just keep smiling and remember that vessel you are—and Who's in it!

Ready, Willing And Able

"Now unto Him that is able to do exceeding abundantly above all that we ask or think, according to the power that worketh in us."

Ephesians 3:20

Vinny Terranova
Evangelistic Chairman,
"Cops for Christ"

God blesses me with His willingness *and* His ability to do for His kids. How many people have you met who are willing, but not able to do much good? And how many are able, but not willing? Isn't it wonderful to know that our God doesn't have either problem?

He's the sovereign God, with all things under His control. And He's given *us* all that power through Jesus Christ! We have the keys to the kingdom, with rule and authority over all the power of the enemy. And with all that power at our disposal, He is able to do things in our lives that are beyond our wildest dreams.

What kind of power? The Greek word is "dunamis," like dynamo or dynamite. The nature of it is that the more you use, the more you get.

When we were kids in Brooklyn, we'd get large tires from big trailer trucks. We'd start to roll them from the top of a hill, then we'd see how fast we could run in front of them before they caught up with us. We'd do all right for about halfway down the hill, then, brother, get out of the way, because when those things picked up momentum, they had the speed and power to do us some damage!

God's power is like that: the freer you let it roll, the more it gains strength in your life. I can just see this big steamroller, being the Holy Spirit, starting at the top of the hill with us riding it. At first, it moves slowly, and we don't think God's going to get anywhere with what He's called us to do. But all of a sudden, we gain speed and power, and before you know it, we're flattening unimaginable obstacles. God has placed no limit on what He can do with your life. So as you go out to face today, don't place any limit on yourself!

On The Lookout For Good

"And we know that all things work together for good to them that love God, to them who are the called according to His purpose."Romans 8:28

Joe and Nancy Cruse
Music Artists

Travelling around with the Cruse Family, we've had ample opportunities to see strange things work out for good. Just recently, we were singing at a Bible Conference. Most of the other musical groups there were of the old-time gospel tradition. As a contemporary group, we were booked near the end of the program.

The audience had been sitting there sweating for about nine hours, and when we came on with our up-beat style, people started getting up and leaving in droves. By the time we finished our set, only a fraction of the listeners were still there. We'd had cold audiences before, but this was a new experience for us. We thought we had ministered our best musically so it would have been easy for us to have gotten bitter or discouraged over this.

But through this experience as we prayed, the Lord showed us some important lessons. We needed to understand that our success was a gift from Him—for all our hard work, He was the Master of the results. God turned the situation which appeared to be disastrous on the surface into a blessing. Late that evening, we as a group, sought the Lord for consolation and direction and He really blessed with spiritual refreshment. It just made our ministry the next time that much more effective and showed us we needed to seek Him more.

Be on the lookout for all kinds of good to come from God. It may not be the good you expected; you may not even recognize it as good at first, but it'll always be what you need most in God's timing.

Three Foundation Stones

". . . Ye believe in God, believe also in Me. In My Father's house are many mansions . . . I go to prepare a place for you . . . I will come again, and receive you unto myself . . ."   John 14:1-3

Dr. Herbert Lockyer
Author/Bible Teacher

Just before He went to the cross to shed His blood for our redemption, Jesus gave these precious words, which multitudes have pillowed their heads upon all down the ages. In these verses are three foundation stones of faith on which we may rest our lives, whatever our age or station in life.

The first of these "stones" is faith in Christ. Christ and trouble can never exist together. Where the Lord Jesus is received in all His fullness, there is always peace and joy and contentment in this life.

Then, in the second verse, is the second "stone": faith in Heaven. This is in logical order because we will never see the inside of Heaven unless the Lord Jesus is our personal Savior. As our lives quickly pass by, Heaven becomes to us who believe in Christ more and more a reality though we linger in this world of sin and need. As the old hymn so eloquently says, "The things of earth grow strangely dim in the light of His glory and grace."

Finally, the third, "stone" is faith in Jesus' return. Here Jesus is giving us the first word in the New Testament concerning His return for His own—the rapture of the Church.

So, we have faith in Christ, and that makes it possible for us to look forward to Heaven and the return of Jesus for us. Rest today, in the assurance that this threefold bulwark offers. Sink your faith deep into these boulders and reach out for the redemption that is yours—now, soon to come, and forever.

God Loves You—Faults And All

"A new commandment I give unto you, That ye love one another; as I have loved you, that ye also love one another." John 13:34

Pam Thum
Singer

Jesus' love is not like man's love. It's unconditional and unchanging. My Jesus loves me when I have bad breath and stinky feet and dirty hair because I've been too busy to wash it for two days. He loves me just like that.

And I think that in the Body of Christ, He wants us to love each other like that. He wants us to put aside our fear of rejection and our insecurities and our hurts and fear of being misunderstood. He just wants us to love each other just as He loves us.

It's funny how differently people will treat you if they think you're a somebody. A lot of times in the Body of Christ, I'll walk up to somebody and say, "Hi, I'm Pam Thum." And they'll maybe reply "Hi" kind of mumbly and then walk on. But then someone will tell them in a whisper. "Hey, that's Pam Thum!! She's an upcoming new artist, you know. Her albums are doing real well!" And back they'll come to gush a little and shake my hand. That's not the way it should be in the Body of Christ.

We should love each other just because we're sisters or brothers, and not because we smell good, or look good, or have a well known name. People could tell that Jesus loved them. Remember that drunks, lepers, blind men, sinners and tax collectors sensed that love so strongly that Jesus didn't have to go to them—they came looking for Him!

And when you came looking for Him, He accepted you, too! And now, He expects you and me to accept one another. Lord, help us to see with Your eyes and to love one another with Your kind of love.

Forget the Blueprint

"Jesus said unto him, I am the way, the truth, and the life: no man cometh unto the Father, but by Me." John 14:6

Dr. Howard M. Ervin
Professor/Author

Perhaps we spend more time and spiritual anguish than is necessary trying to determine something that is really quite simple: what is the will of God for our lives? Our frequent attempts at wrenching a blueprint of the future from the mind of God can rob us of rest in God, and even misguide us by causing us to grab at the first definite-seeming answer we receive.

When I was in my first year of seminary, God dropped this verse very quietly into my heart. Since then, it has remained the guiding word of my life. For I understood by it that God was not going to lead me by showing me a specific way every time I needed to move ahead. Nor would He inscribe a definite "truth" on my mind each time I needed to make a judgment. Nor would He lay out before me His entire plan for my life. Instead, He had given me His Son Jesus, Who would be within me, the way, the truth, and the life.

There is no will of God for any Christian but that Jesus Christ live His life freely in that believer's heart. There is no approach to the Father but by Jesus' presence within. All of the uncertainties of my life and future were brought to rest when I understood this. All that God required of me was that I remain faithful to my commitment to Jesus and trust the future to Him. How true He has proved! Not once has He failed me in my 63 years of life.

Nor will He fail you, if you will merely trust Jesus' abiding presence in your heart and rest your future with Him. Oh, that you may realize what this means: no more futile searching, or anxious worrying. He is within you right now. Let Him dwell there richly today.

Love Your Enemies Today

"Then said Jesus unto His disciples, If any man will come after Me, let him deny himself, and take up his cross, and follow Me."

Matthew 16:24

Sonny Gibson
Actor

After the Lord met me in prison, He told me to make a big wooden cross in the shop and keep it in my cell. I was serving a life sentence for one of a number of crimes, and the Lord wanted to remind me to be the new man He'd made me in Jesus.

Carrying a knife in prison came naturally to me, because most men there do, for protection. Killing was simple for me because I'd done that. Hate was easy to have; it seemed like the normal reaction to being hurt. But to pray for someone who had done me a bad turn, to turn the other cheek when somebody hit me, that was hard.

For my first few years as a Christian in prison, I carried a knife. Having to use it caused me to end up in the hospital. When I got out, the Lord told me it was time to give up the knife and start trusting Him. He set that cross in my cell as a way of telling me that I no longer had the right to hate, to look for trouble, or to seek revenge. Instead, I had to start loving my enemies, even the ones that were a physical danger to me in that evil environment.

If you love your enemy, you won't cause violence against him. You may be thinking right now "Well I've never murdered anyone, and I'm not in that kind of danger, and I've never carried a knife." No, you may not have a blade in your pocket, but do you carry one in your heart? How did you feel that last time someone cut ahead of you in a grocery line? What did you say in your heart when somebody on the road made you swerve to avoid an accident?

Do you still carry a root of resentment or hate in your heart? It would be easy to hold onto it. But the Lord wants you to deny the luxury of hate and take up His cross of love. Will you follow Him in that today?

Never Alone

"Fear thou not; for I am with thee: be not dismayed: I will strengthen thee; yea, I will help thee; yea, I will uphold thee with the right hand of my righteousness."
Isaiah 41:10

Rev. Sandra Torres
Evangelist

Are there ever times when you are frightened because you feel all alone? Have you ever become discouraged by problems or circumstances that seemed too great for you? Have you felt weak, helpless, or unable to carry on?

Then do not miss the message of this verse. For in answer to each of these needs, God wants you to know that He is always present to meet them: "I am with thee, I am thy God, I will strengthen thee, I will help thee, I will uphold thee!"

These promises could not be more positive. If you will receive them, they will strike at the root of your every fear and inadequacy. For the message of the gospel is that God alone is trustworthy, and that He will never fail you. Friends may forsake you, enemies may beset you, situations may overwhelm you, but if you have the Lord, you will never be alone.

My daughter's near-fatal neck injury taught me this. Doctors' opinions conflicted, friends disagreed with our stand in faith for Ruth's healing; I was ridiculed as a fanatic, and subjected to discouragement at every turn. But in all these things, the Lord said to me "Look only to Me; I alone can save, I alone am in control."

The Lord wants you to look today to the right hand of His righteousness, and Who is at the right hand of the Father? It is Jesus Who is waiting for you to release your fears, doubts, discouragement, and weakness to Him. Whatever your problems are today, let them go, and set your feet in the strong hand of the Almighty—Jesus the King.

Strength For Today

"I will love Thee, O Lord, my strength."

Psalm 18:1

Ruth Sebastiano
Student/Author

Two years ago, when I was 14 years old, my neck was broken in a diving accident. Doctors gave me only a 30 percent chance of survival. There was no movement or feeling in my body, nor any hope of my being ever able to function as a normal child again.

Since I was very small, the Lord Jesus has been very precious to me. So when this happened, I wasn't discouraged; my heart filled with love for God all the more. My mother and many believers from our church lifted me up to the Lord, and miraculously, all the feeling in my body was restored almost immediately.

But still, I had no strength or movement. That is when this verse became very real to me. I said in my heart, "The Lord is my strength. I may have none of my own, but He is within me, caring for me." And faith sprang up in my heart from that moment that the Lord would heal me.

Soon afterwards, movement in my body began to return. The more I drew upon God as my strength, the more I was able to do. As His power flowed through my body, control came again to my hands and feet and gradually to all of me from head to toe.

My heart is certain that it is God's strength within me that is now enabling me to walk again, to use my arms and hands freely, and work skillfully although this has been called medically impossible.

The Lord will be your strength also today. He will bring physical ability to you, as He did to me, if you reach out to Him in faith. He will also be your spiritual and emotional strength as you draw upon Him alone to fill all your need.

God Will Perfect Us

"Being confident of this very thing, that He that hath begun a good work in you will perform it until the day of Jesus Christ." Philippians 1:6

Rev. Billy Roy Moore
Pastor

If you were an employer, would you be willing to hire an applicant for a position in your organization who had a history of starting a lot of jobs well, but never finishing any of them? The record of a person like that wouldn't inspire much confidence, would it?

Paul says here that God has begun a good work in us, and that we can be confident that God will complete that work. If we lack confidence in our walk with God, it must be either because we fear that He can't finish what He started, or we fear that He needs our assistance and that we're unreliable.

That job history I used as an example above sounds quite a bit like our past lives, doesn't it? Unfinished projects, good intentions never carried out, stumbling along in frustration, not much grounds for confidence there. And this is why God took mercy upon us and began His good work in us because we could never get it started on our own. This is also why He has promised to finish it because we could never keep that work going on our own.

Now let's consider God's job history. "There hath not failed one word of all His good promise" (1 Kings 8:56). Jesus was able to say to His Father "I have finished the work which thou gavest me to do" (John 17:4). God assures us that His "counsel shall stand, and I will do all my pleasure . . . I have purposed it, I will also do it" Isaiah 46:10-11.

How much more worthy of confidence is He then we? If you will merely love Him today, and thank Him for the work He is doing, your anxiety will flee, you will rest and let Him bear you along to glory. For that's how long He has promised to perform that work—until you see Jesus face to face.

Choosing What Is Important

*"That I may know Him
. . ."* Philippians 3:10

Margaret Cole
Missionary/Author

Paul had been a Christian a long time when he wrote this verse, yet he still cried out his desire to know Christ better. I also had known Jesus for many years, since age 13 until age 66, when I was led to take the deeper steps that were necessary to draw me closer to Him.

At that time, about seven years ago, my husband died. I had to make a decision about what to do with my life from then on. These thoughts crossed my mind: "You belong to a lot of clubs: the women's club, the literary club, the homemakers' club. Are you going to spend the rest of your life going around to teas and luncheons and entertaining? Is that what's important?"

And as I tried to examine myself, I asked, "What do I have to offer Thee, Lord: Talent, abilities, preparation or training? No, I have none of these to give. I only have a widow's mite: a very little to put on the altar. But Lord, I have two desires: I want to know you better, and I want to go to the mission field." This last had been my desire since I was baptized at age 15.

The Lord opened the door very quickly. I served with the Wycliffe Bible Translators in New Guinea, and in numerous other places all over the world. There, God began to do a work in my life that could only have been meaningful apart from the comfortable life of materialism that had covered my childhood wish to be fully used by Him. Through it I came to know Him as never before.

It is never too soon, or too late, to reach out to Jesus, and get to know Him better. Never can we exhaust the riches of His grace and love. If you desire to know Him better, let Him use you now, in a fresh way.

The Builder of Men's Lives

"I am crucified with Christ: nevertheless I live; yet not I, but Christ liveth in me: and the life which I now live in the flesh I live by the faith of the Son of God, Who loved me, and gave Himself for me."   Galatians 2:20

Rev. Mack Evans
Pastor/Author

Jesus is a people builder. Whenever He touches a life, it begins to appreciate in value. This is a very personal verse, written as Paul strove to explain the dramatic change which knowing Jesus had brought into his life.

Paul had been a Pharisee of the Pharisees, bound up in a rigid code of statutes and regulations. After Jesus met him, he became a free man, constrained only by love. Paul had been a murderer, a man filled with violence and anger. The touch of Jesus turned him into a man whose greatest desire was to bring others to new life through Christ. Paul had been a critic and persecutor of others, bent on the destruction of the Church, hostile to nationalities foreign to his Israelite heritage. He became by the transforming power of Jesus a great builder of churches and was used by God to spread the gospel to the Gentile world.

Consider also the changes in Peter, from impulsive braggart to great leader of the early church; in the apostle John, from "son of thunder" to writer of the words "God is love;" in Mary Magdalene, from demon-possessed prostitute to faithful follower of Jesus.

And what of your own life? Take time to think for a moment of all the wonders God has wrought in your life since you first felt Jesus' touch.

Think of how deeply your life has been changed by His presence. Perhaps as you do, you will, as Paul did, come to recognize that you have been built up in all that you are because He Himself has done even more than merely touch your life—He has come to indwell your life, and claim you for His own.

He's Calling Your Name

"But now thus saith the Lord that created thee, O Jacob, and He that formed thee, O Israel, Fear not: for I have redeemed thee, I have called thee by thy name; thou art mine."   Isaiah 43:1

Felicia Kundrat
Heritage School Student

This verse is so personal! I cherish the Lord so much—to think that when He called, He knew my name, out of all the billions on earth. And He knows your name, too.

Look at all that He's done for us! He created us, and formed us, redeemed us through the blood of Jesus, called us, and then made us His very own. No wonder He can tell us, "Fear not." Would He have done all this just to discard us for any little reason? Oh, no! He cares so much, more than any father or mother ever could.

Think of how much love and concern a little child's parents spend on him during his first few years. They encourage him, shower affection on him, correct him when he needs it. Think of all the mistakes he makes and how hard he is to put up with. Sometimes he cries all night, he gets into messes and gets grouchy. But the love of his parents doesn't stop, though it sure gets tried.

Now imagine how much God, whose love never changes, who never loses patience, whose discipline is always perfect, whose care is never-failing, is able to lavish your heart with all that's best for you. He will never let you go!

Oh, how much this has meant to me at times when things have happened to me that have hidden His beautiful presence. I've cried out to Him, "Please, Lord, show me that I'm still Yours!" And He has, just like you would take your own tiny child in your arms, if he was hurting.

Sometime today, you may be tempted to think that God doesn't care about you. Pressures may pile up, things may not go well. But just remember, Jesus has called you, and if you listen, even in your trouble, you'll hear Him calling, calling your name. If you answer, He'll help!

Make Your Thoughts Pleasing

"Let this mind be in you, which was also in Christ Jesus. . . ." Philippians 2:5

Darlene De Haro
Prison Worker

Coming into Christ from a lifestyle without restraints, I experienced difficulty with being renewed in my mind. So many sinful old memories and habits crowded my walk with God, that at times I seemed to take twice as many steps backward as I took forward. This caused me so much anguish that I almost wanted to give up.

This was because my mind was still being allowed to dwell on the old things. I loved the Lord but did not know that His mind had to replace mine, that His thoughts had to become mine. Finally, the Lord showed me this verse, and for days and nights I wept before Him and begged Him to take the old mind out of me and give me His.

Then He showed me how He was going to accomplish this: I was to direct my thoughts to "whatsoever things are true, honest, just, pure, lovely, of good report, virtuous, praiseworthy things," that Philippians 4:8 exhorts us to think about. Every time a thought came to my mind that wasn't pleasing to Him, I pushed it out with a thought that I knew would please Him. His words and His thoughts began to cleanse my mind from evil and steady my walk with Him.

Did you know that you are not a victim of the thoughts and desires that pass through your mind? The Scripture says, *"Let* this mind be in you . . ."* The devil would try to deceive you into thinking that your thoughts are as uncontrollable as dead leaves blowing in the wind, but this is a lie. Thoughts that are pleasing to God, if you will fill your mind with them, will stand as firm barriers against old thoughts and desires that Satan can use to plague your mind. Resolve today to lift up the banners of Godly thoughts and march in victory behind them.

Setting Your Hand

"The Lord shall command the blessing upon thee in thy storehouses, and in all that thou settest thine hand unto; and He shall bless thee in the land which the Lord thy God giveth thee."

Deuteronomy 28:8

Howard Hite
Farmer

Being a farmer, there's one thing I know for certain: if I don't make an effort to plant a crop, I'm not going to reap a harvest. That's plain old common sense in the day to day world, but a lot of Christians seem to throw their sense out the window when it comes to the things of God. We get to thinking we can just pray, then sit down on a rocking chair on our front porch and never do anything and God will bless us. Well, I'll tell you, it isn't going to happen.

I had this idea for awhile, that God was just going to rain it all down out of heaven. I think a lot of Christians are in this bondage. But this verse says that God expects us to do our part, and then He'll do what He said He'd do. He will bless everything we lay hold on and start to do.

But if Christians don't make an effort, for example, to get a job and sustain their lives and support their family, they're not going to be blessed financially. God's not going to make counterfeit money and give it to them. But when as a farmer I buy my seed, plant my crop, fertilize it, prevent the insects from gobbling it up, and make preparations for harvesting it, I know that everything I do is blessed. That means that I have secure grounds for faith, I'm established in God's Word, and He's going to sustain me.

Maybe there's something in your life you'd like to see happen, but you've been waiting around for it just to drop out of the sky. You see now that it won't come that way. Maybe you've been afraid to step out because you think you might fail. God's Word says you won't. Now, make up your mind that you're going to set your hand to that thing today and then you'll see God add His blessing of success!

The Pure In Heart

"Blessed are the pure in heart: for they shall see God."
Matthew 5:8

John Gilman
Movie & T.V. Producer

Have you ever tried to see to the bottom of a stagnant pond that was covered with some slime and greenish algae? All of the filth and impurities make it impossible to see clearly. How much more pleasant to view a crystal clear sea or sparkling clear mountain stream. In the same way, perhaps the most important thing we can achieve in our lifetimes is to become pure, transparent before God, and before one another.

How much we cloud others' vision of Jesus by our pretense and hypocrisy. When we give a compliment, we're often not completely sincere. When we ask someone how they are, we don't really want to know. We pretend to care about others because we ought to, not because God's spirit is caring through us. Thus we almost unknowingly spread sludge over the well of God's love in us.

"The pure in heart will see God." Everyone wants to see God. But the only way we will see Him is through purified hearts. God in His mercy has searched our hearts and known them. He knows every falsehood, every blemish, and yet He loves us. And he has placed His Spirit in our hearts to remold them into the heart of Christ.

And what is a pure heart? One that doesn't need to say "Oh, should I say this or that?" One that doesn't strive for power and influence over others. One that doesn't dwell constantly on past accomplishments or future achievements.

Oh, to be like Jesus who rarely premeditated a thought. Jesus just was, free to be wholly in God's presence and to say, "Not My will, but Thine be done." Oh, to be free to say, "He who has seen Me hath seen the Father." Lord, make me that pure and clear, that Your glory in me might be seen, as I see You unhindered by self.

Love One-On-One

"By this shall all men know that ye are My disciples, if ye have love one for another." John 13:35

Dr. Alan McGinnis
Psychologist

The hallmark by which Christians have always been known is their love. As a psychologist, I'm especially interested in the potential of Christians' love for others because a lot of patients with whom I work are in psychological trouble because they don't have enough love in their lives.

This hunger for love opens up tremendous opportunities for us as Christians. I believe that a lot of psychiatric offices like mine would be closed if more of God's love were shared in our society. And this is where we, who have that love in our hearts, could make the difference to a world starving for love.

The noted psychiatrist, Karl Menninger, has said, "Love is the medicine for the ills of mankind; we could all live if we had love." The head of the psychiatric hospital where I'm a staff worker said that he felt that 85 percent of the patients who were there would not need to be admitted if they had the support system available to them that the Body of Christ is supposed to offer.

Jesus, Himself, is our model in showing love. He was an artist at relationships, treating every individual tenderly, caringly, and uniquely, according to the specific need He faced. Jesus never dealt with people routinely or with preconceived theory. His deep insight always led to loving one-on-one encounters. Just as Jesus did, we should consider accepting into our lives a few troubled, even neurotic persons, people who will probably take more from us than we will receive in return. I believe that in sharing Christ and our lives with them, we can help to love them back to health.

God Loves The Weak, Too

"We then that are strong ought to bear the infirmities of the weak, and not to please ourselves."   Romans 15:1

E. Judson Cornwall
Teacher/Author/Conference Speaker

Americans are almost obsessed with a desire to be strong, whether it be physically, emotionally, financially, or politically. Weakness is viewed as failure, as our strong competitive instincts abhor defeat. We don't relish being even number two! But Paul was realistic enough to admit that life is filled with contrasts and opposites: tall-short, bright-dull, success-failure—and strong-weak. And in the Body of Christ, though these are opposite poles, we must come to see them not as differences that divide us, but as tensions within the unity of Christ.

Too often the strong take advantage of the weak, or at best, simply ignore them. Even Christians may forget that while the Scriptures speak of some who are "strong in faith" (Romans 4:20), and others who are "weak in faith" (Romans 14:1), all are included in the "household of faith" (Galatians 6:10). Paul says that the strong have a responsibility to help the weak. This is true whether the weakness is physical, financial, moral, or spiritual. Just as Christ's strength has been repeatedly made available to us in our moments of weakness, so our strengths must be shared with the other members of the Body of Christ, each of us supplying what is needed for a healthy operation of the whole (Ephesians 4:16).

But isn't there a right and wrong way to share our strength? I was carrying my tool box one morning to a volunteer job during a "work day" at the college where I teach. A misstep caused the catch on the toolbox to slip, spilling assorted screws, washers, bolts, nuts, nails, etc. all over the floor. What a mess! A passing student began to help me pick up, while at the same time giving me a little "spiritual" lecture. A school administrator passed by with the comment, "There's nothing spiritual about being a klutz." But during this entire time, a faculty member was on her knees under the stairway, silently retrieving my spilled items. She didn't quit until the box was filled and fastened and I was on my way again. To this day, she hasn't mentioned the incident to me. She neither teased nor lectured; she shared her strength without underlining my weakness. Cannot we do the same with one another?

"Dear Lord, I thank You for the strength You've given to me. I know that it's undeserved and unearned, for it's You who strengthen me. Show me how to share that strength without being condescending to the weak. Help me to resist the urge to lecture on weakness. Help me to simply give what is needed. May I never put down the weak by my actions, or become proud in my attitudes. In Jesus Name I pray. Amen."

Supporting God's Servants

" . . . And how shall they believe in Him of whom they have not heard? and how shall they hear without a preacher?"   Romans 10:14

Oral Roberts
Evangelist

The only future you have is in God's Word. Anything in today's world that means faith, healing, hope, or love will only come to you by hearing and receiving the Word of God. "Faith cometh by hearing, and hearing by the Word of God," (Romans 10:17). And while God sometimes "speaks" from the pages of the Bible as we read it privately, He has especially chosen the human instrumentalities of preaching and brotherly fellowship to deliver His mind to His people.

This is because He knows best that only through human instruments can He fully express the tender compassion of His heart for people in need. When Jesus, the Son of God walked the earth, He spoke His Father's words with a tongue that really knew the thickness of thirst. He trod the dusty roads with feet of flesh and blood. With warm hands He embraced little children, touched the sick and the helpless, and shared bread with hungry multitudes. With eyes that had known the heaviness of sleep and the sting of sand, He wept anguished tears over the city of Jerusalem. The same heart that had quickened while trudging the hills of Galilee and beat softly in the ear of His beloved disciple John, spilled forth water and His precious blood for our salvation. He hurt where we hurt, He knew first hand rejection and hatred, joy and sorrow, abundant health and cruel death. In God's beautiful plan, we've been given each other. In place of Jesus' physical presence, God's servants each have a portion of His great heart of love, to minister to these same needs today, through words, touches and deeds, from hearts of compassion.

I thank God for the many people of God who have touched me with His love. No one deserves your support and love more than God's servants. Be faithful in ministering to them through your prayers, giving and loyalty.

A Proper Balance

"Beloved, I wish above all things that thou mayest prosper and be in health, even as your soul prospereth."
3 John vs. 2

Paul Olson
Pastor/Author

When I was a child, friends would ask me what my church believed in. All I could tell them was what we did not believe in. We didn't believe in dancing, going to movies, playing cards and a lot of other things. I knew all the "don'ts" but could not tell then what was fun or exciting about being a Christian.

Because of this, I thought of God as a "You can't do this" God; and I always felt I could not live up to all the "don'ts." I had learned more about the fear of the Lord than I had about the joy of the Lord.

The day I discovered 3 John vs. 2, I realized that God really loved me and wanted good things for me. In the verse He calls me His "beloved" and says more than anything else He wants me to be happy and well.

When I searched the scriptures to learn more about the joy of the Lord, I found promises like "The joy of the Lord is your strength" (Neh. 8:10) and ". . . the God of hope fill you with all joy" (Rom. 15:13).

Today, every chance I'm given to tell others why I am a Christian, I begin by sharing what a loving God I have. I tell them about all the good things the Lord has done for me, and that by obeying the principles and rules of the Bible, I realize His love more everyday.

I believe it is important for Christians to obtain a healthy balance of joy in Christ and respectful fear of His commandments and power. If you are a Sunday School teacher, parent, or simply a witness for Jesus, make a point of sharing God's love with others. Help them realize God loves them and He wants to be their Best Friend.

Unceasing Prayer

"And He spake a parable unto them to this end, that men ought always to pray, and not to faint." Luke 18:1

Arthur Blessit
Evangelist

A lot of Christians have been perplexed by this scripture and another one like it "Pray without ceasing" (1 Thess. 5:17). Being in prayer constantly sounds like a fine way to live one's life, but how is that possible with all the duties and responsibilities that crowd our lives these days?

The real meaning of this verse to me is that we are to be in a spirit of communication with God constantly. When they pray, some people begin, "Dear God, this is So-and-so . . . ," and when their prayer is done, they close with "Amen" and they just "sign off." In their minds, there's no further communication with God until they start again, whether an hour later or the next day, or that night.

But isn't this a strange, formal way to treat Someone who is supposed to be "a friend that sticketh closer than a brother" (Prov. 18:24)? When my wife and I are travelling together across the country, I don't keep introducing myself every time I start to make a comment. We don't have to talk constantly in order to be in communication with one another. We know that we are together in one another's presence, in close relationship even if we're silent.

And that's the way we should live in our relationship with God. God wants to share in all the little thoughts and actions and experiences that come to us throughout the day, as our Friend.

Feel free to laugh with the Lord, cry with Him, talk to Him, have fun with Him, just live with Him as a constant companion, not only by your side but *within* you, sharing in and being with you in all that you do and are.

Give God Your "Impossibles"

"He that spared not His own Son, but delivered Him up for us all, how shall He not with Him also freely give us all things?" Romans 8:32

Dr. Larry Ziemianski
Dentist

With God, there are simply no impossibilities. Many things may seem to stand in the way of what we'd like to see done. An unsaved relative may have a hard heart. You may have a habit that you just can't seem to break. There may be problems in your home or job or church or school that just seem to have no solution. But God not only has answers to all of these troubles so difficult to us, He is ready and willing to give us His best solution to each as a free gift.

God's problem-solving ability was demonstrated most fully in the giving up of His own Son Jesus to death for our salvation. To atone for our sins, Jesus did the only thing that was possible: take our sins with Him into death, and rise again to bring us new life.

Can God bring anything good out of our "hopeless" situations? Yes, He can! To the world's eyes, there was never a worse act than the putting of Jesus to death. Yet from it, God brought salvation to the world. God did it for my wife and me, taking a marriage on the verge of divorce, with nothing going for it, and making it beautifully alive by His Holy Spirit.

Can God make His Church around the world all one? I've been tempted to look at all of the denominations and divisions and give up hope. But Jesus believed it could be done: He prayed for it in John chapter 17, and I know that the Father heard Jesus' prayer. And I see it happening right now through the pouring out of the Holy Spirit.

Can God take charge of your "impossibilities" and give you good things in their place? Yes, He can! And He will, if you'll just get out of the way and let Him. So from now on stop saying, "I can't."

The Gift Of Love

"Wherefore they are no more twain, but one flesh. What therefore God hath joined together, let not man put asunder." Matthew 19:6

Marjorie Ziemianski
Helpmate

Before my husband Larry and I found Jesus, we fell out of love with each other. In fact, I asked Larry for a divorce. I just couldn't face the prospect of living out a life without love.

But when he came into a living relationship with Jesus, and was baptized in the Holy Spirit, Larry fell in love with me again. About a week later, I met the Lord, too. I was deeply touched, but my love wasn't completely restored. That night, a young priest prayed that God would give us a gift of love for each other. He shared with us the scripture above, telling us that from the beginning God had intended husbands and wives to be inseparable. The only reason why the Old Testament had allowed divorce was due to the hardness of people's hearts. Jesus' disciples were stunned and wondered aloud whether they ought never to get married! Jesus' answer in this scripture was the reason why this priest had prayed for us. Jesus said that this saying could only be received by a gift of revelation from God.

With that prayer, my husband won back my heart completely. I believe that today, as marriages all over this country are under attack, that we need to receive the supernatural endowment of this gift of married love that Jesus talked of. One woman, for whom we prayed to receive this gift, ran home and found that her previously unsaved husband had met Jesus once she had been filled with this love for her spouse.

This gift can be yours, too, if you'll ask God for it. Even if you're not married, you can pray that married friends whom you love will receive it. As never before, we need to pray that God will uphold the marriage bond among His people. Intercede on behalf of your marriage or a loved one's, right now.

Talking To Jesus

"For where two or three are gathered together in my name, there am I in the midst of them."   Matthew 18:20

Rosie Black
Professional Softball Pitcher

If you're a softball pitcher who's just given up back to back home runs, you usually find yourself in the center of a conference at the pitcher's mound. The catcher comes out, the manager has a few words to share, and several other players gather around to listen, while you kick up clods of dirt with your head bowed down.

The object of this little talk is to find out what's wrong, to calm you down, or to give some advice or encouraging word to help restore your confidence. As Christian ballplayers, the "Queen and Her Court" often share unsettling situations in prayer, right there on the mound.

But isn't it comforting to know that no matter what you do or where you are, when you huddle together in prayer with others of like faith, Jesus is right there in the midst of the huddle?

Sometimes after a game, people share with us about their problems. And there've been times when I've suggested that we pray together right there about them. Some people feel uncomfortable or embarrassed. So I say, "There's no need to be uneasy. Jesus is right here, and you don't have to be inside a church to talk to Him. You can pray anywhere. Let's talk to Him right now."

Some people don't know that they can actually talk to the Lord. They think that if they pray to Him anywhere but in church, they might be sacrilegious.

But brother or sister, this just isn't true. I keep in contact with the Lord on the softball field; Jesus as He walked the hills and dales of Palestine kept in constant touch with His Father. So be sure and take time out for that "huddle" if you need it today. And rest assured that Jesus will be right there!

Trust, Delight, Commit

"Delight thyself also in the Lord, and He shall give thee the desires of thine heart. Commit thy way unto the Lord; trust also in Him; and He shall bring it to pass."
Psalm 37:4-5

Honeytree
Singer

Not long ago, I sang at a prison for about 100 inmates. I was a little scared beforehand, but the sweet special love of the Holy Spirit came down on us, and it touched me very deeply.

I began to pray earnestly that the Lord would enable me to get into prison ministry more often. I knew of Chuck Colson's prison outreach, and I really wanted to work with him. My faith wasn't very great, but I committed this wish to the Lord and then just sort of forgot about it.

Well, soon thereafter at a convention where I was singing, Chuck Colson was the featured speaker. I put aside my shyness after the final banquet and caught up with him just before he left the building. "Mr. Colson," I burst out, "I want to sing in prison—can I help you?" He kindly invited me to join him in an upcoming visit, and I've been working with him regularly ever since in prisons all over the country.

It's such a temptation, if you have a ministry that you think the Lord wants you to do, to get anxious and strive and try to open doors for yourself; but I've found out that you don't have to do that. Just seek the Lord, and hand it over to Him and let it go—almost forget it. God will open the door because He definitely wants us to serve Him. He needs every one of us He can get! And He loves surprises, so why try to figure everything out for yourself?

The Gates Of God

"Enter into His gates with thanksgiving, and into His courts with praise . . ."
Psalm 100:4

Luis Gloria
Pastor/Bible Teacher

Until we learn to enter the Lord's "gates" thankfully, we cannot really start to serve God. Do I mean the ivory, pearl, and gold gates of Heaven? Eventually, yes, but the "gates" I mean are placed by God before us from day to day, the opportunities and circumstances that confront us, drawing us into the things of God.

I have seen the gate of heaven come before a man through the death of his mother. He had steadfastly resisted the gospel, but upon his mother's death, he wept bitterly and repented. It seemed difficult at first for him to enter that gate with thanksgiving, but he did at last. Now there are two souls present in the kingdom of God instead of just one.

How often we thank God for an "open door" to better employment or financial situations. But I've also seen a man dismissed from an executive position, whom God desired to preserve from evil done by subordinates. Not all of God's gates are beautiful or easy to accept.

The death of a child, failing crops, physical weakness; all of these, as well as the doors of material and spiritual blessing, must be entered with thanksgiving. If we truly believe that everything that happens or moves is in His control, then we will give thanks to Him in all things that concern us. Then we will bring to Him the fruit of our lips, our praise, which grows from our total trust in Him.

Are there gates that you have entered in life without thanksgiving? God would have you right now to give thanks to Him. In so doing, you will recognize that all His gates are lovely, as they all lead to His presence.

The Good Book

"Then said I, Lo, I come: in the volume of the book it is written of me, I delight to do Thy will, O my God . . ."
            Psalm 40:7,8

Ross Whetstone
Evangelist/Conf. Speaker

God has a diary! And in it are recorded all the thoughts, acts and conversations of people down through the ages who have feared and served Him. This portion of Psalm 40 has long been considered to reflect the desire and confession of Jesus Himself, as the Holy Spirit spoke these verses through David. Yes, God has a volume, written for His own enjoyment, and you're in it!

You see, God really takes pleasure when people serve and speak of Him with praise and thanksgiving. Malachi 3:16 also talks about this book which God likes to look at: "Then they that feared the Lord spoke often to one another: and the Lord heard it, and a book of remembrance was written before Him for them that feared the Lord, and that thought upon His name. 'And they shall be mine,' saith the Lord of hosts, 'in that day when I make up My jewels; and I will spare them, as a man spareth his own son that serveth him.'"

Think of it: every time you share the Lord with another child of God, your words are written down just for Him to read. Every time you think a tender thought about Him, it's recorded forever. Every action of yours that glorifies Him is inscribed in this book.

Think of the glorious passage that was written in this book about Jesus when He walked the earth! What a record of continual praise and love and obedience to the Father! No wonder Jesus deserves to be crowned with many crowns.

And what has been written in this book about you? How much of adoration and loyal service according to the will of God may be left when the wasted moments, the idle words, and the neglected opportunities are subtracted from the record? Pray that the Lord will so order your life and words as to make you a shining jewel in Jesus' crown.

You're A Whosoever

"For God so loved the world, that He gave His only begotton Son, that whosoever believeth in Him should not perish, but have everlasting life."　　　John 3:16

Derek de Cambra
Artistic Dir./Christian Arts, Inc.

It's possible to think you're a Christian, but never know Jesus. And it's possible to remain in that ignorance until you're really shown your need of Him.

Some people say, "There are many brands of Christianity." I had mine: I was a nominal Christian. But that brand somehow didn't meet my need when I faced imminent danger and death in a dark foxhole one night in Korea. While shells and small artillery fire burst all around me, I thought to myself that there must be more to existence then merely living for 21 years and dying like an animal one night far from home in a land whose people spoke a language I couldn't understand.

My grandmother had shared her deep abiding faith with me when I was a small boy. She would always say to me, "Whenever you're in trouble, whenever there are problems in life, you turn to Jesus, you go to Him."

Then she would read to me the words of John 3:16. She'd say, "Jesus came to earth to show us the way, and He died on that cross for our sins. And He rose again so that we can have eternal life, if we just accept that great gift of His sacrifice on the cross."

And while the guns flashed before my eyes, I thought again of that phrase, "That whosoever," meaning you and me, "believeth in Him." It was the hardest thing in the world for me to put my name in place of that "whosoever." But I did it that night in Korea, and Jesus saved me.

And why am I sharing this with you, as part of a devotional guide? Because you, too, may have heard the things of God and been a part of church life since childhood, but have never known Jesus Christ personally. Do you know for certain today that God's "whosoever" includes you? If not, place your name there right now, and make Jesus your own.

Godly Meditation Equals Success

"This book of the law shall not depart out of thy mouth; but thou shalt meditate therein . . . for then thou shalt make thy way prosperous, and shalt have good success."   *Joshua 1:8*

Willard Cantelon
Author

The secret of the success of Joshua, David, and of our Lord Jesus Himself was their deep knowledge of the Word of God. The Lord here promises similar success to every believer who will follow this single verse.

There are two conditions presented in this verse for the receipt of this promise. First, that God's Word should continually be upon our lips. For this reason, since my mother inspired me many years ago to memorize Scripture, I have continued to acquire it little by little. The secret to scripture memorization is not so much in learning large amounts at once, but in consistent learning over a period of time: a verse learned every day will add up to ten chapters in a year.

Whether spoken before learned audiences or lowly, the "It is written" of the Bible is heard as truth and authority. He who has the Word of God on his lips bespeaks the integrity and power behind that Word.

Secondly, we should meditate upon the Word. Meditation brings memorization into living truth in our lives, for in meditating, we chew over the Word, and digest it into part of our being. If God's truths thus become mixed inseparably with your life, you will find it more natural to believe God for great things than to doubt.

To carry truth, authority, power, and living faith with you throughout life is to ensure success. According to Luke 16:17, "it is easier for heaven and earth to pass than one tittle of the law to pass." Build the eternal foundation of the Word of God into your life, and you will become established securely in Him and in all that is His. Begin by committing this scripture to memory, if you've not already, *today*.

The Second Wind

". . . let us run with patience the race that is set before us . . ."   Hebrews 12:1

Earl Paulk, Jr.
Pastor/Author

As a jogging enthusiast, I especially relate to Paul's analogy of the Christian life and a race. Both require daily discipline and both offer great rewards in the present and future.

Jogging requires a proper diet, rest, and daily exercise. To be spiritually healthy I have learned I must feed on a diet of God's word, rest in His love and promises, daily exercise my faith by obeying God's commandments and share my faith with others.

My life's a course to be run and as Paul says, it requires patience. In jogging I have to find my pace and run in it. If I push myself beyond it, I over-expend my energies and become exhausted before the end of the race is in sight. If I run beneath my proper pace, I don't run at my best potential and may lose the race.

As a Christian, learning to run the race set before me has meant finding God's pace for me and staying with that pace. Where the pace I might set for myself would be too fast or slow, God's pace is perfectly suited for me. The more I discover and live by God's pace for me, the more fulfilling I find life to be.

Running the race with patience also requires my learning to be patient with others and realizing the pace God has given them is different from mine. Just as God knows what is best for me, He knows what is best for my brother or sister in Christ.

When I become impatient with the course my life is taking or the direction I see someone else going in, I remember Hebrews 12:2, that Jesus is the "author and finisher of our faith." Whether I am discouraged or tired, Jesus is always my second wind.

Agree In Prayer

"Again I say unto you, that if two of you shall agree on earth as touching any thing that they shall ask, it shall be done for them of My Father which is in heaven."
Matthew 18:19

La Donna Manning
Student

The Lord cares about everything that concerns you, and if you'll let Him, He will help you with everything in your life, no matter how small it may seem. Even a teenage crush.

My mother was a little worried that I was going to find the wrong sort of boyfriend. We live in a small Illinois town, where boys (at least to a 16 year old on the lookout!) seem pretty scarce. So my friends and I tried going to discos and parties to find boys. But being Christians, we weren't really happy with the ones we found.

So I got together with Mommy, and we agreed in prayer that the Lord would send me a Christian boyfriend. Well, he didn't come right away, and I was tempted to think, "Oh, this just isn't working." But my Mom encouraged me to have faith and keep waiting.

Not long after that, an evangelist came to our church and preached. About a month later, I met his son. Wow! Barry and I really love each other and have a lot of fun together.

So now, when my friends come to me and say, "You really have a nice boyfriend," I tell them how he came to me. And you know, while my boyfriend and I were talking, I found out that he had been agreeing with his Dad for a Christian girlfriend. Isn't the Lord good?

The secret is to hold on and believe God. It doesn't make sense, when you think of it, to try to solve all your problems yourself, if you've got a great problem solver like the Lord on your side. If you'll just agree together with someone who loves Him, He'll be glad to do all the doing, if it's in His will (and you'll just have patience)!

In God's Eternal Family

"He that spared not His own Son, but delivered Him up for us all, how shall He not with Him also freely give us all things?" Romans 8:32

LaRissa Manning
Student

This verse became really important to me when I was quite small, only six years old. That was when my mother died, and I wondered who was going to take care of me. I was worried and sad, but soon I knew in my heart that God wanted to give me all the things I needed. That meant a new mother too, so I now have one!

There are a lot of things we wouldn't get so upset about if we just believed this verse. There isn't anything, really, that God gives us because we've earned it. He didn't give us Jesus because we were good enough to deserve Him. In fact, God had to send Jesus because we were sinners. We had to have the gift of Jesus to have eternal life.

I've been here in the United States for three years now. Though I was born in India, my way of speaking is very American, because my adopted family is American. My new mom and dad gave me their name and gave me a part in their family. Everything belongs to me that belongs to everyone else in the family. Even an American accent!

And just like that, God gave me His name and gave me a place in His kingdom and a new life. He's given me a new way of speaking, praising and giving glory to Him.

I believe that everything that's ever going to be good in my life will be a gift from Him. I really feel that there's no use getting down on myself when I feel sad or weak, or even when I get tempted and fall because I can't make anything good happen to me. I have to receive my whole life from His hand, just like birthday presents.

Expect God to give you good gifts today. He loves you. You're His child. He gave you Jesus. Why shouldn't He give you everything else you need, too?

Ears That Hear

"And in that day shall the deaf hear the words of the book . . ."   *Isaiah 29:18*

Tom Showers
Minister to the Deaf

Some people, like those I minister to, are born deaf. Others are, in the words of an old saying, "deaf to that which they don't wish to hear." The above verse has meaning for both kinds of people, because without the revelation of the Holy Spirit, all of us just don't hear the Word of God very clearly. But in "that day," whatever day God chooses to open our ears to what He is saying, His insight trumpets in our understanding and we wonder why we missed it before.

You may, like I have, read a certain scripture hundreds of times and taken for granted that you knew all it was saying. But one day, you glance at it once again, and a word or phrase practically shouts at you. I'll never forget the day I was reading John 20:22 and suddenly got the picture presented there of Jesus *breathing* upon His disciples. What a strange, yet down to earth way of imparting the Holy Spirit to them! How it spoke to me, of Jesus' being in the world, yet not of it, expressing the supernatural through His resurrected, yet still physical, manhood.

It was as if a person hard of hearing had just activated a brand-new hearing aid, and after many years of struggling to make out the conversations around him, could now really participate fully in dialogue once again.

Will this be a day in which God will open your ears to something new in His Word? If you will faithfully read the Bible and pray for God's revelation, God will speak to you. He will turn up the "volume" on your spiritual "receiver," and make you continually able to be enriched by His Word. If you've been spiritually dry, ask God right now to anoint your ears as you search His Word.

Love-In Deed And In Truth

"But if anyone has the world's goods and sees his brother in need, yet closes his heart against him, how does God's love abide in him?"
1 John 3:17 RSV

Julia "Mom" Taylor
Director, "Pass It On" Ministries

My strongest temptation is not to love people—because there're so many to love and the needs are so great. I refuse to yield to this temptation as the Lord quickens my heart with these scriptures and I find myself giving lots of things away.

This ministry really started many years ago when I was a little girl in the Tennessee hills giving away what little we had during those hard depression times. I'd enjoy helping out my young black friends down the street, so giving and sharing on an equal basis is not just theology but is something that's been built into me all my life.

Giving to one another is a part of the gospel that is much neglected in our society. Under the Old Testament Law, God's people were commanded to take care of their own and you know that tradition has so prevailed among the Jews that in Israel today, there are no destitute. How much more as Christians, we ought to supply each others' needs. I don't believe welfare programs are a part of God's plan.

Jesus said, "I only do what I see the Father doing," and He did good and met needs wherever He went. What will you be doing all your life that you saw your folks doing? If you have children, what will they do that they see you doing?

John's answer to that in verse 18 can make you think hard: "My little children, let us not love in word, neither in tongue, but in deed and in truth."

Overcomers!

"Ye are of God, little children and have overcome them: because greater is He that is in you, than he that is in the world."   1 John 4:4

Coy Barker
Pastor/Evangelist

This tells me who I am: I am God's, His child, born again into His possession. That means a lot to me. It helped me when my mother and father died, when I had leukemia and my wife had cancer, to realize that I was God's, even if I was in the middle of all those problems I knew that regardless of what came or went, He would watch over me, and that gave confidence to my heart.

Christian brother or sister, we are overcomers. We're winners, not losers, and all through the Bible, we're told that we're to be the head, not the tail, on top, not on the bottom. When we're shoved or knocked down, we'll get up. Traveling to heaven and living for God can be rough, but we'll overcome because we keep the faith.

We haven't overcome because of abilities or backgrounds, but because of Who is in us. Jesus Christ has actually come and made His abode in us, and He's greater than the devil. In 2 Corinthians 6:16 it says that we have become the temple of God. So God actually dwells, acts, speaks, and moves with every step I take.

So there need be no fear in us, but great courage because we are aware that He lives inside of us. It's Jesus in your life that's dispelled dread, that's given you courage to go forward when everything around you said, "Give up!"

Now, may be a time in your life when things in the natural seem absolutely impossible. Now is the time when you can say to God, "Lord, You're in the middle of this, and You're inside of me, and You're bigger than every problem that's facing me." Believer, say it along with me right now: "I *will* overcome today, because my God is greater!"

The Renewing of Your Mind

" . . . Present your bodies a living sacrifice, holy, acceptable unto God, which is your reasonable service. And be not conformed to this world: but be ye transformed by the renewing of your mind . . ." Romans 12:1-2

Carl Bunch
"Singing Security Guard"

"If a man can only control his thoughts, nothing will be impossible to him." That's what the self-help books and teachers told me. And I really believed it and tried to practice it before meeting Jesus. But still, my life wasn't successful. Because God wasn't in my life, my mind wasn't new, my body wasn't under control, and my old self just couldn't get life together.

Then, for two years after I got saved, my life was still pretty much a mess. I knew that I was on my way to heaven, but I didn't see my mind as really being new or my body as really being acceptable to God. I saw myself as being just the same old wreck with a ticket to glory. When God got me up in heaven, He'd clean me up, but there wasn't too much hope for me the way I was down here. You see, I didn't really know what salvation meant in the *now*.

But this passage of scripture changed my life in God. It was saying, "It's not that you're going to be acceptable to God someday, you're acceptable to Him *now*, just as you are. It's not that you're going to get a new mind some day: you've got a new mind *now* and you've got to start thinking with it, instead of with your old attitudes." Wow! *Re*-newing my mind meant that I had to have a new mind to begin with. Presenting my body to God was giving Him something that He had already accepted because of what Jesus did on Calvary! I just had to keep letting my mind become *more* new, and give my body, so He could make it become even *more* acceptable. Now I'm doing it daily and getting victory.

My friend, if you know Jesus Christ, you don't have to live in the failure and condemnation of the past! You are new and acceptable in God's eyes already! So today, just be that new person. You can do it!

Yea And Amen

"For all the promises of God in Him are yea, and in Him Amen, unto the glory of God by us."
2 Corinthians 1:20

Joe Parkhill
Author and "Honeyologist"

There are hundreds of promises in the Bible, but if you want to get the blessings of them all, there's really only one you have to claim, and this is it! Are you a Christian? Then you're "in Him," in Jesus, and you can take all God's promises for yourself by faith. It's just that simple: take God at His Word, and don't worry about anything, and God will keep all His Word to you.

Jesus said not to worry about yesterday or tomorrow. Did He really mean that? How much time do you spend regretting yesterday and trying to plot out tomorrow? What tomorrow? How do you know you're going to have another five minutes? James learned this from his brother Jesus, and he put it very well in his little letter: "Go to now, ye that say, Today or tomorrow we will go into such a city and continue there a year, and buy and sell, and get gain" (James 4:13). He knew what Jesus knew, that you can't live in what you haven't got!

I believe God wants us to put the whole question of our welfare out of our minds. That's why He's given us all these promises, and then made them yea and amen, positive and final, so we can stop worrying over how we're going to keep alive, and spend the time God gives us bringing life to the rest of the world. I just believe God's going to take care of me no matter what. Some people say I live "devil may care." Well, the devil *may* care, but I *know* God cares. And that's good enough for me.

How about you? I just want you to know right now how much God loves you. He wants to take every worry and care from your mind. Why claim the promises one by one? Just accept this one, relax, and let your loving Father nurture you with all the infinite abundance He's got!

The Gift of Giving

"Give, and it shall be given unto you; good measure. For with the same measure that ye mete withal it shall be measured to you again." Luke 6:38

Joe Bias
Singer/Evangelist

Let me make one thing clear to start with: I don't believe that our receiving from God is dependent upon our giving. God is by His own nature good and loving to us. He takes delight in meeting our needs, and even before we ask Him, He knows "that ye have need of these things"(Matthew 6:32). But he has given us the joy of giving to bless others and ourselves and guarantees that if we become givers, He'll add a rich fullness and abundance to our lives. So why not enter into the giving spirit?

Just today, during my visit to PTL, the Lord exercised His "giving-back guarantee" again in a special way for me. I have had several nice Bibles which I have treasured. Recently I found that, by accident, one of them was left in Paducah, Kentucky, where I was ministering. The other one I gave just the other day to a young man who was staying at a halfway house in Nashville. He needed a Bible, so I was glad to part with it. Well, I no sooner walked into the guests' lounge at PTL just before the show than Phoebe Conway, one of PTL's gracious hostesses, came up to me and gave me a hug and put a beautiful new PTL Club Bible into my hand! "Brother Bias," she said, "I just felt you could use a Bible, so there you are." Now, isn't God good?

You know, that wasn't a really big thing, but it sure blessed me. God could have said, "Oh, he doesn't need a Bible, he'll get that one back from Paducah soon." But God cares about small things, and He's true to His Word. It doesn't matter whether you give a lot or a little, God will get it back to you, and He'll even use people to do it. Is there a need that you know of that you could meet for someone else today? Give what you can to help meet it. Then watch God give it back!

The Path of Light And Life

"Jesus saith unto him, I am the way, the truth, and the life: no man cometh unto the Father, but by me."
John 14:6

Michael Christian
Artist/Cartoonist

A man became hopelessly lost in a swamp of despair. There was no certainty that his next step would not plunge him headlong into the sucking bog. Even if he remained on solid footing, he faced the entrapment of hanging vines or the lurking stillness of alligators lying in wait in the mossy gloom. Florida's Great Dismal Swamp is such a place, though even there, some men have chosen to live their lives.

Such a man chanced upon our unfortunate victim. "My friend," he called out, "I cannot help you, but you can get out if you have enough faith." But the lost man did not dare move from his spot of immediate safety, and the speaker soon disappeared into the darkness.

Then another happened by and cried, "If you have enough love, you will find the path." The wretched victim tried to step in the direction of the voice, but he immediately began to sink, and struggled back to his solid mound.

Several other would-be helpers came and shouted advice and vanished into the heavy mists. Finally, the victim was so tired of all the futile suggestions, that he resolved not to listen to another, but just to await death with as much courage as he could muster.

Then another man approached with a companion. He said quietly, "This man is Jesus Christ; if you follow Him, he will lead you out." Somehow the light in this Companion's eyes inspired confidence. The victim arose, and began to follow.

The covering of leaves above has thinned; the sun is beginning to shine through. The ground is more solid now, the path wider, your footsteps more sure. With every step, you are becoming more sure. Yes, He knew the way; He told the truth, and to live was to be with Him!

The Pitfalls of Zeal

"And he said, I have been very jealous for the Lord God of hosts . . . and I, even I only, am left; and they seek my life, to take it away."
1 Kings 19:10

Dr. Gerald T. Sheppard
Seminary Professor

The story of the prophet Elijah clearly illustrates for us the pitfalls, as well as the glories, of religious zeal. The verse above is part of Elijah's answer to a startling question from God: "Elijah, why are you here?"

Elijah had just been used mightily by God to overthrow the priests of Baal as fire from heaven consumed his drenched offering on Mount Carmel. But here, because the nation of Israel had not returned to the Lord as Elijah had hoped, he fled, hid himself in a cave, and prayed that God would take his life.

Elijah's great zeal for the Lord was wonderful; but he made the mistake of thinking that he was indispensible to the work of God. He had a true vision of what God would someday accomplish in Israel. But when he wasn't able to bring this into being himself, he lapsed into self-pity, imagining himself to be alone and the work of God to be at a standstill.

The Lord informed Elijah later in this chapter that there were thousands of others still faithful to Him in the land. Eventually, another generation passed, and God used another man, Elisha, to finally drive Baalism from Israel.

We ought to be zealous for the things of God, but we must never think that God cannot get His work done without us. Let your zeal be mixed with joy in what *God* is doing through you. And let it be restful as your certainty grows that He *will* bring His word to pass—with or without you. Let it be compassionate, as you reflect upon the tenderness God showed Elijah, and has for you, too, when you falter.

Faith That Works By Love

". . . Our God whom we serve is able to deliver us from the burning fiery furnace . . . But if not, be it known unto thee, O King, that we will not serve thy gods."

Daniel 3:17-18

Rusty Goodman
Singer/Composer

The three Hebrew children about to be thrown into King Nebuchadnezzar's fiery furnace showed an attitude toward their God in this bold statement that went beyond mere belief to holy love. The Apostle Paul's famous "love" chapter 1 Corinthians 13, says that it's possible to have "all faith," enough even to "remove mountains"(vs.2), yet amount to nothing in God's kingdom without His love.

Now, what do I mean? Am I teaching against faith? No, faith is tremendously important: without it, it's "impossible to please God" (Hebrews 11:6). And it's obvious that these three servants of God possessed enough faith to secure a miraculous deliverance from death, as the Biblical account goes on to tell us.

But do you see how strong their love and loyalty to God was? They were able to say that even if God for some reason chose not to deliver them they still would not bow down to the king's image. I believe that God's loving heart desires to know of each believer whether we love Him, not for what He can do for us, but for Himself.

There have been times in my life when I've been "up against the wall." And I knew the Lord could see me through. Yet in His wisdom I've realized that His way of dealing with the problem might not agree with mine. What I might be asking might not be for my good. So I became willing to serve Him even if He didn't work things out my way.

Do you know in your heart how much the Lord really means to you? Would you be willing even in the face of inescapable danger to choose to serve Him? That kind of love would need to be supernaturally given to you, wouldn't it? But our God can supply it. Will you ask Him right now to search and know your heart, and release in you the kind of love that pleases Him?

Availability Over Ability

*"But Jesus beheld them,
and said unto them, With men
this is impossible; but with
God all things are possible."*
Matthew 19:26

Ron Hollings
Heritage School Student

God didn't have a whole lot of raw material to work with when I was born. I was premature, weighing less than three pounds, affected by a borderline case of cerebral palsy. Though the Lord saw fit to preserve the lives of my twin sister and me, for a long time, I didn't see how I could be of any use to Him.

Not being able to walk right, being small and slight, with eyes that didn't work so well, what purpose could God have for my life? All I could think of was the many things I couldn't do.

But when I became a teenager, the Lord "beheld me,"and He said the words above to me. He said, "Yes, with you, it's impossible, but I don't look on the outward appearance. I'm not concerned with your physical body. I'm not worried about what you think you can't do. I don't need your ability, because all of the possibility is in My hands. All I need is for you to become available for My use, and I can do wonders through you."

I said, "Yes, Lord! With me, it's impossible to even walk right, but You will walk through me. With me it's impossible to save anyone, but You're going to use me to lead many to You. With me, it's impossible to heal the sick, but with You, I can lay hands on them, and they'll get well. I can't love of myself, but You can love others through me!"

No matter what you might think your handicaps or limitations are today, Jesus is looking past them right now, straight to your heart. All He wants to know is, are you willing to let Him be everything it's possible for Him to be through you! Pray right now, "Use me, use me Lord! Just as I am, take me and spend me for others today. I'm yours! Amen."

Lift Jesus Higher

"And I, if I be lifted up from the earth, will draw all men unto Me."   John 12:32

Mrs. Elna Smith
Founder of The Great Passion Play

Many years ago, when the Lord spoke to my husband and me about erecting a large statue of Jesus to overlook our town and countryside, we never suspected that He would create a ministry that would draw millions to hear the gospel.

After the statue was in place, standing 70 feet high, with its arms spread 65 feet apart, my husband and I stood gazing up at it. "Honey," he said quietly, "wouldn't it be wonderful if someday we could put on a great play depicting the last week of Jesus' life, for visitors from all over the world to see?" Just then the sculptor, who'd overheard this question, said with surprise, "It's strange that you should say that. I have a friend who has for many years hoped to see that very thing happen in his lifetime!" Thus, the Great Passion Play was born.

God has used the Passion Play, the statue of Jesus, the museum and art gallery to draw thousands of spectators to Christ. Over two million visitors have attended performances of the play. And this beautiful statement of Jesus is always spoken by the actor portraying the Savior, for all to hear.

It may not ever be your part to participate in such a large undertaking on behalf of Jesus. But the Lord expects you to lift up Christ continually in your conversation and life and work. Daily, you need to be sure that He is seen, with His arms of love outstretched, reaching out for lost souls, through your compassion and care for those around you. Pray that you may lift Jesus up and draw souls to Him today.

Crisis Working For Good

"And we know that all things work together for good to them that love God, to them who are the called according to His purpose."Romans 8:28

Jamie Buckingham
Melbourne, Florida

It was a time of deep thanksgiving when the word came down from the Operating Room that the lumps in my wife's breast were benign. Shortly afterwards, my friend, Costa Deir, wrote Jackie a note. In it he gave us all a first class handle on facing crisis. Costa's concept: "Going through—with God—results in our maturing always, though we may not realize it at the time."

Such a word always brings a feeling of gladness to spiritual people. It encourages them to realize God is at work in all events. And when it comes to those people known as "The Called," then we can be confident that all these things work together for good.

Who are "The Called?" Jesus told his disciples, "You did not choose me. I chose you." They were called. Peter told the crowd who gathered at Pentecost that the promise of the Holy Spirit was not only for them and their children, but to "all that are afar off, even as many as the Lord our God shall call" (Acts 2:29). That includes everyone chosen by Jesus to be in the Kingdom.

So, when crisis comes to The Called, it is for a purpose. According to Costa, any difficult situation, especially crisis offers three things: (1) A lesson to be learned (2) A divine purpose to be realized (3) A fresh revelation of God to us.

It sounds like God has good things in store for each of us, no matter how dark the night or intense the crisis.

The Law Of Life

"Behold, I set before you this day a blessing, and a curse." Deuteronomy 11:26

Barry McGuire
Music Artist

This is Moses' charge to the nation of Israel before they entered the Promised Land. The blessing would be theirs if they obeyed God's law; the curse would come upon them if they neglected to obey it.

Outside of Christ and into the drug and rock music scene, Satan had us twisted into thinking the opposite was true. I was convinced that the Judeo-Christian tradition was a "curse" and a shackle to keep me from becoming the "free" spirit of my dreams.

But then I began to see that those people who indeed unshackled themselves from God's laws and became "free" became monsters, like Charlie Manson. When we radically depart from God's moral absolutes, we become sometimes less then human and "cursed" from the rest of society.

The laws of God are like the natural laws of the universe in that if defied, certain consequences are bound to follow. An airplane, for example, not flown according to the known laws of flight, is bound to crash. God's laws are the most intricate, delicate instructions for the operation of the human system ever devised, and if they are followed, a person can function freely, to capacity.

To us as lovers of Jesus, His laws are also like a life-support system, such as the astronauts wore on the moon. From day to day, we live in an anti-life environment of hate and lust and greed. God's law, as it's written on our hearts, is our protection from the soul-death being dealt around us. Learn to appreciate God's law, and meditate upon it. It'll become freedom as you live it from your heart.

Adorned With His Gifts

"And Isaac went out to meditate in the field at the eventide; and he lifted up his eyes, and saw . . ."
Genesis 24:63

Maynard Ketcham
Missionary

This lovely scene falls near the end of the touching account in scripture of God's provision of Rebekah as the suitable bride for Isaac. As you probably remember, Isaac's father, Abraham, sent his eldest servant, bearing rich gifts, back to his country and kindred in search of the wife of God's choice. You remember that the Lord led the servant to Rebekah, who was willing to tend to the thirsty camels and to return to her waiting groom, sight unseen.

A clear allegory can be seen here, with Abraham representing a type of God, the Father; sending the servant of God, the Holy Spirit; to prepare Rebekah, a type of the Church; the Bride of Christ, to meet Isaac, or Jesus Himself. As Rebekah had proven herself a worthy choice to be Isaac's bride, so Christ's Bride will be worthy to meet Him, "without spot or wrinkle or any such thing."

As Isaac in our text looked up and saw Rebekah coming, I like to think that he was able to recognize her because she was wearing the gifts that Abraham had sent for her. Someday, Christ will be looking over the battlements of Heaven, waiting for His Bride to come. How will He recognize us? We will be wearing His gifts of righteousness, holiness, purity, compassion, tenderness and love.

Isaac gladly took Rebekah to himself as his wife, and they became the mother and father of many nations. As you and I allow the Holy Spirit to adorn us with His precious gifts, we will be fruitful; Jesus will recognize us; and we will spend a glad eternity with Him.

God Wants To Use You

"And Moses said unto God, Who am I, that I should go unto Pharoah . . . ? And He said, Certainly I will be with thee." Exodus 3:11-12

Gladys Ketcham
Missionary

In the service of God, it doesn't matter who you are. It didn't matter to God when He called Moses, and it doesn't matter now, as long as you are willing to serve Him.

God didn't really answer Moses' question directly, did He? But think of all the answers He might have given: "Why, Moses, I've prepared you for 40 years for this job, you're just the right man!" Or: "Moses, you were raised by Pharoah's daughter—you'll have an enclave right to Pharoah's heart." Or perhaps: "You've been taught all the wisdom and learning of the Egyptians—who could be better qualified for this task?"

No! God didn't tell Moses how great or qualified He was: He told Moses that He, the Lord God, the Great I Am would be with Him. For this is the only truly important thing—that God, with all His power, and wisdom, be with a believer in any endeavor.

All God needs is an empty vessel through whom He can work. You may be rich or poor, big or small, old or young, shy or outgoing, an orator or a stutterer: God can use whatever you are.

Oh, so you don't think you're a suitable vessel? Well, everyone may praise the lovely platter a tasty dish is served on, but the pretty platter didn't make the tasty dish. That trusty old frying pan back in the kitchen performed that service. Heaven will be full of surprises, I think. There, the truly important vessels will receive their praise.

No. Moses was nothing, and you are nothing. But God Who is with you is everything. If you, like Moses, ask Him, *"Who* am I?" He will give you the same answer. Why not answer Him instead: *"Here* am I—send me!"

Poured Out Wine

"... Emptied from ves-
sel to vessel ..."
Jeremiah 48:11

Robert Gass
Pastor/Evangelist

The land of Moab, to whom this oracle was addressed, was a country where winemakers lived. Rich vineyards grew there, and the Moabites well understood the term "emptied from vessel to vessel." This referred to a process in winemaking that began to take place after the grapes had been crushed under the women's feet in a vat until the sticks, seeds, and sediment settled to the bottom and the grape juice could be poured off into another vessel, leaving the impurities behind. After remaining in this vessel for some time, the juice was transferred into a different vessel, then another, and another, each time leaving behind other impurities. Ultimately, after having been poured from vessel to vessel, the wine was ready to be poured into a glass for the king's table.

The Christian life is also a process of being poured by God from experience to experience. Each time God changes your "vessel," you leave behind in the last one all the things God was trying to remove from your life. Whether these experiences involve being misunderstood, having our lives made "open books" before others, enduring dark trials, or having to follow strange guidance from God, it is He who is continually perfecting you in whatever "vessel" contains you.

You cannot change yourself, so God needs to prepare unique vessels to mature you. But He will never allow you to stay in that vessel longer than the purpose it is designed to serve. Some of us can become comfortable in any circumstance, so God brings into our lives the brokenness that makes us easy to "pour" and launches us out for the next stage. God's ultimate goal is to bring us from glory to glory, from the vineyard to the King's table, forever to be enjoyed by Him.

Old And New

"Thereford if any man be in Christ, he is a new creature: old things are passed away; behold, all things are become new."   *2 Corinthians 5:17*

Pat Terry
Vocalist

Eight years ago when I met Jesus Christ, my life was completely turned around. I suddenly didn't want to do things I had always done, and I found myself wanting to do things that had never appealed to me.

I went from doing the "in" things and doing without peace in myself, to doing things that I had always defined as "out-of-it" and getting the joy I had never found doing the "in" things.

In these eight years I've had some real struggles that have sometimes made me doubt I was getting any help or support for believing in God as my source of strength. At times I have looked at myself and said, "Just who do I think I am saying I'm born-again. I'm still a mess. Look at this sin area and this one." I've pulled an imaginary blanket of unworthiness and self-disgust around me and soon found myself smothering in self-condemnation.

Then I remember 2 Corinthians 5:17, "if any man be in Christ, he is a new creature." Looking back I can see the reality of how Jesus has changed me to become more and more the person He wants me to be and who I like being.

Year by year I can see how the Holy Spirit is working in me to make me more like Jesus. It amazes me to realize how many "old things" like bad habits, attitudes, and weaknesses have actually died in me and I am a new person with new beginnings happening every day in my life.

Today, thank Jesus for how He's made you a "new creature."

Discover God In Your Trials

"When thou passest through the waters, I will be with thee . . . when thou walkest through the fire, thou shalt not be burned; neither shall the flame kindle upon thee." Isaiah 43:2

Judge Helen D. Dodge
Evangelist

Before I went to Russia in 1976, bringing Bibles and tracts with me to give secretly to people while I was there, the Lord gave me this verse. Because I had it in my heart, I experienced no fear when a companion and I were arrested at the Russian border for smuggling Bibles. God was with us at every moment.

I had tried to make my passport and papers completely clean of the title of "Judge," but the Lord knew better. The authorities there were having some trouble deciding our fate. The penalty for smuggling Bibles was 15 years in prison. But we were also accused of possessing rubles, and the penalty for that was death. Somewhere in two little folded up papers were two newspaper articles with my name and picture that identified me as a retired federal judge. The border officials couldn't decide what to do, so they called Moscow. And Moscow said, "She's a retired federal judge from the United States? Give them their bus ticket and luggage and set them free. Better get them out of the country rather than create an international incident!" So we were sent on our way. I had 400 tracts on my person and Bibles strapped to my legs. Later I heard that these ended up in the Christian underground in Lapland.

When you're facing death or great personal danger, the assurance of God's presence alone is strong enough to bring you peace. All kinds of questions can occur to you at such moments: what did I do wrong to get me into this mess? Is this the end for me? Lord, are you going to bring me out of it? At times like these, to know in your heart that He is with you is answer enough. Remember in your waters and rivers and fires that He will always be there with His peace.

Give Him Time

"And it came to pass, in process of time, that the king of Eqypt died . . ."

Exodus 2:23

Ralph Wilkerson
Pastor, Melodyland Christian Center

God can heal any of the problems you face, if you'll just give Him time. God's got all the time in the world. We're creatures of eternity and realizing that can teach us a lot about patience.

In one of my first churches, I had preached that certain things would take place, and that God would vindicate my ministry, and He didn't. I couldn't understand that and was confused. But God impressed upon me that I was wanting the problem solved in my time frame rather than His. In every area of Christian living, we need to learn about God's timing.

It may be that God has promised you something or given you a vision, or planted a word in your heart and that thing just hasn't seemed to come to pass. It may be that there's a problem you've prayed and prayed about, but the answer hasn't come. The temptation to get discouraged can easily overtake you.

But this verse tells you that when the time is right, God will work out the problem. You see, I hadn't realized that God had planned in the course of time to move some people out of that church, move others in, and lift my vision to a higher plane. When the church and I caught onto God's timing, He accomplished a work there that was better than anything I had foreseen.

Get a hold of God's eternal point of view. Just give Him time, and He will move your Pharoah out of the way, too.

God Is Still The Great Creator

". . . And the Spirit of God moved upon the face of the waters."   *Genesis 1:2*

Dan Betzer
Host of "Revivaltime"

God is still today creating things out of nothing, just as He did at the beginning of time. Just as the Spirit of God brooded over the waters at Creation, He is brooding over the hearts of men, waiting to create in them what is needed to do His will.

The Lord demands a great deal of us as Christians. Many of us shrink back from God's will in our lives because as we face it, we just don't feel adequate. When I was first asked to follow the beloved Dr. C. M. Ward as host of "Revivaltime," my inadequacies all came to stare me in the face. Who could possibly take the place of such a mighty and talented man of God? For awhile, I could think of little else but how little I had to offer.

But God showed me that He had not called me to this work because I had all the ability needed for it already. He had called me in order to create in me the things that would make me able to do it.

God has not called you to follow Jesus because you are anything special in yourself. "But God hath chosen the foolish things of the world to confound the wise . . . the weak . . . the mighty . . . and things which *are not* to bring to nought things that are" (1 Corinthians 1:27-28). How can God do this? Because He Himself, by the same power with which He made the world, can create in you the ability to be useful to Him.

Yes, you can do "all things" through Christ. Ask the Lord right now to reach down into your lacks and to create ability. Enter into the day ahead of you confident that He will make you sufficient for all its requirements.

Angels

"The angel of the Lord encampeth round about them that fear him, and delivereth them."   *Psalm 34:7*

Carl Richardson
Radio/TV Director

Often in exchanging details of a close brush with death or some precarious situation, I've had people say to me, "Your guardian angel must be looking out for you." I'd accept their comment in passing until one day I discovered Psalm 34:7.

This verse sparked my interest in the ministry of angels to the believer. In studying the Bible I found accounts of angels delivering messages, fighting battles, guiding God's people out of danger and carrying out God's orders on behalf of His people. I have also interviewed people who have had encounters with angels and have myself recognized God's assistance through the intervention of angels.

There is so much preoccupation today with the spiritual world of demons and the occult. I believe Christians should be just as outspoken about God's angels. I want the news to get around that angels are real and minister at the command of God to instruct, warn, encourage, bless, protect God's people and execute His judgment.

In studying about angels I have learned the importance of knowing and speaking God's word. Psalm 103:20 says God's angels, ". . . do His commandments, hearkening unto the voice of His word." This means His angels listen and respond to the spoken word of God.

I love the descriptions of angels given in the Book of Revelation. Their beauty and power are more than I can ever comprehend. Yet, as a child of God, I believe in them and praise the Lord for their protective care.

Seeing Beyond

". . . whatsoever things are true . . . honest . . . just . . . pure . . . lovely . . . of good report; if there be any virtue, and if there be any praise, think on these things."
Philippians 4:8

Rhonda Stegall
Singer

If the words of our lips can be snares to our souls (Proverbs 18:7), then our thoughts are the bait our lips consume. This is why it's so important to learn to direct our thoughts towards the things that are pleasing to God: for as a man "thinketh in his heart, so is he" (Proverbs 23:7).

When our minds are not focussed in the right direction, we tend to see only the problems in our lives and not what God is doing to solve them. Once I had been praying for a certain young man to receive the Lord. After sharing the things of salvation with him several times, I almost became discouraged, because he just seemed like a stone wall. The only response he gave was to ridicule and belittle me. But I finally said to the Lord, "All right, Lord, I'm just not going to look at all the negativity anymore. Instead, I'm going to keep on believing you for a miracle."

So after starting to ignore his taunting replies, I began to see how the Lord was working with him. He was putting up such a fight because he was under a deep burden of conviction! And the more I started praising the Lord, the more I could see this boy's salvation coming to pass. Soon the rest of his resistance let down, and he was able to receive Jesus.

You see, God wants our attention directed towards praiseworthy and virtuous things: in other words, the things He is working for His glory. The enemy may try to convince you today that he has the victory in hand. But keep your eyes on what God can bring about in the situation, and He will bring that bright new picture into view!

Unashamed

*"For I am not ashamed of
the gospel of Christ: for it is
the power of God unto salvation to every one that believeth . . ."*   Romans 1:16

Jack Mitchell
Pastor

As a young man when I accepted Jesus Christ and His call on my life
to be a minister of the gospel, I was met with great opposition by
members of my family. They could not understand my desire to spend
my life serving God.

They tried to discourage me from entering the ministry, but the
new-found reality of joy, peace and love that Jesus brought into my life
was stronger than all their arguments and persuasions. God's grace had
saved me and I had to tell everyone I could that His grace was available
for them, too.

Romans 1:16 describes how I believe Christians should feel about
sharing the gospel. Remembering my own salvation, it took someone
willing to share Christ with me, for me, to know of God's love and how
to receive it. When I accepted Christ, I was not ashamed of the gospel. I
needed the good news of salvation for the forgiveness of my sins and
power of the Holy Spirit to make me a new person.

If I do not share and live out the gospel in sight of others, there is a
possibility they may never discover God's love for themselves. In my
many years of ministry, I've seen so many people like I was, who are
hurting and lost with no hope, peace or love in their lives. I want them
to know God offers all three through faith in Jesus Christ.

Romans 10:17 says faith comes "by hearing, and hearing by the
word of God." I know that in sharing the gospel, my faith is
strengthened as well as the faith of those with whom I share.

Share the good news of the gospel so others can find Jesus!

Christ In You

"I can do all things through Christ which strengtheneth me."
Philippians 4:13

Jerry B. Walker
Evangelist

As a believer in Jesus Christ, I am part of Him, and all that He is doing. And being part of Him, there's nothing that I can't accomplish this day. Jesus has mixed His life so thoroughly with mine, that I've been made a partaker of His "divine nature" (2 Peter 1:4). Thus, I'm capable of anything Jesus could do while He was on earth, and "greater works than these" (John 14:12), since He went to heaven and His Father sent the Holy Spirit to empower me.

The popularity of the "Bionic Man" and "Bionic Woman" television shows today is interesting. In these adventure series, many of the natural parts of the bodies of the hero and heroine are replaced by mechanical parts that render them capable of remarkable feats of strength and agility. They can knock down walls with the swing of a fist and rip the doors of safes off their hinges. Though their bodies look normal on the outside, inside, they're an incredibly complex blend of flesh and blood and electronic circuitry. Could it be that these space-age fantasies are merely reaching out for a weak shadow of the divine empowerment God has offered to His children, if they'll just let Jesus be Lord in them?

Christ's strength in us means that we no longer have to worry about today's problems or the future's. We can do anything through Him. For instead of the power of steel and wires, we have the Almighty power of God Himself available within us. Just the knowledge of this should begin to produce faith that will move us out of defeat and into victory.

In whatever challenges confront you today, Jesus in you is your strength and your Partner, and all the help you need to meet life face forward with confidence. Flex your "muscles" and move out in Him.

Wheel And Deal Or Delight?

"Delight thyself also in the Lord; and He shall give thee the desires of thine heart."   Psalm 37:4

Chico Holiday
Singer

If all the desires of your heart are being fulfilled today, you must be placing Jesus first in your life; but if your life seems somehow to be unsatisfying to you, it may be that you have let your desires crowd Him out of first place.

Perhaps you've said to God, "I think I've put you first in my life: why aren't all those good things happening to me that you promised?" Brother or sister, maybe in a subtle way those things when they're all totalled up, come to more than Jesus is in your life. Let me explain how this can happen.

If you make a list of the things that are important to you, I trust that if you're a Christian, Jesus will be at the top. But if you go down the list, by the time the seconds, thirds, fourths and fifths are added up, they may outweigh Jesus' place in your day-to-day thoughts. All told, there may even be more desires on the list than Jesus wants!

It's only when Jesus becomes all and everything to you that all of your desires will be fulfilled; because until He has first place in your heart, your desires won't be perfectly in tune with His. When He's in first place, the Holy Spirit will give you the wishes He wants and truly, every one of them will be granted.

Friend, I had to learn this the hard way. For two years after I was saved, I wheeled and dealed with God and men, trying to make good things happen in my life. When I finally got too tired to scheme anymore and let Jesus take first place and put His desires into my heart, I came to know real satisfaction. That's why I know that if you do the same, you'll find fulfillment, too.

Prayer Unlimited

"The centurion answered and said, Lord, I am not worthy that thou shouldest come under my roof: but speak the word only, and my servant shall be healed."
Matthew 8:8

Sister Briege McKenna
Nun

How pleased Jesus was with this centurion's demonstration of faith! Jesus would have been glad to go personally to the place where the sick servant lay. But His presence there was unnecessary because the centurion understood something about God of which we all need to be reminded: that God's ability to do His work is not constrained by our limitations in time and space. The power of prayer is unbounded.

Just recently, I was participating in a very important gathering when a call came requesting prayer for a priest who was in a nearby hospital dying of cancer. Since I am recognized as having a healing ministry, several people there assumed that I would have to leave. Not feeling led to leave then, I joined the group in prayer. At that moment, the Lord spoke to a priest there and said, "I don't need Sister Briege at the hospital; but I need all of you to be aware that *I'm* there." About six months later, we learned that the priest was totally healed.

The Lord desires that we reach out with this level of faith, beyond the presence of men (even those we revere as ministers) to the Source of healing and power, Himself. With this understanding, I have prayer for the healing of many by telephone, some as far away as Australia, India and other distant parts of the Earth.

You need never fear that your prayers are limited: Jesus is always present with you, and His power is available to move at all times and in all places. Release your faith to Him, and His compassion will reach beyond the miles and hours to heal and deliver just as it did with the centurion.

Trust God's Word Now

"My son, attend to my words; incline thine ear unto my sayings . . . For they are life unto those that find them, and health to all their flesh."
Proverbs 4:20-22

Keith Johnson
Pastor

In this day and hour, more and more people are realizing the importance and integrity of the Word of God. I believe we're seeing such great growth in Christianity today because believers are giving the Word of God its rightful place in their lives.

As a minister, I emphasize reading the Word of God, and getting established in it. The Bible isn't just a book of good advice. This verse tells us that it is literally life to those who are rooted in it, and physical health to the whole of their bodies.

You can build upon the Word of God so that when the storms and tests of life come, you'll stand. Now, if you do take a strong stand on God's Word, the enemy may bring all kinds of thoughts of failure to your mind. But you can stand steadfast and win the victory.

The enemy once tried to afflict our daughter Amy with appendicitis. We felt led to hold onto the promises of God for her healing. It was a real struggle for two days, but as the Lord gave us grace to stand, the manifestation came. The power of God literally filled our house and administered divine healing to Amy's body. She was perfectly whole.

God didn't do that just because I'm a minister. And it wasn't because we had special favor with Him that day. The Word of God says that we all have favor with Him every day, and if you're a believer, this means you. If you will make a firm decision to stand on the Word of God, it will never fail you or let you down. If you can trust Him at all, why not trust Him right now with everything you've got? Let God's Word be more than just words to you; stand on it and let it be life and health, too.

Let's All Be One

"That they all may be one; as Thou, Father, art in Me, and I in Thee, that they also may be one in Us."
John 17:21

Dr. Karl D. Coke
Pastor/Teacher

Perhaps this ought to be called the Lord's Prayer rather than the one we usually say. The prayer we've given that name was given to us by Jesus for our use; the prayer above was prayed by Jesus Himself. It shows the intense desire of the Lord for all Christians to be one. This was the prayer of His heart, just before He began His sufferings.

God has given me a great burden for the unity of the Body of Christ. I'm not against denominations, I think strength can come from our differences, provided that we all unify around the common denominator: the Lord Jesus Christ and His wishes. But we need to see an end to "denominationalism" in the sense of our fighting and opposing one another. We can all learn from our different emphases on the message of the gospel, but they should never keep us from fellowshipping with Jesus and one another.

The apostle Paul used the illustration of the human body and its many parts to illustrate the many different kinds of believers who make up the bride of Christ. And I believe that even today, every church can be a New Testament church. This doesn't mean that they have to drop all their distinctive procedures and programs, just that they shouldn't get locked into them. The important thing is that the people needs of the congregation be kept foremost in mind, and every part of worship and doctrine be examined in the light of New Testament principles. If that's kept first in mind, we don't shut each other out.

So whether you're from an old line denomination or a new charismatic fellowship, don't shut everyone else out of heaven! Let the Lord's prayer be your prayer also, and let it be followed by reaching out and touching people of God of every denominational persuasion.

The Real Life

"Jesus said unto her, I am the resurrection, and the life: he that believeth in Me, though he were dead, yet shall he live." John 11:25

Bill Baird
Race Drivers' Chaplain

Men keep busy with all kinds of things to ward off their fear of death. Money, fame, sex, possessions, and occupational pursuits can fill up their lives and give a sense of warding off the inevitable. But none of these things can create additional life or make a person's span of time on earth really worth living.

In this verse, Jesus gives us the reason for this: that Jesus Himself is eternal life. We can say, "My life is this way or that way." But we're only fooling ourselves to think that out life is our own. Whether we know it or not, we belong to somebody. And if it's not Jesus, what we really have is a living death. If we have Jesus, we have real life.

My ministry is to race car drivers, men who often face the prospect of quick and violent death. They can be driving along and find life slipping away in an instant of ripping metal and searing gasoline flames. Most of us don't think about life getting cut short like that. But every day, age creeps up on us. Every time we feel sickness, we sense our mortality. And the thought of unforeseen personal tragedy can haunt the happiest life.

That's why knowing Jesus personally is the greatest assurance we can have. To have laid hold on Christ is to have life secured forever. To have Christ is to see death as just a stepping stone to a much greater future than we can imagine. Do you have that eternal life in Jesus? Then let your life today be richer with the peace of His presence.

Chosen To Bear Fruit

"Ye have not chose Me, but I have chosen you, and ordained you, that ye should go and bring forth fruit, and that your fruit should remain . . ."　　John 15:16

Keith L. Winrich
Evangelist

Aren't you glad that Jesus chose you? I surely am, and I like what He chose me for, too: that I might produce fruit, the kind that remains. But I almost didn't "remain" long enough after Jesus saved me to bear any fruit at all! Right after receiving the Baptism in the Holy Spirit at 14 years of age, I was run over by a combine while working in my father's field.

God spared me from immediate death by keeping the machine from running over my head or heart. But a doctor told my parents that I'd never live to reach the hospital. Eleven more told them when I got there that I couldn't live the night. My injuries included a paralyzed arm, broken ribs, a punctured lung, a broken collar bone, and complications because of the lung that were causing a massive infection sapping my life by the minute. Our Spirit-filled church joined in prayer.

The lung was scheduled to be removed, but on the appointed morning, the specialist decided to take one more x-ray. A few minutes later, the doctor leaped into the room with the x-rays shouting, "You have a brand new lung in your body!" There was no trace of infection, no holes in the lung, and the bones had been perfectly knit together. Ten days after the accident, I was home, and five days after that, God healed the paralyzed arm while I slept. Three days later, I knew that God was calling me to the ministry.

What God chose and ordained me for, I'm now doing, preaching the gospel and helping churches raise funds. Now, you may not know how much God's choosing you has spared you from. You may have a lot to thank Him for in avoided accidents and enjoying good health. But the purpose for His choosing you is not just for you to give thanks for your salvation. It's to bear fruit. Have you started sprouting yet?

Stone Into Flesh

"A new heart also will I give you, and a new spirit will I put within you: and I will take away the stony heart out of your flesh, and I will give you a heart of flesh."
Ezekiel 36:26

Judge Kermit Bradford
Jurist

Soon after my conversion and Baptism in the Holy Spirit, I became aware that for all my love for God and desire to serve Him, I was lacking somehow in the great self-sacrificial love for others that Jesus had so completely demonstrated. It wasn't that I didn't strive to meet the needs of others, but I always kept my own interests foremost in my mind.

Then the Lord began to show me that there was an even more excellent way (as Paul puts it in 1 Corinthians 12:31) to walk with God than even in the exercise of the gifts of the Spirit. These were much to be desired, but not as meaningful as walking in the holy love of God and learning in all things to put others first, expecting nothing in return. I began to cry out to God to help me find that way, as it was obviously impossible for me to attain it in my own strength. I asked God to show me where the resistance lay in myself, and He led me to the verse above.

He showed me that even though I had Christ dwelling in me and the Holy Spirit baptism, when it came to expressing God's all-giving love, I still had a stony heart that got in the way and needed to be dealt with. God wanted me to ask Him to remove that old heart and replace it with His heart of love. As an act of faith, I claimed this promise and soon felt a supernatural infusion of that love that now began to flow as I extended myself towards others. Finally, I was free to love as Jesus loved.

Have you ever felt distressed, as I was, with your inability to love others as Jesus commanded you to: as He loved, without reservation or self interest? You needn't be—your discouragement comes from trying to love with your love, which is imperfect. Ask Jesus to get your stony heart out of the way and share with you his own tender, giving heart, whose love is without measure.

Your New Last Name

*"I have even called thee
by thy name: I have surnamed
thee . . ."*   Isaiah 45:4

John McPhee
Minister

Born a McPhee in Scotland I grew up under social scorn because of my last name. Being a McPhee labeled me a descendent of tinkers, workers of tin, which in Scotland is considered the lowest of occupations.

Gypsies are also considered undesirables, and I was of a family of gypsy tinkers. This made the social prejudices even greater against me as I grew up. Over the years I felt trapped by my heritage, branded by my name and of little worth to the world or God or even to myself.

I met the Lord Jesus when I was twenty-two and knew myself to be beloved of Him and a child of God, but I still resented my last name for all the rejection and hatred that was directed at me because of it.

One day in a fit of complaining and self-pity, my wife and I prayed for the Lord to remove my bitterness and show me why I was born a McPhee. The Holy Spirit led us to read in Isaiah 45 and there the Lord says, "I have even called thee by thy name: I have surnamed thee."

This verse showed me that God had arranged for me to be born a McPhee. I can now value myself and my family in the eyes of God. As a pastor I have a greater ability to counsel with others who have suffered society's scorn. I share with them God's answer to their feelings of inferiority, bitterness, or self-pity.

Jesus says in John 15:16 "I have chosen you, and ordained you." You *are* God's special child. Believe and enjoy His love.

Serving Vs. Striving

"But they that wait upon the Lord shall renew their strength; they shall mount up with wings as eagles; they shall run, and not be weary; they shall walk, and not faint."   Isaiah 20:31

Bud Zimmerman
Psychologist/Educator

This verse contains such an attractive promise. We'd all like to soar high enough above our problems to see them clearly, to have the strength to run our assigned course in life, to gain the attitude necessary to walk in God without discouragement. But a lot of us fail to reach this level of life because we are seeking to get there without waiting on God.

Try as we might, we cannot come to the renewal of spirit that leads to this victorious plane until we give up striving to get there and learn to stand still so God can tell us what He wants us to do.

In these modern days we live in, we've forgotten the meaning of the Old Testament concept of personal service. To serve, or wait, upon a king meant to stand in his presence and attend to his wishes. A servant was committed to remaining in his place before the king until the king gave him orders to act upon. After the servant had been commanded, he moved with diligence to fulfill his master's wish.

Just so, we need to see ourselves as in the presence of a mighty King, whose proper place is to rule and reign over our hearts and lives. We need to understand that He is our leader; we are not His.

King Jesus knows exactly the place you hold in His court. He knows your needs, your fears, and the way you should go. He has chosen you for His personal service. Wait upon Him, and in the design He has for your life, you will find the vision, the strength, and the zeal you long for. "Be still," and you'll know.

Bearing And Caring

". . . for he hath said, I will never leave thee nor forsake thee. So that we may boldly say, The Lord is my helper, and I will not fear what man shall do unto me."
Hebrews 13:5-6

Murray McLees
Pastor

The Lord once gave me a dream of a beach stretching out toward the ocean, with jutting rocks and rolling sand dunes touching the surf and footprints embedded into the distance. He led me to know that this beach represented my life, with all its obstacles, storms, highs and lows, and that the footprints were mine and His as we walked side by side.

The Lord showed me, from a vantage point high above, all of my life's highlights in a moment. As my life lay below me, I noticed a very curious thing: that at the low points and in the difficult places, there was only one set of footprints on the sand. I asked the Lord, "Why is this? I thought you promised never to leave me nor forsake me." Jesus tenderly answered, "Murray, I never left you: those places where you see only one set of footprints were the places where I picked you up and carried you!"

At trying times in your life, God's presence may not always be obvious to you. Especially in times of persecution or suffering. The intensity of the immediate experience may hide your consciousness of God's presence. But the wonderful message of this promise is that He is still bearing and caring for you, even when you seem to be struggling all alone.

Learn to acknowledge His presence, even when you don't feel it. When you are able to say boldly the truth, that the Lord *is* present, you will find your fear and loneliness crumbling in the circle of His everlasting arms.

God Cares About Vitamins

> *"Let Him have all your worries and cares, for He is always thinking about you and watching everything that concerns you."*
> *1 Peter 5:7 (LB)*

Lillie Knauls
Singer/Disc Jockey

Do you let the Lord have *all* your worries and cares? I mean even the ones that don't bother you much, that you don't think to trouble Him with? It might surprise you to discover that God would like to take those off your back, too! He's just so good that, if you will let Him, He'll relieve you of *all* your worries and cares.

Once while on a three week singing tour, I ran out of my supply of Vitamin C. If there's one thing a singer tries to avoid, it's catching a cold, and research has shown that regular doses of that vitamin can help prevent colds. So I asked the pastor at the church where I was ministering if he had a representative of my favorite vitamin dealer in his congregation.

He said that he did and made a quick phone call. She came to the church carrying what I needed, with happy tears in her eyes. She explained that when she went to pick up her last order, the Lord told her to get an extra bottle of Vitamin C. This had puzzled her, because she didn't really need it. Now she knew that God had anticipated my visit and my need.

Wasn't that nice of the Lord? Before I even left home in California, God had opened the way for me to get those vitamins in Memphis, Tennessee! So you see, God's answer doesn't always have to be something super-spiritual. No matter what it is, if it concerns us, it concerns Him.

Why don't you start today to give God some of those pesky little worries and cares that you've been toting around? He wants you to stop fretting about them and let Him start settling them right now!

Love And Suffering

"Jesus answered, 'Neither hath this man sinned, nor his parents: but that the works of God should be made manifest in him."
John 9:3

Ralph Showers
Minister/Author

This verse is part of the familiar Bible account of Jesus healing the man born blind. Jesus is answering here the question asked by His disciples about the possible cause of the man's blindness: "Did this man sin, or his parents, that he was born blind?"

As a minister to the handicapped, this passage has special meaning for me. First, it says that with God it doesn't matter if you can't hear or see well, if you can't run and jump, or even if you can't think as quickly as most people. God loves each person He's created, and each person has value and meaning. Each person has a distinct purpose and calling in life to fulfill. You may consider your limitations as obstacles to your being useful in the service of God, but Jesus here declares that God has works which can be done through you if you will give yourself to Him, just as you are.

Second, there's a loving rebuke in Jesus' words. You may be among those who consider themselves without handicap or limitation. Jesus reminds you not to be judgmental about the apparent flaws of others. It is a mistake to assume that every misfortune that befalls certain individuals is a result of sin on the part of that person or someone close to him. God's ultimate purpose in any man's life ought not to be the subject of our scrutiny: "His ways are past finding out."

Approach others' suffering and your own with love, compassion, and reassurance as Jesus did. Don't dwell on the misfortune or its cause. Be encouraged to look to Jesus for the revelation of His purposes, His glory, His loving and healing touch in the situation.

Preparing For His Coming

"Therefore, my beloved brethren, be ye steadfast, unmovable, always abounding in the work of the Lord, Forasmuch as ye know that your labor is not in vain in the Lord." 1 Corinthians 15:58

Earl E. Williams
Bible Teacher

Let's try to look at doing the Lord's work the way a farmer views running his farm. He can't expect to get a crop in the summertime or fall unless he does certain things beforehand. He must ready the soil, plant the grain, and see to it that it's taken care of. In some places, that requires irrigation, or even, as in the Orient, flooding.

Time goes on, and then the harvest day comes. In the work of God, just as in farming, we can look expectantly for that harvest day if we've been faithful. We don't get paid for our faithfulness day by day. But if we've been weeding and watering, pruning and fertilizing, we'll have every right to expect abundant fruit.

We must always keep our relationship to God in perspective: He is the owner of the farm, the Lord of the harvest. He loves us, but we are His servants. As such, we need to work steadily, punctually, and responsibly. And even if it seems we're plowing a boulder-filled field, work, without complaining, is the joy of the Lord.

Abounding in the Lord's work, I liken to being a full sponge. Now, if you put a sponge in your hand when it's dry, it's hard, rough, and not very useful. But when you put that same sponge into a pail of water, it fills up, and there's no way you can touch it without getting water on yourself. We as believers in Jesus can be so saturated by Him, filled with the Holy Spirit, that when people touch us or talk with us, Jesus Christ exudes out of us and changes lives. In that condition, we're very useful, dripping with Jesus in God's hands!

So get out into those fields, and get drenched with the Holy Spirit. There are barrels full of harvest up ahead!

Freedom From Fear

"For God had not given us the spirit of fear; but of power, and of love, and of a sound mind." 2 Timothy 1:7

Morris Sheats
Pastor/Author

There are some fears that are pretty wise to have! It's best to be afraid of standing in front of a moving truck, for example. But abnormal fear of the unknown, or an undefined anxiety that constantly follows a person through life, is not given by God or pleasing to Him.

Usually this type of clinging fear is the result of too much preoccupation with past failures in life or future uncertainties. Jesus, knowing this, has given us some very practical advice in telling us that "Sufficient unto the day is the evil thereof" (Matthew 6:34). I loosely translate this to mean, "There are enough problems for one day at a time—don't borrow more for yesterday or tomorrow!"

The way to get free of fear is through the power that comes from meditating on the Word of God. By this I mean, thinking about, digesting, absorbing from the conscious mind into the inner spirit, the promises, qualities, acts, and commands of God as revealed in His word. The medicine of God's Word, as we are saturated with it, is the sure antidote to every kind of fear known to men. When fear is conquered, peace in the spirit results. Then, without the crippling of fear, we receive *power*: explosive, concentrated strength for daily needs. We experience *love*, the Bible kind that expects nothing in return. This can happen because our attention is no longer crowded with dread over our past or future. Lastly, our minds are cleared of fear, so we can make sound, reasonable decisions about life and how to live it.

Today, you need to begin replacing those nagging anxieties with the assurances of God's Word. If you've been neglecting your reading of the Word, re-establish the practice. Learn, meditate, and grow!

By God's Spirit

". . . Not by might, nor by power, but by My Spirit, saith the Lord of hosts."
Zechariah 4:6

Bertha Holt
Director
Holt Adoption Program

Aren't there times in your life when you start doing something for the Lord and then wonder whether He really called you to it? That fear of being out of the will of God that you may experience is a kind of reminder that this verse is true. You know in your heart that you won't succeed unless God goes with you.

My husband was bound over in Tokyo, Japan, on the way to Korea, where he was to meet the eight children we were going to adopt into our family. Sitting in his hotel room, he began to have doubts. Was this his own doing or the Lord's? Would God supply the great needs for material provision and love that these children would need? Before he got too deeply into this pit of doubt, he stopped and asked the Lord for a word. The Lord led him directly to Isaiah 43:5-6.

"Fear not," the passage said, "for I am with thee: I will bring thy seed from the east; and gather thee from the west; I will say to the north, Give up; and to the south, Keep not back: bring my sons from far, and my daughters from the ends of the earth."

In a flash of revelation, my husband realized that, although it was he who was journeying to receive those children, the Lord was energizing and motivating him by the Holy Spirit to bring the little ones, so that they might receive true sonship in Jesus Christ! Yes, the Holy Spirit was doing His work, through my husband's will.

Although you might not always discern His presence in your daily activities, God's Spirit is always at work to do His will in you. And remember that it's not your might and power that's going to get the job done. So just stay in touch with Him today, and He'll order your doings.

Changed For Good

"He brought me up also out of a horrible pit, out of the miry clay, and set my feet upon a rock, and established my goings. And He hath put a new song in my mouth . . ."
Psalm 40:2-3

Rev. Jerry Kaufman
Pastor

Thank God that He doesn't just pull us out of sin and then let us flounder. He establishes us in a direction for life and gives us purpose along with the joy of a personal relationship with Jesus.

I knew the horrible pit of drugs and living in a New York City ghetto. As a mainline addict for 2 years, I ended up living in the streets, frequently riding the subway all night. I was in and out of jail six times, sometimes barely free for three weeks straight. They say there's honor among thieves. Don't you believe it. Even in the streets, you live with your back to the wall for fear of other addicts. You know what it means to be "miry clay" when nobody wants you or cares about you anymore, and all you are is part of the dirt of the city.

But God took me out of drugs and set my foundation on Jesus Christ and gave me the ministry of building a large church right in the Bronx, where I used drugs for all those years. And He gave me a "new song" to sing, about the gospel of Jesus Christ. Not long ago I went to see a guy in jail whom I'd grown up with on the street. I led him to the Lord, and one day later when I visited him, he started to cry. I asked him why, and he told me, "Jerry, when you were on drugs and I saw you coming down the block, I used to cross the street to avoid you. Now you're visiting me and helping me get to know Jesus."

Before, I was a junkie. Now, I have joy. And from the solid foundation I stand on, I can pull others out of that clay. How about you? Are you singing a solo from your safe perch? Reach down and pull up some of those around you. Get a little "group" started, maybe even a choir. Look around today for a hand reaching out for help.

His Sweet Care

"Behold the fowls of the air: for they sow not, neither do they reap, nor gather into barns; yet your heavenly Father feedeth them. Are ye not much better than they?"
Matthew 6:26

Leo Mascitto
Music Director
Circus Maranatha

If we would only accept with child-like hearts the simple sense of what Jesus says there, how different our lives might be! How much evil has been committed in the world because men have worried and striven and even murdered to take by force the abundance that God would gladly give as a gift, if we'd only trust Him.

Why would we rather earn or take than merely ask God to supply our needs? We would be kings and lords of our own lives, self sufficient and proud. The philosophy of "the survival of the fittest" is pleasing to the fleshly part of us, because it allows us to remain in charge.

For a time after meeting Jesus Christ, I did not make a complete commitment to Him. I wasn't too certain of what God wanted to do for me. Salvation of my eternal soul was enough for me. I did not even know that God was at all interested in my day to day existence.

But soon after I began seriously reading the Bible, I discovered this verse, and Matthew 7:7. Jesus told me through these two verses that He loved me so much that He wanted to take the burden of my material needs from my shoulders, and that He wanted me to ask Him to do so. Praise God, I was struggling financially at the time, and so was willing to ask Him for help. He answered my request and has continued to meet my needs unfailingly ever since.

If you have not entrusted the Lord Jesus with all of your material needs, you cannot know the tremendous breadth of His love. Stop struggling to be the master of your means. Place them in God's hands. Taste of the sweetness of His provision, and abandon yourself to a new dimension of His loving care, today.

You Are God's Choice

"According as He hath chosen us in Him before the foundation of the world, that we should be holy and without blame before Him in love."   *Ephesians 1:4*

Roy Brown
Pastor

How beautiful it is to recognize that it wasn't by works or color, poverty or riches, nationality or status, that the choice of salvation was made. And it wasn't left up to man to make the choice!

Not long ago, while returning by plane from a Bible conference which I'd been an invited guest, I was sharing a testimony with a fellow minister. I was glorying in the fact of what I had done: how I decided to make Jesus my choice and give my life to Him, I this, and I the other. But this brother began to share with me that it wasn't really my doing, but God bringing me to the point of meeting Him, long before I even knew of His movement in my life. In fact, God had chosen me to be His before my life even began!

For three months, I went into tears, after recognizing that God had selected His people. They had not just popped up and decided to follow Him, they had been brought to the point of salvation by the deliberate drawing operation of the Holy Spirit. Just as every other bit of creation stands within the direction of God, so man's activities stand under God's ordination also, planned in His wisdom.

Yes, our being a part of God's Beloved was *His choice*. And it was for a glorious purpose. We did not come because we desired to stop sinning or give up our vices, but at His appointed hour, He pricked our hearts through His Word, causing us to surrender to Him—that we might live in holiness and blamelessness before Him Who loved us so much! No, it's not our holiness, but His, in which we can rest.

Oh, prove Jesus' loving choice of you today, by allowing Him to live freely through you! And praise Him, for choosing you to belong.

Invest In Jesus

". . . Yet lackest thou one thing: sell all that thou hast, and distribute unto the poor; and thou shalt have treasure in heaven: and come, follow Me."   Luke 18:22

Teddy Huffam
Gospel Singer

Jesus never guaranteed that salvation would be all steak and potatoes. This rich young ruler was like a lot of other people who want eternal life but want to keep a hold on the world's goods, too.

Brother or sister, you just can't do it! Leaving all that behind is a hard decision to make. It's so hard that Jesus said a couple of verses later that with men it's impossible. But let me tell you that with the Lord, all things are possible!

Take a look at a beautiful promise that's hidden there in these orders: "thou shalt have treasure in heaven." How about that! Here's where the young ruler missed the boat. He didn't see that every shekel he gave to the poor was going to end up banked in a moth and rust proof vault in God's heaven! If you've got your Bible out, look down a few lines to the 29th and 30th verses. There, Jesus says that God will multiply back all that we "give up" *in this life*. That young man should have stuck around for a few more minutes!

And I hope you're still with me. I met the Lord many years ago, and that decision faced me back then. Oh, I ate beans now and then for a while, but let me tell you, God kept His word. God's given me some things now, but they're not really mine, they're His. And I'm happy to leave it that way, because now I don't have to worry about them.

Let's get serious now. Is there any thing or person or position in your life that you haven't turned completely over to God? Riches is not just money, it's anything that you'd choose in your life rather than God. Is the Spirit of God speaking to your heart? Let Him have His way right now. Nothing will ever top the "interest" that last "investment" will bring you.

The Power Of The Tongue

"*A wholesome tongue is a tree of life . . .*"
Proverbs 15:4
"*Death and life are in the power of the tongue: and they that love it shall eat the fruit thereof.*" Proverbs 18:21

Don Hughes
Evangelist

The most powerful force in all the world is the spoken Word of God backed by the force of faith. It was by God's spoken word that the earth was made and all the creatures in it.

As Christians, God dwells within us, giving us His power to preach the gospel of Jesus Christ, cast out demons and command mountains to move in His name. The Holy Spirit in us is the authority of God Himself. With a gift of such power, God expects us to use it responsibly and constructively.

With your tongue you can speak life or death. Salvation is ours through confession of our sins and acceptance of Jesus Christ, (Romans 10:9). The person who confesses and forsakes his sin will receive mercy, but "He that covereth his sins shall not prosper" (Proverbs 28:13). When we confess Christ before men, He will confess us before God in heaven. If we deny Him before men, He will deny us before God.

The principle to "Give, and it shall be given unto you," (Luke 6:38) applies to what you say as much as to what you do. Speak faith and you will receive faith's results. Speak doubt and you will receive your doubting expectations.

Solomon declared that through a wholesome tongue you can be a tree of life. David said in Psalm 1, that this tree will be planted by rivers of water and will prosper in everything. You can be that kind of tree. You can prosper in all you do. So be wise in your conversation. Using one comedian's popular but true phrase, "What you say, is what you'll get."

The Battle Is The Lord's

*". . . Thus saith the Lord
unto you, Be not afraid nor
dismayed by reason of this
great multitude; for the battle
is not yours, but God's."*
2 Chronicles 20:15

Vince Montano
Singer

These were the words of the prophet Jahaziel to King Jehoshaphat on the eve of a great battle against the Moabites and the Ammonites. No matter who or what your enemies are, these words of God are also for you today.

The battle never really is yours in the Christian life. The battle aways belongs to the Lord. That's why, if you try to fight it in your own strength, you will lose. Notice that God through the prophet pointed Jehoshaphat away from consideration of the multitude assembled against him. Men's eyes reason according to appearances and numbers. God's eyes reason by faith, and He asks us to depend upon faith for our victories, not human reason.

To prove that the battle was His, God fought it the next day by His own rules. He actually sent singers out in front of the army, praising and worshipping His name. As they went forward, the enemy was put to flight even before Judah's armies reached the field of battle.

How many battles we face might be settled before we ever entered the fray, if we, too, would only let the Lord do the fighting for us! Praise God, in today's world, the problems and challenges we face are becoming so great that we're having to depend upon Him more and more. When we allow him to undertake, we know the victory will be ours.

Have you been trying to reason out a solution to an insurmountable problem that's facing you? Have you gotten bogged down in a multitude of obstacles that seem to be standing in your way? God can see a winning strategy ahead! Let your praises go ahead of Him, place the problem in His hands, where it belongs, and take the spoils of victory for Him!

You and Jesus Can Do It!

"I can do all things through Christ which strengtheneth me."
Philippians 4:13

Glen D. Cole
Pastor

Jesus always found His Father's grace and strength sufficient in His life, and you can always find it enough in yours. Whatever challenge, whatever circumstances you face, Jesus found God's help equal to it in His life, so as He lives through you, you can expect Him to succeed for you.

Your inadequacies and weaknesses may be very real to you, but when you find the strength of Christ and His resources, there'll be no circumstance you can't tackle or circumstance you can't face. Jesus is active in you, and there's no limit to what you can do.

A scientific experiment was performed in which both a heavy steel bar and a small bottle cork were both suspended from a ceiling by wires, side by side. The bottle cork was swung, in rhythmic motion, like a pendulum, and struck repeatedly against the solid steel bar, again and again, for hour after hour. For a long time, nothing seemed to happen. But suddenly, on one stroke, the steel bar began to swing from side to side, too.

The experiment proved that if you hit anything rhythmically for a long enough time, it will eventually move, no matter how large or powerful it is.

Science proved it, and you've got proof, too, right here in the Word of God. There is no problem you will face today that's so great that you and Jesus can't move it if the both of you just keep hitting it hard enough and long enough and often enough. Praise God!

Speaking Into Reality

"Whosoever shall say unto this mountain, Be thou removed, and be thou cast into the sea; and shall not doubt in his heart, but shall believe that those things which he saith shall come to pass; he shall have . . ."

Mark 11:23

Vicki Jamison
Evangelist

God hasn't just told us that we're overcomers in Christ. He has given us the tools we need to be overcomers in this life. These tools are the faith He's placed in our hearts and the words of our mouths.

At the beginning of all things, God spoke the universe into being, seeing by faith that all He spoke would then appear. And with this verse, Jesus announced that He was putting this same power into the hands of all who would believe in Him!

Imagine how excited I was when I first heard this taught 13 years ago! Yes, this was for even me, a nobody. I didn't need to have great gifts or strength or anything but Jesus Himself in my heart. What a thrill it was to realize that now I could look up at those mountains in front of me without fear!

No longer did I have to live with them. With just a spoken word, mountains called Despair, Poverty, Fear, Hatred, and Disease all would have to uproot themselves and move. I didn't have to yell or scream at them, I just had to tell them quietly to get out of the way.

Recently, mountains of unbelief and discouragement tried to prevent me from starting a home for young women who've been involved in drugs and prostitution. I experienced delays and opposition, but I kept the faith for this vision God had given me and kept confessing that it was a reality regardless of the circumstances. And now it is!

Pray this simple prayer with me now, will you? "Jesus, I trust You, and I believe You and Your Word will work for me! You are not partial; You can work through me, as well as anyone on earth. Let me speak Your Word with faith and power today, and move mountains for Your glory! Amen."

Are You In Church?

"Not forsaking the assembling of ourselves together, as the manner of some is." Hebrews 10:25

Bobby Allision
Stock Car Driver

Assembling for worship or fellowship with other Christians on a regular basis is so important to nourishng your walk with God. The writer here takes the time to say, and I'll give you my own free translation, "Don't skip church, as some do!"

My mother and father raised me, along with nine other children, in a strong spiritual atmosphere. All of us attended church every Sunday, and we were encouraged to pay attention and really get something out of it. And even when I left home and started my career as a race car driver, I always kept up with church attendance and the habit of personal prayer that I'd been taught.

Race driving is a tense and tiring occupation. By the time I was through racing on a Saturday night, I'd just want to dive into a motel and sack out. But before turning in, no matter what part of the country I happened to be in, I'd find a phone book or ask somebody where I could find a church in the area. And except for rare occasions, you'd always find me there on Sunday morning.

Yes, growing up with God as a big part of your life is very important. The foundation of fellowship, prayer, and Bible teaching never leaves you completely. But if your trust in God is going to grow, you have to nourish it, with the fresh ministry of God's Word and the sacraments, and with the strengthening company of other people who share your faith.

Let me urge you, if you possibly can, to get into a good church fellowship, and be faithful to attend services. Get to know the pastor and your fellow members. If you're shut in, ask someone to visit you regularly. You need the love of Jesus that other people can give. Reach out today and make sure that you receive the help you need.

Certain Disciples

"And there was a certain disciple at Damascus, named Ananias; and to him said the Lord in a vision, Ananias. And he said, Behold, I am here, Lord. Acts 9:10

Hank Walker
Pastor

Ananias wasn't one of the great heroes of the Bible. He didn't perform any great exploits or preach to thousands of people as far as we know. He merely was called by God after Saul's Damascus road experience to lay hands on the future great apostle Paul, that he might receive his sight. Ananias isn't described as dynamic or courageous, he's simply referred to as "a certain disciple," whose only recorded accomplishment was to touch the life of another man.

It's not hard for most of us to relate to Ananias. He wasn't super-spiritual; he expressed some anxiety about the reputation of Saul. But he was willing to obey God and minister to this man in need.

The Lord needs more "certain disciples." However, many of us are overcome by a passionate drive to be someone extraordinary, something more than we are. I'm all too prone myself to be like Joseph, a dreamer, hoping to become something I'm not, because deep down inside, I'm not really satisfied with what I am. The Lord has been dealing with me, to help me to rest in Him. He's telling me that, just as I am, I'm special to Him, and I should treasure that relationship I have with Him and cultivate it. Through this relationship He can use me as He sees fit.

You need not have a world-encompassing ministry to be important in the service of God. As a housewife, you can be that "certain disciple" and minister to your family's needs. As a father, you can be that "certain disciple" who brings God's love to your son. You can be that "certain disciple" as a millworker, sharing with his supervisor the miracle of salvation. Like Ananias, whether you reach few or many in your lifetime, you may never know how your touch today may be multiplied for eternity's sake.

Strength For Today

"I can do all things through Christ which strengtheneth me."
Philippians 4:13

Sen. Alan Trask
U.S. Senator from Florida

Have you ever felt almost overcome with inadequacy? I have, especially at those times in the Senate when I've been listening to the debate going on and trying to formulate what I need to say when it's my turn to get up and address that group of distinguished men.

But it's encouraging just to get on the floor and start speaking about right and truth instead of what's politically expedient. Then it seems that a hush comes over the whole Senate body, and everyone listens because Christ Himself is speaking through me by the thoughts he quickened in my mind. That's certainly something I couldn't do on my own.

Things like that have given me the strength and boldness to go on. When I was first a Christian, I was very timid about one to one witnessing, while my wife Jan was courageous! But over the months and years, God has worked that forthrightness to share about Him into me.

A lot of other things in life are difficult to do, but we can face them all through Christ. Like losing everything and still greeting the world with a smile. Like having to tell creditors that you can't pay them now, but you will. I couldn't have endured that without Christ. That's tougher than the Senate. But with Him, I did.

That's one of the most wonderful things about being a Christian. That confidence shines through, and people can see it. Has anyone ever asked you, "How do you keep going? What keeps you cheerful?" Isn't it good to be able to answer, "It's the Lord Jesus!" When nothing else can sustain you, He'll always be there. Look to Him first, always.

Life More Abundantly

"I have not seen the righteous forsaken, nor his seed begging bread."
Psalms 37:25

Jan Trask
Wife/Real Estate Agent

Loss in man's eyes can be victory in God's. In 1976, we suffered the loss of all of our possessions except our house. God provided the funds to redeem that, and then started us on a total faith walk that has lasted more than 3½ years.

During this remarkable time,we have not been in need for anything. God has taken care of shelter, food, clothing, vehicles, and to all outward appearances, we have prospered. We have no credit whatever in man's world, but we don't operate in man's world; we are living in God's world, where this scripture has come to vivid life.

When we first began sharing this testimony, we were in the very middle of this difficult financial situation. People sometimes told us, "That doesn't sound much like victory." But in Jesus, there is victory, even in what appear to be our defeats. Yes, we may have failed, but His goodness and abundant supply to us didn't fail. He neither forsook us nor sent us out begging. The peace, joy, and new strength we have gained through this experience has meant the greatest victory of all for us: Jesus' victory over our smug self-sufficiency, and His leading into our total dependence upon Him.

We praise God that He doesn't have to use situations like ours to teach all believers to depend upon Him. But whatever your need, His message is the same: the answer is not in you, but in Him. And the way to receive it is this - don't plead, don't prod, don't push, just pray. Your need is really His need, and He has all the supply in the world. Press on into His abundance. Never fear - hold tight to this promise, and you'll find that it's all yours as His gift of love.

Jesus Reproduced - In Us

"As a man, He humbled Himself, and became obedient unto death, even the death of the cross. Wherefore God also hath highly exalted Him, and given Him a name which is above every name."

Philippians 2:8-9

Father Frederick Buckley
Radio Broadcast Producer

This is God emptying Himself, Christ humbling Himself and appearing among us as a man, without ceasing to be God. In order for the Word to become flesh, to dwell among us, and to share our life, He had to give up all the heavenly glory He knew.

Then as a man, He had to be obedient in carrying out His Father's plan, which was to die, even on a cross. And because of this emptying and obedience unto death, the Father has exalted Jesus and placed His name above all others. This is the gospel, telling us of the emptying, the death, and then the glorification of Christ. It is a wonderful story, the epitome of heroism, the grand design of the ages executed by God.

And yet, it is not complete, unless prefaced with what Paul has placed at its beginning in verse 5 of this chapter: "Let this mind be in *you*, which was also in Christ Jesus..." For Jesus' life was never intended to be merely admired, or even to be imitated. It was meant to be reproduced in us by the indwelling of His Holy Spirit.

Today, Jesus' work will have little meaning unless you and I are also in the process of emptying ourselves, of our sin, of our selfish desires, of our hold on this world's possessions. Jesus' obedience will be for the modern world but an inspiring tale if we are not in obedience to God, living lives of holiness, doing the works He did and greater, pouring ourselves out for the lives of others, and laying our lives on the altar that souls might be saved. And unless He is exalted in and through us, unless God is glorified because of our faithful walk and giving of self, the world will not see Him. How will your life be spent for Him today?

Tuneful Praise And Glory

"The trumpeters and singers were as one, to make one sound to be heard in praising and thanking the Lord; and when they lifted up their voice with.. instruments of music, and praised the Lord.. then the house was filled with a cloud . . ."

(2 Chronicles 5:13)

Reba Rambo Gardner
Musical Artist

This glorious scene took place at the dedication of Solomon's Temple in Jerusalem. The finest craftsmen and builders in all Israel had labored for many years to complete this magnificent structure in which God's presence was to dwell. A huge crowd from all points of the nation had assembled, headed by the elders and heads of all the tribes of Israel, with King Solomon presiding. The glistening of gold and the shine of brightly polished wood had flashed across the ark of the covenant as the stately priests slowly carried it to its place.

Then trained singers and instrumentalists, spotless in white linen, burst as one into music and song, and the glory of the Lord descended upon the temple as a cloud, with the praises of the musicians.

Today, the Lord has again raised up a host of servants devoted to praising Him with music. We no longer have to seek His presence in stone buildings: God has chosen to make His temple the hearts of men and women who love Him. But the Lord has still ordained the praises of His people as His special habitation. The worship leaders of ancient Israel praised the Lord beforehand for the great things He would do in their midst, and their praises brought the cloud of glory down. How much more today, now that the Temple's veil has been rent in two, will the Lord's glory visit us if we'll praise Him: He's promised us His glory will cover the earth as the waters cover the sea.

Always, before a concert, we praise the Lord for the great things He is going to do. And you can praise Him, also, for all that He's going to do in your life. Give Him the praise He's worthy of and, bring His glory down where you are.

Man's Greatest Power

"And it came to pass, that, as He was praying in a certain place, when He ceased, one of His disciples said unto Him, Lord, teach us to pray . . ." Luke 11:1

Rev. Fred Hall
Evangelist/Pastor

This is my favorite verse simply because I believe that prayer is the highest position God has allowed His creatures to enter. Both sinners and saints can approach Him in prayer, and in that humbling find from the very beginning of their Christian walk a position of power, prestige, authority, and joy.

Prayer makes us a part of what God is doing in His world. He's allowed us a part in the very creation of souls by the new birth. We have been given the high privilege of praying souls into the kingdom of God.

God places such importance upon prayer that in Luke 18:1 Jesus urged us *"always* to pray." If we don't pray, we will miss out on the greatest thing God has given us to do. We have abdicated the power in prayer that He's given us over all things. For He said, "All things are possible to him that believeth" (Mark 9:23).

Without prayer, we just cannot do the work of God. In Mark 9, we read that the disciples of Jesus could not cast the evil spirit out of a child brought to them. When they asked why, Jesus answered that their faith was deficient without enough prayer and fasting.

Yes, we need greatly to be taught by Jesus how to pray. We live so much of our lives in unnecessary struggling and frustration because we have not stayed close to God in prayer. We haven't discerned His will because we have kept out of touch with Him. We have not been used by Him to the fullest because we have not been empowered by His personal touch through prayer. And we have not known the depths of His love because we have not let Him embrace us through prayer. Lord, today, teach us to pray!

He Brought Us In

"And He brought us out from thence, that He might bring us in, to give us the land which He sware unto our fathers." Deuteronomy 6:23

Jerry Horner
Theologian

It was never God's intention simply to deliver Israel out of bondage in Egypt and then abandon them. God doesn't just put us on the road to heaven and point out the right direction and say, "Now I've forgiven you of your sins, and it's all up to you. You go the rest of the way in your own strength." And He doesn't just pat you on the back and say, "It's a long rough road, and I hope you make it. If you do, I'll see you at the other end."

No, He not only brought us out, He brings us in. He's with us every step of the way. And God doesn't intend that we just wander around in the wilderness, either. He brings us right over Jordan, right into Canaan, the Promised Land. He brought us out, "that He might bring us in."

Too many Christians are living below the level of their possibilities. Ephesians 1:3 tells us that God *has* blessed us with every spiritual blessing in Christ. That's not a future tense, God *will* bless; that's a past tense, He *has* blessed. These shortsighted believers remind me of an old farmer who eked out a bare existence on poor soil and went to his death bed, lamenting that he had so little to leave his sons. The sons, thinking the land was worthless, sold it for nearly nothing to a group of men. The sons didn't know it, but the buyers discovered that there was a treasure of minerals underneath that soil.

I think we make a mistake in thinking that Canaan just means heaven. No, it's here and now. And God swore to our spiritual fathers that it was ours: to Paul, to Isaiah, to John. He's still promising it today, if we'll just accept His whole will. Start taking God at His word today, and don't be content with less than God wants for you to have.

God Likes A Full House

"And the Lord said unto the servant, Go out into the highways and hedges, and compel them to come in, that my house may be filled."
Luke 14:23

Ernie Eskelin
Missionary Evangelist

The Lord likes a full house. So does a preacher, which is why I've encouraged hundreds of churches with this verse to go out and get the souls that'll bless God's heart.

Here's how I've done it: I've stood before a congregation and challenged them with this verse, while a big banner was spread across the platform spelling out these words - "THAT MY HOUSE MAY BE FILLED." I would talk about this verse and recruit the people to pledge themselves to filling a row of seats. Then we'd tack a piece of paper with their names on it on the edge of that row, and by next Sunday, they'd get that row filled. I'd take a pew in the church, too, and all together, we'd fill that church the next Sunday.

This wasn't a giveaway, there were no prizes given. The only inspiration was from the Word of God. After Sunday school, when the church was packed to the door, I'd follow with a sermon entitled "What it takes to get to heaven," from the third chapter of John, where Nicodemus asked Jesus, "How can I be born again?"

In 38 years of working to fill churches, the results have been great. One church had 300 one week and 625 the next and never went below 600 again. But people of God need to make a commitment to fill their church for Jesus.

How about your home church? Is it full every Sunday? Have you ever taken this parable of Jesus seriously? If there's a lot of room in there, prehaps God is nudging you right now to think about it, and pray about it — and do something about it!

Happiness Is

"For David, after he had served his own generation by the will of God..." Act 13:36

Tommy Barnett
Pastor

Someone described King David as "a bundle of life." How David managed to be so fruitful while spending so much time fleeing persecution and waging war is a mystery. Yet he is blessing us to this day through his life's testimony and his sharing in the Psalms. Perhaps the clue can be found in the verse above: David *served* his generation.

The happiest people in the world are not those who've searched for happiness, but those who've introduced happiness to others. One of the reasons why our church has grown from 76 members to over 5,000 is that we try to encourage every member to find a need in the fellowship that his or her ability can supply. Some folks tell me, "But I'm not needed!" I answer, "Then create a need!" Let me give you an example:

An elderly lady in our church heard that I like coffee early in the morning. So every Sunday morning, she comes down to church at 4:00 A.M. when I get there and heats me some rolls and coffee, which I really need to get me going. One day she was sick and couldn't come, and I really felt disappointed and abandoned. You see, she had made herself needed. She became a (positive!) addiction in my life.

There's no reason why anyone should feel needless and helpless when there's so much hurt in the world. Just look for a need around you, concentrate on that need and what you can do about it. A very successful man once said, "The way to become rich is to find the greatest need in the world and fill it." And Jesus is the world's greatest need.

There *are* needs where you are that *you* can fill: a batch of cookies, a kind word, a mended toy. Ask God right now to enrich your life by showing you the need He would have you serve today.

We Have Treasure

"But we have this treasure in earthen vessels, that the excellency of the power may be of God, and not of us."
2 Corinthians 4:7

Judy Chavez
Bible Teacher

Because they have missed a powerful truth contained in this little verse, many children of God are thinking of themselves as "have-nots," rather than rejoicing in the great "treasure" that they "have" within them. Yes, Paul says that we *"have . . ."* in present tense, not will have some day or did have before. We, who have accepted Jesus Christ, *have*, right *now*, a "treasure."

And what is that treasure? It is the life of Jesus Christ, resurrected, all-sufficient, compassionate, and loving. And where do we have it? In "earthen vessels," in these earthly bodies we live in now, Jesus is dwelling, abiding, tabernacling. And by this indwelling, our bodies are made sanctuaries, temples, houses of the Holy Spirit (1 Corinthians 6:19). This is why all of our bodies together are called Christ's body, through which He moves and acts. As Paul says in Galatians 2:20, "I live, yet not I, but Christ liveth in me." Another translation puts it, "the life of another lives in me." So in the present moment of trial or adversity, it is no longer my struggle, my efforts, my striving, or even my tryings. He is within me, the Supplier, as well as the Supply of my needs. I have the Answer already within me, Christ, the Hope of Glory!

And within you also, if you are His. You need to cry no longer, "I am destitute, I don't have, I need, I need, I want, I want!" Instead, you can shout triumphantly with David today, "The Lord is my Shepherd: I shall *not* want, for joy, for victory, for peace, for assurance, for strength! All of these are already within me, because Christ is within me. I need only mine the treasure of Him, and be satisfied. I need only allow His riches to spill forth from me, to meet the hunger and thirst of a needy world!"

Seek His Kingship

"But seek ye first the kingdom of God and His righteousness; and all these things shall be added unto you."   *Matthew 6:33*

Father Victor Affonso
Evangelist

It is so easy to pursue the things you want from God rather than seeking His personal kingship over your life. I well understand this temptation. For many years as a Jesuit priest, I sought through study and discipline and following the teachings of Christ to find inner joy and peace. I gave up everything materially and did all I could to act rightly, but I did not find the fulfillment I sought.

Then the Lord baptized me with His Holy Spirit to make Jesus real to me. I discovered the wonder of knowing the King, not as a distant ruler, but as the Monarch who is also friend and brother.

My heart then filled with the desire to share with every man the simple message of the gospel, and I better understood why we as a church had not been more effective in reaching nations for Christ. We had tried to compete with the many worldly religions in good works, education, and philosophy but had forgotten that people need first to know that Jesus loves them.

All of the things you may do for God and want from Him are good, but never forget the most important thing: that the great love of Jesus be allowed to flow through your heart and touch others with His presence. Only He can add the forgiveness, the peace, the assurance you and this hungry world are seeking.

The Spirit Of God Vs. Fear

"For God hath not given us the spirit of fear; but of power, and of love, and of a sound mind." 2 Timothy 1:7

Buddy Harrison
Pastor/Teacher/Publisher

The atmosphere I grew up in as a boy was full of anxiety and fear; my father was a professional gambler. When I got to be a teenager, I ran around with gangs where everyone acted tough to cover up their fear.

When I came to know the Lord, fear would still try to overtake me. I didn't know that it was a spirit; I was afraid of being a failure, I was afraid of being a success.

When I found the above verse in the Bible, I realized that God had not given me that spirit of fear, but one of power, love, and a sound mind. I began confessing that I had the love of God inside me and soon it became so real that it rose up in me as a mighty force that cast fear out and helped me be victorious in Christ.

I know that the greater One is in me, and this helps me think better. It gives me a sound mind. I don't have to get geared up and pre-plan always because I'm confident He has it all in order.

And I have power because I have ability and authority through the Spirit of God to do whatever is necessary from day to day. So life has become a great adventure for me.

It can be for you, too. Reject that spirit of fear; no matter what form it takes, it's not from God. Start filling yourself with God's Word. Instead, accept His unconditional love for you and you'll see, as I did, that fear melts away.

Weakness Means God's Opportunity

"My grace is sufficient for thee: for My strength is made perfect in weakness."
2 Corinthians 12:9

Rev. Paul R. Gaehring
Executive Dean, Heritage School of Evangelism and Communication

The Apostle Paul has been referred to as "the apostle who shook the world." Yet Paul's own testimony to the Corinthians revealed that weakness, reproach, need, persecution, and distress regularly confronted him. What, in the fact of all these seeming hindrances, was the secret of his success in victorious Christian living? It was a simple, yet profound paradox: "When I am weak, then am I strong" (2 Corinthians 12:10).

Paul didn't need to seek opportunities to expose his weaknesses or to magnify his problems with a false sense of humility. His struggles from within and without were the same real battles that are common to all those who could endeavor to serve God. But Paul's perspective did not leave him paralyzed in ineffectiveness. It rather enabled him to equate human weakness with divine opportunity.

It's been said that, "Man's desperation is God's opportunity." When God selects a servant through which He can manifest His power and reflect His glory, He isn't looking for ability, but for availability. Evangelist D. L. Moody approached his Christian life and ministry with the conviction that "the world has yet to see what God will do with, for, through, in and by the man who is wholly consecrated to Him." Moody concluded, "I will try my utmost to be that man."

Today, inventory your strengths and weaknesses, assets and liabilities. Think about how God might use you for His Kingdom. You may be tempted to be dismayed if your human shortcomings seem to indicate that you're not adequate for the task. Instead, consider as did Paul and D. L. Moody your weaknesses as greater opportunities for God to demonstrate the sufficiency of His grace in you. Pray that He take you as you are, and let His glory shine through your lacks.

APRIL 16

Tuning In To God's Frequency

"Therefore, leaving the principles of the doctrine of Christ, let us go on unto perfection . . ." Hebrews 6:1

A. C. Valdez, Sr.
Evangelist

Perfection in the Christian life is not a matter of having complete head knowledge of the things of God. Oh, a good foundation is important. We should know, the writer of Hebrews says, about repentance, baptism, laying on of hands, resurrection, and eternal judgment. But growing in God is getting to know how to find God's "frequency" in the Holy Spirit, and staying on that wavelength.

This is what Jesus meant when He talked about "abiding" in Him (John 15). You see, everything in nature vibrates, whether at a rapid or slow rate: Animals vibrate, plants vibrate, rocks vibrate, planets vibrate. If we could hear the entire range of nature's frequencies, we'd be astounded. But remember, God has a frequency, too. We can't hear it until we're born again, but with our newborn spiritual ears we begin to tune into it.

Have you ever driven cross-country, and kept your car radio running? As you travel from city to city and state to state, you come within range of many different local radio stations, fading in and out as you cross the miles. To stay tuned to one of them, you have to remain in the locale it's broadcasting from. Now, if you want to hear God's voice, you have to keep your attitudes and actions within His appointed range. To help with this, He's given us His commandments, and the witness of His Spirit within.

But real movement towards perfection means that you walk, live, think, and pray within the frequency of His Holy Spirit at all times and in all places , too: job, school, laundry room, kitchen, workshop, playground, and auto, not to mention church on Sunday. So, if you ever feel "static" creep in, twist that dial, and get tuned back onto God's channel!

Joy For Mourning

"The Spirit of the Lord God is upon me . . . to bind up the brokenhearted . . . to give them beauty for ashes, the oil of joy for mourning."
Isaiah 61:1,3

Ann Murchison
Author

A broken thing that's not been repaired is limited in its usefulness. Musty, gray ashes are a poor substitute for something lovely that's been burned beyond recognition. Mourning can never replace a thing that's been utterly lost.

All of the above things present a picture of a life in desperate need of the touch of Jesus: a broken heart, the ugliness of dead or damaged relationships, a sorrowful spirit. They describe me, before the power of Jesus reached down into the painful memory of a childhood hurt and brought His wholeness to my scars.

Many Christians today are not experiencing fully all that Jesus has for them because deep emotional hurts from the past still need healing. The beauty of Jesus within them cannot shine out, and the oil of the Holy Spirit cannot flow freely from them to bless others. But this verse tells us that healing the past hurts was one of the chief tasks the Holy Spirit has been sent to accomplish.

Jesus read these words about Himself at the beginning of His ministry on Earth. And by His Holy Spirit, He is still reaching out today to heal the hurts in your heart, if you will allow Him to do His deep work.

Ask Jesus to reach into all the areas of your emotions where hurt or anger has shackled your soul. Ask that His healing presence enter each injured place within and make you whole. As He heals you, you will then have a fresh heart for others and the beauty of His presence through which to glorify Him. The overflow of His Spirit in you will bring His healing touch to others in need.

His Love

". . . God is love."
1 John 4:8

Hugo Zerbe
Pastor/Counselor

When the Word of God speaks of His love, it does not mean the shallow sentiment that Hollywood talks about that's rooted in self-gratification and present experience. The love of God is eternal, not changeable, forgiving and healing, cleansing to the depths of the emotions and the soul. It turns the negatives of today's hurting world into the positives of joy and peace. It overflows, as this Love Prayer did from my heart, into the lives of all around us. The Lord gave this prayer to me one night as I was meditating upon the beautiful description of His love found in 1 Corinthians Chapter 13. I hope that it may also become your prayer as you seek to serve Him.

Love Prayer

God give me love . . . That is patient, loving, and kind,
Forgiving and helps me place the past behind.
God give me love . . . That does not demand its own way,
The love that helps others find a new day.
God give me love . . . That is humble and without pride,
Never selfish or rude, where hate is denied.
God give me love . . . That is never boastful, envious or jealous,
That gives me strength for others to be zealous.
God give me love . . . That is never irritable or easily hurt,
It holds no grudges, is never curt.
God give me love . . . That will always be sincere, loyal, and true,
I really want my life to be a reflection of You.
Amen

Working For Others

"Let him that stole steal no more; but rather let him labor, working with his hands the thing which is good, that he may have to give to him that needeth." Ephesians 4:28

Jim Rutledge
Pastor/Evangelist

The apostle Paul gives a fascinating reason in this verse why a Christian who had been a thief should turn from stealing and work with his hands. The first reason that would probably occur to most of us is that the former thief should work in order that his own needs be met honestly. But the reason Paul gives goes far beyond that. Paul writing in the Holy Spirit puts foremost the motive of being able to give to meet the needs of *others first*.

When I was about to be released from the prison term I served for robbery, another inmate who was serving a life term, came up to me in the prison yard and placed a dollar bill in my hand. He said, "Jim, every time you look at that dollar bill, remember who your god once was." Though we no longer acknowledge money as a god once we've met Christ, it's not too difficult to replace our concern about getting money with a preoccupation with getting our own needs satisfied.

That taped up old dollar bill is still in my pocket, reminding me not only not to steal any more, but that any money I receive belongs to God first, and to the needs of others second. For my own needs, there's always that little oft-forgotten inscription on the back: "In God We Trust."

You may never have been a thief, but God in this verse is asking you, too: "Why are you working?" Is it to meet the needs of others first? Perhaps in God's eyes there is a quiet measure of stealing in too much concern with the needs of self. Ask God right now to perform a miracle in your heart, so that you would work first in order to be able to give.

God Tries Harder

"And we know that all things work together for good to them that love God, to them who are the called according to His purpose."

Romans 8:28

Marvin E. Gorman
Pastor/Author/Radio Host

No situation can ever arise in your life that God isn't able to turn into something good. Now, you may doubt that statement. You might even say, "Well, that man just doesn't know how bad my circumstances are, or he wouldn't say that." But let me tell you about my boyhood. Then you'll know why I affirm this verse with such confidence.

I wanted to follow Christ very badly as a boy, but outward circumstances made it very hard. My father was an alcoholic who stood against all churches, and he made sure I couldn't attend church on the regular basis I wanted to. But because I wasn't free to go to church and Christian meetings, my spirit got all the more hungry for the Word of God. So I got deep into the Word on my own, and that's when this Scripture became especially real to me.

It was hard for me to understand why God didn't change my dad's heart or make it easier for me to have fellowship. Often, I cried out to Him, "Lord, when are you going to do something about this?" Then this scripture would come back to me, and He would whisper to my heart, "Son, I know what's best for you. Accept it, and learn to draw upon Me." Then such a peace would fill me, even in the turmoil of my home life.

Because I believed this verse, and acted upon it, the Lord caused me to grow faster and stronger than if I'd had an easy road. I had to try harder, and God knew that would strengthen my love for Him.

Whatever it is, God is using that situation you're in to make you grow up perfectly in Him. Ask Him right now to start showing you the good He's making of it. And look for that good all day today.

Sent For Peace

"Peace be unto you: as my Father hath sent me, even so send I you."   John 20:21

George Stallings
Conference Speaker

There I was in my kitchen wrestling with the old devil. I knew God had called me to the ministry, so I'd sold my business and most of my possessions. Now I had my house on the market and was ready to move to the place God had shown me.

Enter Slewfoot: "God hasn't called you—you're just hallucinating. Now look, you've still got the time to get another business together here; but once you sell your house, you'll have no place to come back to. You'll fall flat on your face and look like a fool."

He sounded so reasonable. I desperately cried to God, "Give me something I can hang onto!" I grabbed my Bible and let it fall open to those words, "Even so send I *you*." That *you* burned straight into my heart and brought the peace. It was *me* He was sending. I put the devil behind me and packed my bags.

Every believer in Jesus Christ has been *sent* into the world. I say "believer" because that's what God has called us to be—to believe that we're in the world to do what Jesus did. You and I are sent *as* the Father sent Him: to set captives free, to heal the sick, to do good.

Are you a believer? You won't find real peace until you, too, see yourself as sent personally by Jesus and do the work He's got for you in this world.

It's Wise To Win Souls

"The fruit of the righteous is a tree of life; and he that winneth souls is wise."
Proverbs 11:30

Joe Panzino
Evangelist

There's a T.V. commercial being broadcast that says: "You only go around once in life, so grab all the gusto you can get." To a mind set on the things of this world, this might seem to make a lot of sense. Live it up, get ahold of everything you can that this life has to offer, and enjoy it to the fullest. God's word doesn't agree with this philosophy of life to the Christian. God says, "Real wisdom lies in winning all the souls you can while you're here."

All of the things this world has to offer are going to pass away and the desires for them, too, according to 1 John 2:16. Only the souls of men are eternal in God's eyes. To seek the world's goods, approval, or fleshly satisfactions cannot be wise for this reason. When eternity dawns, none of these things will still be around. This world is rather like a Christmas tree several weeks after the holiday is over: all the pine needles have fallen off, and it's only fit to be thrown out or burned.

But the fruit of souls won by a Christian will grow and grow forever because they're on a "tree" planted in eternity's soil. The Christian who has won souls will forever enjoy their fellowship and love. This "fruit" is the treasure Jesus desires for you to lay up in Heaven: eternal lives to love and cherish always.

Do you see now why it's *wise* to win souls? The only time angels get excited, according to Scripture, is when they see souls saved. The message of the gospel you share today could put another piece of fruit on that tree of life. Be *wise*, win a soul, and get all the angels excited today that you can!

The Love That Brings Life

"For God so loved the world, that He gave His only begotten Son, that whosoever believeth in Him should not perish, but have everlasting life."   John 3:16

Earl Banning
Pastor/Counselor

In this one verse is a summation of the whole dynamics of the gospel message and that is God's love. For God so loved that He sent Christ, that we through Christ might have love with which to love others. Love is the motivation of grace. Love is the power of grace. Love is the redeeming element of grace. God is love.

There is so much more in this one verse than we usually realize. It *is* the power of God unto salvation, the whole gospel in one verse. It's the reason for grace, the truth of God, the exposure of God, His opening and revealing of Himself to us in one verse. If this were the entire text of the Bible, it would be enough.

This verse is commonly associated with the altar experience alone, but its message reaches from the beginning to the end of the Christian life. In times of my greatest stress and need, people have come to me and compassionately identified with me in love. Their love for me, Christ's love that flowed through their love, has been the greatest source of healing I've experienced, aside from the Word of God itself. And as I've ministered to people with unanswerable questions, who've suffered unexplainable tragedies, where I found no words, the Lord Jesus used moments of silent empathy and love to powerfully express His perfect, tender understanding.

Your salvation only began at the altar. Your need for the saving touch of God's love will be just as real this day as it ever was. And as His wonderful love is reaching out right now to lift you into the great fullness of everlasting life, reach out to someone else today, and extend that rescuing love to their need, too.

Be Not Ashamed

"*For I am not ashamed of the gospel of Christ: for it is the power of God unto salvation to every one that believeth; to the Jew first, and also to the Greek.*"

Romans 1:16

Bubba Chambers
Singer/"Hope of Glory"

The brother who guided me into the things of God was very forceful about never being ashamed to share the good news of Jesus with others. Our group's ministry has been a soul-winning outreach, but we've seen a need to pass on to others in the Body of Christ the urgency we feel about sharing the gospel.

Why does Paul tell us in this verse that he was not *ashamed* of the gospel? And why are so many Christians hesitant or fearful about witnessing to others?

I believe that *shame* can come in if we don't see where the *power* of sharing Christ is. Too often we think that being an effective soul winner means being able to talk well, to answer sinners' clever arguments, to have a Bible scholar's knowledge of the Word. So we get discouraged from telling people about Jesus because we think that the power has to be in us to make them believe it.

But it is not our power or eloquence or wisdom that brings Jesus into anyone's heart. *The gospel itself*, the good news of what Jesus Christ has done, is the *power*. The power is in the message itself and not in the messenger! Yes, the message itself is the power of God that draws men to salvation. This takes all the weight off of my shoulders, because now I don't have to put confidence in myself or my great ability to speak for God. You can put your confidence in the message you're sharing, because God guarantees that the power of that message is going to save souls.

Lord, forgive us for not sharing You with others, and looking for power in ourselves. Give us someone to share the gospel with today.

Possess By Professing

"Jesus saith unto her, Said I not unto thee, that, if thou wouldest believe, thou shouldest see the glory of God?" John 11:40

Larry Lea
Evangelist

Today, God's Spirit is bringing His people to a place where we can possess the things we are professing. We ought to be walking in what we say we have. But too often, we're saying one thing and experiencing another.

The classic case of this in Scripture is Martha's doubt at the tomb of Lazarus. Martha had what I call a faith for yesterday and a faith for tomorrow, but she didn't have a faith for right now. Before she and Jesus got to the tomb, she said all the right things: "Lord, if you had been here, my brother wouldn't have died." Jesus answered, "Your brother will rise again." "Yes, I know," she replied, "that he'll rise again in the resurrection *at the last day*."

She missed the point, you see. Jesus turned to her and said, *"I am the resurrection and the life . . . Do you believe this?"* And she said, "Oh, yes, of course I do." "All right," Jesus said, "Let's go to the graveyard." But then she held back: "But Jesus, he's been dead for four days; he stinks by now!" That's when Jesus rebuked her with the words above and went on to raise Lazarus.

But isn't this too often true of us? We say we trust God, but when a real life situation comes along, we forget God and try to solve it on our own. And we accept so many things about our own personalities that need changing because, sort of like Martha, we say to God and to others, "Oh, I can't change, I've been this way too long, I stink too much. God will clean me up on the last day, but He can't now."

Jesus is crying out to you today, "If you believe, you'll see the glory of God!" He's still the resurrection and the life—*your* resurrection and *your* life. *Will* you believe Him today and start taking possession of what *He* says is yours? Begin truly trusting Him, now.

The Key To Perfect Peace

"Thou wilt keep him in perfect peace, whose mind is stayed on Thee: because he trusteth in Thee." Isaiah 26:3

Elwood Coggin
Dir. PTL Phone Counselors

So many people in this world are not at peace with themselves, God, or anybody else. The unreliability of feelings within and relationships, and circumstances without does not contribute to a peaceful state of mind. This is why we need to be reminded constantly of the unchanging nature of God's love, regardless of variable personalities or circumstances.

Do you remember the first question God ever asked man? It was in the garden of Eden, after the disobedience of Adam and Eve, recorded in Genesis 3:9. "And the Lord God called unto Adam . . . 'Where art thou?'" Now, Adam knew where he was, physically. And God knew where Adam was. But Adam didn't know where he was in relationship to God, spiritually. This question was God's way of pointing out to Adam the position he'd come to. God is constantly asking us this same question: are we in right relationship with Him?

After his sin, Adam's peace was gone. His mind was no longer stayed upon God. In fact, he tried to hide from God, even though he knew in his heart this was impossible, just as we sometimes try to hide from God after we've disobeyed Him. But not only was Adam's relationship with God broken, his sin caused a breach in his relationship with his wife. In his shame, he tried to blame it all on Eve. Guilt will always drive us into a turmoil of unrest, between God and our fellowmen.

The initiative in restoring peace is always taken by God as He asks us, where are we? Are we in the right relationship of trusting Him? Are we loving one another? His love is always extended to us. The key to perfect peace is in our extending our hearts to love and trust Him and in reaching out to touch others with His love.

Step Out, God Will Supply

"My God shall supply all your need according to His riches in glory by Christ Jesus." Philippians 4:19

Bill Baize
Evangelist

When God called me to the ministry, I was in secular entertainment as a background singer for Elvis Presley, making an excellent salary. I fought that call for several months because I was afraid of the financial future and not being able to meet my obligations.

Through these months, I became very despondent. Finally, God faced off with me, His will against mine. He said, "Listen, Bill, I'm God, and I've got all the riches in the world. If you'll follow me and sell out totally, 100%, I'll supply all your needs. Why do you need to depend on Elvis Presley's riches when you're a joint heir with My Son to all there is in the universe?"

Well, I had just bought a new home and was especially preoccupied with the payments on it, but God's kind of logic was very persuasive. I decided right then and there to totally devote myself to Him, let house go, let car go, let it all go. I'd just serve Jesus. That was three years ago. God have mercy on him, Elvis isn't around anymore. But my God is, and He's supplied every need. I haven't missed a payment on anything; my financial shape's better than it's ever been. The shape of my body's better, too. I've lost 30 pounds, and from all over, Christians have given me new suits. Somebody just gave me a trip to the Holy Land.

Is Bill Baize anybody special? No, this has happened because my entire being, every thought, action, penny, everything in my life belongs to God. It's working for Him that counts: if God comes first, everything else we need will come to us as "fringe benefits." It's simple, and it'll work for you, too. If you've been holding anything back, why don't you just sign it over to God right now? He'll multiply it, take good care of it—and of you, too!

Working For What?

"And when Jesus departed thence, two blind men followed Him, crying, and saying, Thou son of David, have mercy on us."

Matthew 9:27

Thomas Farrell
Businessman

When Jesus was on earth, He was moved with compassion for the multitudes who walked through life like sheep without a shepherd, or as blind men, who couldn't see. I wonder how He feels when He looks down on the masses today; our "shepherds," our business and political leaders are struggling just as blindly to try to get a grip on the world, with the help of money, prestige, and alcohol.

No, I'm not a doomsayer or down on America—but I was one of them. "I did it my way," as that strutting pop song boasts. I learned, and most men learn who are in the business world and don't have a spiritual base, to believe in myself. No matter what the situation, I would prevail. Nobody had better tangle with me or get in my way. I was going straight to the top, and I was doing it "my way."

Many successful men and women have gone through their whole lives that way, into eternity that way. But before they pass on, they all have to face an immense, gaping hole in their lives that money, prestige, and power just can't fill. One powerful man I know gets drunk every night, and often ends up staggering to his safe, pulling out his stock certificates, and pleading through his tears, "What more could a man want?" Blind, miserable, and he doesn't even know why.

Only Jesus can fill that emptiness. I thank God, Jesus loves rich young rulers, too. Pray that God will save ours today.

And if you're a Christian in the business world, make sure you never forget for Whom you are working. And what kind of riches God wants you to store up. Thank God you've got a Good Shepherd—and the joy and privilege of doing it His Way.

Hold Your Ground

"If the spirit of the ruler rise up against thee, leave not thy place; for yielding pacifieth great offences."
Ecclesiastes 10:4

Bill Woods
Evangelist/Crusader

God never intended for His people to be apathetic. When the forces of evil or oppression come in at us like a flood, we Christians ought to stand our ground against them.

Our nation was founded by men who feared and loved God. But today, many Christians seem to be apathetic about their rights and duties as American citizens. This scripture is telling us that if our political leaders take themselves out from under the guidance and direction of God, we ought to stand forth and hold our ground, demanding our rights in God.

Some Christians might plead that Jesus said, "Turn the other cheek." But this verse in Ecclesiastes isn't advocating physical violence. It's reminding us of the many prophets, apostles, and martyrs all throughout the Bible who stood strong against ungodly rulers and protected what God had given from evil men who would have taken it away.

In Acts Chapter 5, when the rulers of the synagogue commanded the apostles to refrain from teaching in Jesus' name, Peter and John had to hold firm and tell them, "We ought to obey God rather than men." We should be subject to those in authority over us. But God will not hold us guiltless if we condone by our silence or inaction things contrary to His will.

In medieval times, Christian crusaders fought to preserve the world for God's people. Today, God is using crusaders like Jim Bakker, Pat Robertson, Oral Roberts, Cecil Todd, Vicki Jamison and many others who are standing on what God's Word says. Perhaps right now God is calling you to stand in the breach for Him. Take a moment to silently ask Him to show you *your* part in the fight for Truth.

The Ash-Bucket

"But this one thing I do, forgetting those things which are behind, and reaching forth unto those things which are before, I press toward the mark for the prize of the high calling of God in Christ Jesus." *Philippians 3:13-14*

Cliff Dudley
Author/Publisher

Somebody once said, "The past is a bucket of ashes." It's the used-to-be present burned out, and there's nothing we can do about it. But oh, how we love sometimes to drag that heavy bucket around with us and bend over to sift those ashes through our fingers.

A lot of it's fine ash, pleasant memories and others that don't hurt too much. But there are also clinkers, heavy and sharp, those painful memories we tend to hold tightest to. The past heartaches and insults, the old failures and might-have-beens, the knotted lumps of bitterness left from cruelty we received and dished out. And there are yesterday's fresh ashes too, some of them still hot in our hands.

Forget them, God says. "Listen," you say, "that's easier for God to command than for me to do." Not only is that because the passage of time doesn't really dissolve those clinkers. It's also because to all of us, those clinkers sometimes seem like the only warm things left in our lives.

I carried my share of them for a long time. My upbringing was strictly religious, though Christ wasn't in it. I never realized there was such a thing as forgiveness. So when I was betrayed by people I trusted, I didn't know how to forgive. Instead I turned around, lashing out at and climbing over others. Then the Lord came and said, "Forget it." I said, "Why?" "Because none of those things behind you were your goal," He said, "I'm your goal."

What's happened in your past that you're still bitter about? Who have you hurt or failed? Who's hurt or failed you? Would you rather have those ashes—or Jesus? It's that simple. Ask God right now for the grace to forget the past. And trade that dirty old bucket for a clean suit of praise, and walk tall in it all day long!

Cleansing

"If we confess our sins, He is faithful and just to forgive us our sins, and to cleanse us from all unrighteousness." 1 John 1:9

Ray Mossholder
Evangelist/Bible Teacher

Jesus never *healed* any lepers . . . He always *cleansed* them. If Jesus had only *healed* lepers, they would have still had a terrible problem . . . deterioration. If leprosy had already led to the loss of a nose, fingers, toes, etc. . . . those parts would have been gone for life. But Jesus didn't just *heal* . . . instead, He *cleansed* the lepers. When Jesus touched a leper, all missing parts of his or her body grew back!

Does Jesus still do this kind of thing today? Absolutely! In 1977, I met a woman in Auckland, New Zealand. That woman had no eyebrows. Her eyebrows had been eaten away by eczema when she was just a baby. I prayed to Jesus as I laid hands above her eyes and before a large crowd of people, the Lord gave this woman a very bushy set of eyebrows! Her eyebrows grew right out under my hands! That wasn't just healing, that was *cleansing*!

The Bible idea of "cleansing" always includes the thought of complete restoration. And, oh the joy of understanding *cleansing* in the light of 1 John 1:9. In that verse John tells every person who has sinned . . . "Confess your sin" . . . The Greek word "confess" means "to say the same thing." The one who has sinned needs to say the same thing God says about his or her sin . . . tell God they were wrong and desire to break from the sin. That's how to be forgiven by God for *any* sin. But God doesn't just forgive the sinner and leave them locked at the point of deterioration. He forgives and goes on to "cleanse" the sinner "from *all* unrighteousness." God goes about restoring the fallen one to full fellowship with Him and with others, just as if he or she had never sinned.

Have you been ashamed to approach God with some area of weakness in your life? Read Hebrews 4:14-16. Right now, Jesus is waiting for you to confess your sin. Surrender any and all sin to Him, then use His power to break from it . . . and you'll be *cleansed*.

Jesus' Prayer For You

"Neither pray I for these alone, but for them also which shall believe on Me through their word." John 17:20

Henry M. Harrison
PTL Club Co-Host

One day at Christmas time, shortly after I'd received the baptism of the Holy Spirit, a Christmas card arrived in my mail. It was from a beautiful Spirit-filled lady who'd been especially instrumental in my rapid growth in the walk with the Spirit, and inside she had written the words: "Read John 17:20-24."

Upon opening my New Testament and reading this Scripture, I realized that this was what is known as the high priestly prayer of Jesus, which He shared with His Father just before going to die on the cross. Suddenly, it was like a firebrand burning in my heart, for all at once I understood that Jesus was not just praying for His twelve disciples, but for *all* those who would ever believe on Him because of their witness. I realized that *I* was one of those that He was praying for, and His prayer was still reaching down the centuries, saying, "Father, I love Henry Harrison just as much as You, Father, love Me, and I want him to be one with Us, and to share My glory, and to be made perfect—that's how much I love Him." That just literally blew my mind. I dropped on my knees and at that moment received what I've referred to ever since as my "baptism of Love." This experience was the greatest I'd ever had other than the baptism of the Holy Spirit itself. But God didn't mean to give this precious blessing to me alone.

Today, I long to share it with you also, so that you too might be baptized in Jesus' love. Right now, put your name in this passage: Jesus loves you so much—He wants *you* to be one with Him, *you* to be made perfect, *you* to share His glory, and for *you* to be where He is, forever! Bow your heart before Him right now, and let Him drench you with His love, all over.

Tears Are Flowers Of Joy

"They that sow in tears shall reap in joy." Psalm 126:5

Susan Harrison
PTL Club Guest Hostess

There will be no tears in heaven. Tears are for down here, where sometimes things happen in our lives that hurt so much, only tears can bring us relief. Though we don't always understand such things, I believe God allows them to happen, and we can trust Him always to use them in a manner which brings glory to the name of Jesus.

Such a time occurred in my life in 1973, when my only son was dying of Hodgkins disease, a deteriorative kind of lymphatic cancer. Henry and I along with other sincere believers prayed for Jerry for two years. To this day, we don't understand why he wasn't healed. But even in his death, God revealed a purpose and brought a blessing.

As I was in the emergency room awaiting Jerry's admission to Duke Hospital, I met a lovely Christian mother, obviously distraught. Among those who know Jesus, there are no strangers, and she soon shared with me her heart's burden. She also had a son Jerry's age, dying of the same dread disease, who she feared was about to enter eternity lost, without knowing Jesus. The doctors did not expect him to live through the night, and she begged me to pray with her that he might have time before he died to meet Jesus. We prayed, and the Lord preserved his life for three weeks. I truly believe I shall meet him up in heaven.

What a joy to know that even in my grief, the Lord was able to claim an eternal soul! God has since used this testimony to comfort and save multitudes who've heard it. Perhaps it is healing a grief you feel today. Could it be possible that for every tear we shed here on earth, a flower of joy will burst into bloom in heaven?

Not By Chance

"For I know the thoughts that I think toward you, saith the Lord, thoughts of peace, and not of evil, to give you an expected end."Jeremiah 29:11

Gene Hardcastle
Minister/Singer/Author

As Christians, we don't live by a throw of the dice, the spin of the roulette wheel, the draw of the cards, or by signs in the skies. We live by the promise of God to watch over us in every circumstance. God has not left our growth and development to chance, but has given divine purpose to our beginning and glorious end in Christ.

The way God has made you and ordered your life is no accident. If you could see yourself as God sees you through Christ, you would like what you'd see. God sees past the prison house of your despair and the shackles of your sin. He sees you transformed, renewed, born again, a replica of His own Son.

A painter in London once looked down from the window of his studio on the street scene below. He spied a derelict, beggarly man, with dim eyes, sad countenance, stooped shoulders, and sagging limbs. As the artist looked at this pitiful man, he wondered, "What would this man look like If I drew a sparkle in his eyes, smoothed out the furrows of his brow, and put a smile on his lips?" As he imagined, he drew. He straightened the shoulders, set the man solidly on his feet, and made his posture erect. When he had finished he tore the sketch from the drawing board, ran down to the street, and showed it to the forlorn man. With wondering eyes, the man asked, "Do you really see me that way?" "Yes," the artist replied, "I do." "Then," said the beggar with new hope in his voice, "That's the man I'll be!" And off he strode, with a spring in his step, a glitter in his eye, and a smile on his face.

If you will see yourself as God sees you, you will find it easier to be all He wants you to be. Ask Him now to show you who you really are!

Confessing Christ

"Whosoever therefore shall confess Me before men, him will I confess also before My Father . . . But whosoever shall deny Me before men, him will I also deny before My Father . . ."
Matthew 10:32-33

Efrem Zimbalist, Jr.
Actor

Watching Christian television afforded an amusing way to combat my long bouts of insomnia. Or so I thought. I'd discovered a Christian channel while flipping around the dials, and for several weeks, the strange behavior of these believing preachers and musicians could always induce at least a broad smile to lighten my nights.

But after a while, my grin started to level out. The unabashed sincerity of these people started to get to me. I began to listen intently to their stories of changed lives and new joy. It wasn't long before I knew that I wanted what they had, to fill up the emptiness and futility of my own soul. I knew there was only one step for me, and I had to take it: my life had to be surrendered to Jesus Christ.

It wasn't an easy decision to make. Once made, it was an even harder one to make public. After all, everyone knew who I was. I might be exposed to ridicule, my career might be affected, I might lose friends. But again, the fervency of the people I saw on television affected me. They weren't ashamed to tell the world they belonged to Jesus. I knew that I was denying Jesus by not confessing Him. One night, this feeling crystallized till I couldn't keep it in any longer. I reached for the phone and confessed my commitment to Jesus.

I hope these verses become imprinted in your heart. Jesus knew very well when He said them what it would cost His disciples to acknowledge Him as Lord. He knows what it will cost you to unashamedly proclaim Him to everyone where you work or shop or study. I'm not sorry I took my stand for Him. And you never will be either. Pray right now that you'll have the boldness to be fully His and let everyone know it.

Prophesying

"And Moses said unto him, Enviest thou for my sake? would God that all the Lord's people were prophets, and that the Lord put His Spirit upon them!"

Numbers 11:29

Dr. Stanley M. Horton
Professor/Author

When the children of Israel were wandering in the wilderness, God put His Spirit on 70 elders of the people to help Moses with his task of spiritual leadership. All of these elders assembled themselves around the tabernacle, prophesying before the Lord. But two, Eldad and Medad did not go to the tabernacle. Instead, they remained in the camp, prophesying among the people.

Joshua, then a young man, reported this to Moses, fearing that these two were mavericks who'd stepped beyond Moses' authority. Moses reply gives us an Old Testament glimpse of God's plan for His people from Pentecost to the present day. Moses realized that this was as it should be among God's children; that all should be filled with the Spirit and be used to prophesy for His name's sake.

We find this vision fulfilled in the New Testament. The baptism in the Holy Spirit was meant to be the normal experience for Christians. Many believers have taken it to be a peak or climax of their walk with Jesus, but it's meant to be a basic experience. And Paul goes on to say in 1 Corinthians 14, that there's an even greater edification in prophecy. He substantiates Moses' vision by encouraging the believers, "So that you all may prophesy one by one."

Though God doesn't want us all jumping up to prophesy at once, in a disorderly manner, He desires that we all participate in this ministry of edification, comfort, and exhortation.

So Moses glimpsed it, Joel saw it as the Holy Spirit being poured out upon all flesh, Isaiah saw it and Pentecost realized it. Do you see it now? And have you entered into this vital ministry the Lord has for you?

Breaking Down The Walls

"Under His direction the whole body is fitted together perfectly, and each part in its own special way helps the other parts, so that the whole body is healthy and growing, and full of love."
Ephesians 4:16 (LB)

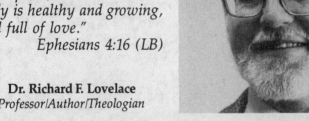

Dr. Richard F. Lovelace
Professor/Author/Theologian

There's a great sense of spiritual awakening abroad in America today. People are coming to the Lord from all kinds of different subcultures in our country alone, even from the homosexual and drug cultures.

Also, there's a sense of God's renewing or awakening in all of His people, the whole professing Church. I believe that it's a special burden upon the heart of Christ that the parts of His Church begin to fit together. How important it is that the different denominations and movements, such as the charismatic movement, the evangelical movement, and those concerned for social action and cultural change, begin to contribute to one another. Then the Body of Christ, not as parts, but as a whole, can cease contending and fighting and putting each other down and really be a witness to this world for Christ!

There are evidences today that this is indeed beginning to take place. A powerful renewing work is going on in the Roman Catholic Church today. A giant renewal is beginning to span many different denominations in Protestantism. The barriers are breaking down— between fundamentalists, charismatics, evangelicals, and even Christians emerging from liberalism. They're all being brought together in a common desire to advance the kingdom of Jesus Christ.

How are you "fitting in" with this "joining" that God is doing? It's easy to get wedged into the little corner of what your church or denomination is doing, to look upon God as merely being contained within the walls of a single point of view. Pray for this great renewal, and be open to what others in the Body of Christ might have to share that is uplifting to Him. See past the "joints" to the Head!

The Path Of Life

"Thou wilt show me the path of life: in Thy presence is fullness of joy; at Thy right hand are pleasures for evermore." Psalm 16:11

Dr. C. M. Ward
Evangelist/Teacher

Heaven has placed each of us on this earth to accomplish something that will tell for time and eternity. Human beings are not atoms or digits, or parts of an assembly line. We are each unique individuals designed by God with dignity for specific destinies that lie on a path that He wishes to show us.

In wandering from this path through sin, we are not merely breaking some sanction or regulation; we are failing to enter into the purpose and meaning that God desires to give to our existence.

Often we do not wish to follow this path because we fear that life lived God's way will be too limiting. This idea is false, because, in reality, the sense of oneness, of peace, of meaning in our lives is brought into focus by God's personal care for our individuality. According to this verse, there will be fullness of joy, as we are in complete touch with His perfectly designed gift of individual life.

Life is not a short run, a miasma of gospel singing, charismatic renewal, a blitz of giving, quickly extinguished. Life is not designed for the short space between diapers and wrinkles—it is for eternity. God's perfect plan does not end with our passing from this earthly scene. The path that He would have us on starts here, brings us into fullness of joy, and stretches on into eternity.

Finally, this path of life is not merely a system in which we are formulated to function. It is a Person: God's only Son, Jesus Christ. To know Him is to be in the path of life. To abide in the center of His will is to know the joy of what you were created to be. Take every step today in His footprints.

Pray About Everything

"Ask, and it shall be given you; seek, and ye shall find; knock, and it shall be opened unto you."
Matthew 7:7

Marolyn Ford
Author/Speaker

To me, the secret of this verse is that little word *"it."* *"It"* can stand for a hundred different things. If you're lonely, frustrated, or needing a friend, sick, having family problems, financial, material, physical, or emotional problems, you can always come to the Lord.

People write me and say, "I've been praying for years; why doesn't God release me from this burden?" I tell them that the Lord wants them to ask and keep on asking. Remember the parable Jesus told about the man who wanted a loaf of bread and went knocking on his neighbor's door after bedtime? The neighbor said, "Go away, I'm in bed!" But the man kept on knocking and knocking until his neighbor got out of bed and gave him what he needed, because he was such a pest.

This is the way it is in your Christian life. Not that the Lord is a grouchy neighbor who doesn't want to give. But He wants you to *keep on* asking and *keep on* talking with Him, about everything. So often you can fall into the trap of feeling like the Lord is a big God up in heaven who's just too busy with big things to be concerned about the little.

But He *is* concerned, because He knows that it's the everyday nitty gritty things that make up the whole of life. So it's not that God doesn't want to answer: He's trying to draw you into constant prayer with Him about *everything*.

Perhaps God has a number of little things He wants to do in your life before He gives you the big things, things that have never been done because you've never asked Him. Like James says, "ye have not because ye ask not" (James 4:2). Yes, those little, annoying problems *you've* been trying to solve! You know what they are. Why don't you start to ask today and keep on asking God to see to those things first?

Overflowing Love

"My prayer for you is that you will overflow more and more with love for others . . . always doing those good, kind things which show that you are a child of God . . ."
Philippians 1:9,11 (LB)

Cher Floria
Studio Singer

Paul's letter to the Philippians is filled with a prevailing joy that sounds like a man writing from the comforts of his vacation cottage, enjoying the beauty and serenity of self-imposed solitude. Yet Paul was in a Roman prison, enduring insults and beatings, receiving scant rations and sleeping on a wet stone floor.

One of the first things Paul mentions in his letter is a prayer that his Philippian brethren "overflow more and more with love for others." He also encourages them to grow in "spiritual knowledge and insight," that they would know right from wrong and be beyond reproach in their behavior, unsusceptible to criticism, "always doing those good, kind things which show that you are a child of God."

These qualities are what I would like to see in myself. It is the greatest challenge to read the first chapter of Philippians and see the supernatural love and strength of character that Paul has in the midst of life-threatening circumstances. His joy and trust in Christ to sustain him until God fulfilled His purpose for Paul's life is an inspiration to all believers.

To become the soldier in Christ that Paul was, I realize I must also be as willing a prisoner for Christ. Only by abandoning my self-serving comforts will I ever know the true comforting of God's Holy Spirit filling me with the same joy, love, and strength I see in Paul.

The wonderful and ironic joy in being a prisoner for Christ is that regardless of our circumstances we know freedom in our hearts, for "where the Spirit of the Lord is, there is liberty" (2 Corinthians 3:17).

Doing Well On Planet Earth

"He that spared not His own Son, but delivered Him up for us all, how shall He not with Him also freely give us all things?" Romans 8:32

Dr. Bill Basansky
Author/Evangelist

It's God that's doing fine on planet Earth today, not Satan. The devil's days are numbered, and that turkey is going to burn, but my Lord Jesus is going to remain forever. And when we as Christians realize the importance of Who our Father is and who we are in Christ, we're not going to walk around defeated. We're going to be "more than conquerors" (Romans 8:37). Not just conquerors, but MORE THAN CONQUERORS!

To me, that says a whole lot. And the reason we are more than conquerors is because Jesus took care of us at Calvary. Because He's still taking care of us, I can relax and praise and glorify God and have a wonderful time in life.

I don't care what the world does. I'm not part of the world. I'm in it, but not part of it. I'm part of a heavenly world, just a representative on this earth. I'm an ambassador for God, and He'll see to it that I always have enough to get around to do my job for Him.

I don't have to drive a tiny car, I can drive the biggest there is. Now I don't want to overemphasize material things. I'm saying that we need to look at God as being the greatest, because He is! God is big, and He's got enough of whatever we need.

You and I are washed in the blood of Jesus. The blood is what the devil hates. God didn't make this world for the devil and his gang. He made it for you and me, to have a good time here and now.

You can say that you used to have problems, but now you don't. You have Jesus to handle them. You've got health in Him. Prosperity in Him. Love in Him. Peace in Him. Joy in Him. You have everything that God's Word offers as long as the Living Word is in you. God gave them all freely. You can take them freely. When are you going to start?

Sharing The Light

". . . I will also give thee for a light to the Gentiles, that thou mayest be my salvation unto the end of the earth."
Isaiah 49:6

Dr. Ralph Winters
Missionologist

As the world's state of affairs are rapidly correlating with how Christ describes the end times, Christians—more than ever before, need to identify themselves with the great commission of Isaiah 49:6.

Our nation has the greatest access to the gospel of Jesus Christ of any people in the world. America has prospered as no other nation in history. God has blessed us in years past for our obedience to His commandment to "Go ye therefore, and teach all nations" the message of God's love made available to all through faith in Jesus Christ.

Only through our continued willingness to live and share the gospel of Christ with others is there hope for our nation. As we lift up the name of Jesus in our personal lives, in our government, by ministry outreach through foreign missionary projects and the use of media airwaves, God will lift up the United States of America.

The principle of giving and receiving applies to the message of salvation. As the United States gives the good news of salvation to the world, we will receive the joy of salvation in our homeland.

It is Christ's commission that you share the "Light" of Christ that makes real the hope and truth of God and His Love for all men. Allow God to use your prayers, financial support, and witness to show a hurting and skeptical world that Jesus Christ is the Lord of Salvation, who loves and cares for them.

Rebirth, Not Repair

"... no one tears a piece from a new cloak to patch an old one; if he does, he will have made a hole in the new cloak, and the patch from the new will not match the old."
Luke 6:36 (NEB)

Frank Constantino
Priest/Evangelist

God is not in the business of giving sinners a second chance. Lest that statement sound cruel to you, let me add to it that He *is* in the business of giving sinners new life. Jesus in this parable is expressing very simply a profound truth: that sinners do not need mending, they need replacing. This is the message I bring to the prisoners where I preach—regeneration, not rehabilitation.

Our prison system today is trying to change criminals through rehabilitation. This involves a system of rewards and punishments designed to alter an already existing lifestyle that society has found undesirable, patching up old behavior patterns to make them more socially acceptable by the world's standards.

But isn't this really like trying to patch up a bucket full of water that's leaking from a thousand holes? While you're patching up the holes, the bucket is still leaking. If you want to hold the water, you need a new bucket to contain it. Sinners need to be regenerated, born again, not rehabilitated or just patched up.

As Christians we also need to be reminded that we are not living a second chance either. We are new creations in Christ. The persons we used to be are now dead and have been buried with Him. The new life we now live is not the old one patched up by rewards and punishments. Morality alone can not bring righteousness or godliness. Learn to draw on the new life of Jesus in you, and get some relief from the struggle of trying to patch yourself up. A new coat doesn't have to try to be new; it simply *is* new, fresh off the rack. Don't you work at being new either. Just put on Jesus; let Him shine through you and enjoy how well you look with Him as your covering.

Are You Persuaded?

"For I am persuaded, that neither death, nor life, nor angels, nor principalities, nor powers . . . nor any other creature, shall be able to separate us from the love of God, which is in Christ Jesus our Lord." Romans 8:38-39

Mike Warnke
Author/Comedian

Having been a Satanist and occultist, I don't know what would have become of me without this verse after I became a Christian. The devil fought me for years, trying to make me believe his lies, like:

"Warnke, you turkey, you know Christianity isn't going to work. God doesn't love you anymore, you're bound to make a fatal mistake. You're not good enough for Him to keep on forgiving you! Nah, nah, nah!"

Well, listen devil, this scripture says that nothing created, (and you and all your demons *were* created, remember) could ever possibly keep me from Jesus' love. Not you and all your uglies, nor how good I can be, nor how lousy I feel, can keep His love from flowing down on me.

And with the love of the Lord, I can do anything, and I can make it, and I can be a success. And I don't have to worry about you coming in and ripping off my salvation, you degenerate old crook.

I can depend on Christ always loving me. Plus notice, devil, that it says "things present or things to come" can't separate me. It talks about now and the future and doesn't even mention the past. 'Cause the past isn't even important after Jesus comes in. It's all been wiped away. So don't even mention the past coming between me and the Lord.

Brother or sister in the Lord, God made the devil let go of this "yours frog-faced truly," that the old snake thought he had tight in his hands. But Satan can't make God let go. That's why I'm persuaded.

Are you?

Ambassadors For Christ

"And for me, that utterance may be given unto me, that I may open my mouth boldly, to make known the mystery of the gospel, For which I am an ambassador in bonds . . ." Ephesians 6:19-20

Leland Schultz
Nat. Dir., Com. Div., Assemblies of God

Unfortunately, many of us in the Body of Christ are reactors rather than conscious actors of God's work through our lives. We react: if someone else smiles, we smile; if someone else speaks, we speak— rather than *we* being the ones to approach people, letting our lives reflect the mystery of the gospel.

Utterance here signifies more than just vocal expression. We communicate Jesus to the world around us through our conduct, our expressions, our attitudes, and our actions. *Boldness* is coming out and through our lives letting people know, not who we are, but who Christ is in us. This is the task of an *ambassador* to be an expressor and communicator of the will of the power that rules him. As a man called to this position, I am *bound* to fulfill this calling. God has yoked me to a different way of expressing this than I had imagined, but my commitment has been to His direction, rather than to my own original wishes.

This boldness can only come through a strong commitment to following Jesus Christ every moment of the day. Our walk with God isn't just something we put on Sunday morning and take off Sunday night, and dust off again for Wednesday prayer meeting. It's a dynamic, active movement through every day, with Christ as our entire life. Not a lifestyle, to be changed with whims and seasons like a suit of clothes, but a life, which is Christ, in the heart, under the skin, on the lips, in the hands. This, Christ in us as our whole existence, is the *mystery* of the gospel!

Lord, let me not just live with You clinging loosely to me, to be discarded when it's convenient. But this day, may I be *Your* garment, worn by You to enhance Your beauty. Let me be bold to let You shine forth!

Blessings Out Of Tragedy

"And we know that all things work together for good to them that love God, to them who are the called according to His purpose."Romans 8:28

Lenor Madruga
Author/Radio Show Host

Can a terrible tragedy cause a life to soar? How but by God's Word could I explain that He has turned cancer, an amputated leg and hip and even drug addiction into means by which He could deliver rich blessings for me!

The Lord had become my personal Savior two years before, in 1972. Weekly Bible studies with an excellent teacher in my home and good fellowship had prepared me for the blow that was to fall. But suddenly, I knew that my successful modeling career was finished, and that everything in my world had changed forever.

Though family and friends were a great consolation to me, there were adjustments I could not possibly have made without the miraculous help of the Lord. First, there was the morphine addiction acquired during recuperation, with its own torment and spiritual disorientation; the Lord enabled me to conquer it almost immediately, cold turkey. Then, the "phantom pain" I suffer in some measure to this day—in the limb that's no longer there! There was also the problem of fitting and learning to use the artificial leg and hip. The Lord solved that so well that today I'm able to do practically anything a normal person can, to the astonishment of doctors. The Lord has given me a new career in radio, and now I'm also able to share through my book and testimony as I travel telling people of what a wonderful God can do. I've never been happier.

No matter what may happen or may have happened to you, the Lord can take it and use it for His glory and your joy. Personal tragedy, such as mine, in the physical body, or in the life or loss of a loved one, or in your own life, certainly contains a hidden blessing, stored by the mercy of God. Have you asked the Lord to reveal it? Do it now!

Look What God Can Do

" . . . His grace which was bestowed upon me was not in vain; but I labored more abundantly than they all: yet not I, but the grace of God which was with me."
I Corinthians 15:10

Jim Conway
Minister/Author

"You can do all things through Christ, who's strengthening you." Who, me? That sounded like the Lord's voice, but He had to be joking. I was insecure and inadequate. I was a failure at everything. I kept getting promoted in high school just so they could move me out. My high school principal told my Dad not to waste money sending me to college, because I'd never succeed. My high school guidance counselors kept telling me, "Why don't you go to trade school and find something useful to do with your hands?" As kindly as they could, they were saying, "You don't have anything from the shoulders up."

So this really was God talking? "I'll never leave you or forsake you. Fear not, I'm with you always." These words from God kept on coming to me. What right did I have on the basis of established potential or accomplishment to step out? Prephaps none, but I couldn't deny that the love and grace of God were pressing me on. It wasn't a result of my I.Q. or family background. It was God's impact on my life.

Look at what God can do with a life! I've been around the world twice, have master degrees in science, psychology, and divinity, doctorates in divinity and pastoral ministries, and am pastoring a church of 2,000 people on a university campus. But I am who I am by the grace of God.

Has God ever whispered words of encouragement to you that you've rejected because you just can't imagine being capable or useful to Him? He may want to favor you with surprises you've never dreamed possible. You are a vessel all the more able to work for Him because you have no confidence in your strength. Do you dare to say to Him, "Yes, Lord, if that's what you want for me, have your own way?"

Jesus Has Paid Your Penalty

"For He hath made him to be sin for us, who knew no sin; that we might be made the righteousness of God in Him."
2 Corinthians 5:21

Terry Law
Evangelist

This explains for us the Divine exchange that happened at Calvary: Jesus took the sin of the whole world upon Himself, and in exchange He offered us the righteousness of God and all that God has.

Billy Graham tells a story about how once, while he was traveling through a Southern state, he exceeded the speed limit a little and got stopped by a policeman. He was politely escorted to a local court, which was to be conducted in a small town barber shop.

Billy went in and faced the judge, seated there in a barber's chair. "How do you plead?" asked the judge. "I plead guilty, your honor," Billy answered meekly. And the barber-judge said, "That's going to cost you $15.00." He looked at Billy quietly for a moment.

"Say," he said slowly, "aren't you the famous preacher, Billy Graham?" "Yes, I am," Billy answered. "Well," said the judge, "that's still going to be $15.00."

"But," he went on, "I'll tell you what I'm going to do. You've been such a great help to me and my family, I'm going to pay your fine." So he reached into his back pocket, pulled out $15.00 and laid it on the cash register and let Billy go. Billy paid nothing.

That's exactly what Jesus did even though we hadn't done Him any good, as Billy had the judge. Jesus paid the penalty. Somebody had to pay the penalty for your sin. God couldn't just turn His back on that sin and say, "All right, you're forgiven—go your way." Jesus paid your penalty. In so doing, He became sin, and you in the process became totally free, forgiven, a son of God! I hope you'll rejoice as much today as you did the hour you first met Jesus, for what He did, and what He gave to you.

Whoever Believeth

"But as many as received Him, to them gave He power to become the sons of God, even to them that believe on His name."   *John 1:12*

M.C.Johnson
Pastor/Conference Speaker

There are people who think that only they and their little group are going to heaven. Doctrines and nationalities and denominations have been Satan's "divide and conquer" tools whenever folks have let them stand in the way of the free message of the gospel.

But God in this word through John would declare to us that there is no exclusive group that's destined alone for heaven. Salvation is free to as many as receive Christ. It's as simple as that. If we open our hearts to Jesus, we don't enter into some second class relationship, we become sons, children of God. Think of that: the God of the universe Himself becomes our Father.

And when we become His sons, according to Galatians 3:29, we are "Abraham's seed, and heirs according to the promise." In other words, every promise God ever made to Abraham is ours also in Christ.

I used to think that only the Hebrews were God's chosen people. I no longer believe that. I believe that *whoever* is in Christ is now an heir of the covenant God made with Abraham, now made complete as an everlasting covenant through relationship with God in Christ.

This verse made me realize that there was no doubt about it. I was included, regardless of my past, my nationality, or my denomination. God didn't say salvation was mine if I'd been good, if I'd bought my way into the kingdom or worked my way in. Just "as many as received Him." And I was one of them.

Have you ever questioned your own salvation—or anyone else's because of the kind of church or brand of preacher that led you to the Lord? Don't judge yourself; if you have Jesus, you have it all.

"Hands And Feet" For Your Faith

". . . All things are possible to him that believeth. . . Even so faith, if it hath not works, is dead, being alone."
Mark 9:23, James 2:17

Rita Warren
Author/Crusader

These two verses must be placed side by side, because if faith has no "hands and feet," it will get nowhere and do nothing. God has chosen for you and me to carry out His work on earth, and that work consists not only in believing Him, but in doing for Him because we have the faith to do so.

You may tell me that you have mustard seed faith to move mountains. But will you then go and put your shoulder against one and start pushing? That would be faith, that is what these scriptures are saying, there is no such thing as faith without works.

Some people think I am a crazy lady because I walk the halls of Congress talking to officials in government so that we can get the right to prayer back into our public schools. But because so many good people have refused to "get involved" in the affairs of our country, Congress no longer opens with prayer, God has been thrust out of the government of our land, and our country's position in the world has declined distressingly.

No, I am not being a doomsayer about America. God never loses a battle. We are fighting today because we are not defeated, we are winning! In my home state of Massachusetts, prayer is back in the schools. God is working in California to restore prayer to the schools there, too.

But He is not working alone. God's people are rising up and starting to be counted for what's right. Are you willing to join God's people like Paul, Martin Luther, John Wesley, and millions of others down the centuries who have striven with Christ to turn the world upside down?

Crucified!

"But God forbid that I should glory, save in the cross of our Lord Jesus Christ, by whom the world is crucified unto me, and I unto the world."   Galatians 6:14

James H. Thompson
Pastor

Separation of believers in Jesus Christ from the world has been one of the most frequently discussed and preached on themes of the Church since its birth. Debates about how far believers ought to stand apart from the world in behavior, dress and character have had Christians chewing over bones of contention for centuries. But Paul in this verse explains the true foundation of the believer's separation as in the death of Jesus Christ itself—not as merely a matter of externals, but as a spiritual, inner reality.

Jesus' death is the most important fact of universal history. Far more than the death of one man was involved. All of humanity was split in two when Jesus died, and this verse tells us that the two halves of humanity, those who would believe in Jesus, and those who would reject Him, became dead to one another. No longer could there be full communication between the followers of Jesus and the citizens of the world system outside of Christ.

Have you ever felt confused about where you belong in the Body of Christ and wondered at times whether, in fact, you'd feel more comfortable back in the world? Did you ever try again to share on a heart-to-heart basis with the old friends you knew before you met Jesus? You probably experienced a gap there, a sense of apartness. This is the effect of Jesus' death, 2000 years ago, on your life today.

If you belong to Jesus, you do not have to strive to be separated from the world; you are already different because you died many years ago with Jesus Christ. His nature is in you, and you cannot be what you once were. Praise God, the separation is already accomplished!

"Digging In"

"Study to show thyself approved unto God, a workman that needeth not to be ashamed rightly dividing the word of truth."

2 Timothy 2:15

Elmer Dringenberg
Ministry of Helps/Usher

Some people think that the responsibility for studying the Word of God rests exclusively upon the professional ministers of the gospel among us. It's true, there are many wonderful teachers of the Word ministering today. And, it's very easy to go from conference to conference, meeting to meeting, just soaking up teaching.

There was all kinds of teaching in the Lutheran Church where I was reared, the Baptist church where I got saved, and the Holiness Bible school I attended. But everywhere I went, I heard different points of view, and frequently, my thoughts became confused. You see, though I was getting fed a certain amount of the Word, I was like a baby bird, eating second hand what its mother had caught and partially digested. A lot of Scripture passed through my brain without my really knowing what it meant. And although I was sitting in church a good deal, my life was still sinful in many areas, and God didn't have my heart.

So after meeting the Lord, I was impressed to study the Bible on my own. There's just no substitute for discovering the riches of the Word for yourself. Now, I never planned to be a preacher, but God makes it clear in this verse that if He is to be pleased, I have to search His Word for heart knowledge as well as head.

In God's kingdom, there's no such thing as a "layman." If you know Jesus, you've been made a "king and priest" (Revelation 5:10), with authority and responsibility to properly carry out God's will. You may never be a preacher, but whatever you do, God's got ruling instructions for you. Start finding them for yourself in His Word today.

Proof Positive

"Trust in the Lord with all thine heart: and lean not unto thine own understanding. In all thy ways acknowledge Him, and He shall direct thy paths."   Proverbs 3:5-6

Dr. Donald R. Witaker
Physician/Surgeon

Being a professional man, all my training channeled me into a life of self-sufficiency. Twenty-four of the 47 years of my life were spent in educational institutions: for 12 years after high school and throughout my internship as a physician, I was taught to depend upon my own abilities, mental and physical.

With reliance upon my own diagnostic and decision-making powers so ingrained in me, it was very difficult for me when receiving salvation to learn dependence upon God in my medical practice. I had to retrain my heart to lean toward God when the pressures of life or death crises bore down on me.

Also, my understanding needed reordering. I had been a professed atheist because I was a highly educated man who would recognize nothing but laboratory proof, and God's existence was not subject to my kind of analysis. God, for me and other scientists, was a myth for the superstitious, the weak, and the uneducated.

God changed my perception by showing me Himself in the wondrous order of nature's patterning of the microscopic atom and the vast universe. When I became convinced of His sustaining power in the functioning of all things, great and small, I began to rest in the faith that He would direct all of my life's events.

Has that faith become settled in your heart? Do you know that as God cares for each subatomic particle and each giant star, He has every particle of your life in His hands? Do you imagine that He who has numbered every hair of your head and watches each sparrow fall has overlooked your needs, though he upholds all else that is?

Put Off The Old, Put On The New

. . . But one thing I do: forgetting what lies behind and reaching forward to what lies ahead, I press on toward the goal for the prize of the upward call of God in Christ Jesus.

Philippians 3:13b-14 (NAS)

Rev. Calvin Bacon
Pastor/Teacher

Most of us are collectors. We have difficulty turning loose of things that we've discarded. We keep our old shoes, old clothes, even our old furniture in the attic when it ought to be tossed away.

So with our minds: We want to progress in right thinking and right appearance, but we don't want to throw away the old and put on the new. But Paul said that he *forgot* those things which were behind. Forgetting is active—something he *made* himself do. So too, we must take action and forget what's behind. We live so far below our true capabilities because we hang onto the old rather than reaching out for the new. Just as we feel better with new clothes on, we act better with a new mind. Salvation, the Bible says, is the renewing of the mind.

All nature believes in the right to new apparel. God Himself gives us an example by causing the trees, the animals, and the birds to put on new clothes as the seasons change. As we've been made in His image, I don't believe He expects us to do any less. I believe we should look and act like we belong to Him.

If you will make preparation for the new, it will come to you almost automatically. You only have to have a need to get a supply. When you make way for the new by discarding the old, God always comes through. Forget those things which are behind you and press forward to those that lie ahead. Today is the first day of the rest of your life. Live it to the fullest in the power of Christ in you!

Right Where God Wants You

"For the kingdom of God is not meat and drink; but righteousness, and peace, and joy in the Holy Ghost. For he that in these things serveth Christ is acceptable to God, and approved of men."
Romans 14:17-18

Ben Swett
Singer

Going to the mission field by faith back in 1960, my wife and I had to depend on man's approval to a great extent to take care of us financially while we were there. Back some years before, when I was first saved, baptized in the Holy Spirit, and growing in God, I didn't think that the approval of men was something I could hope for in this life. But then I found this verse, which told me that if a man is serving God rightly, he will receive, on God's promises, everything he might need in life, including the favor of men.

The righteousness we have to serve God with is not our own, but His. I lose myself in Him. Daily, I commit myself afresh to Him. You know, I like to hand myself over to the Lord before getting out of bed every morning. I tell Him, "Lord, this is a day you've made. I can't do anything without You today. I need Your strength and the anointing of Your Holy Spirit, so I can make the right decisions and react the way You would want me to."

Then whatever heights or depths or struggles or joys the day brings, I have that joy and inner peace at the heart of those experiences. Even in recent grief over the loss of four dear loved ones, that peace has been mine. And the Lord has caused men to look favorably on our ministry, maybe in part because that peace and joy have been so contagious.

Righteousness is just a big word meaning that a person's right where God wants him. You can't go wrong if you just set your eyes on Him and place yourself in His hands. Have you worried about God's accepting you or about how people are looking at you? You just try what I've done, and see if the Lord doesn't take those worries right off your shoulders.

God's RDA'S

*"But grow in grace, and
in the knowledge of our Lord
and Savior Jesus Christ . . ."*
2 Peter 3:18

Richard K. Tanon
Prison Chaplain

Certain foods and dietary substances such as proteins and vitamins are essential for the proper growth and maintenance of human life. All foods purchased in this country must specify on their packaging their ingredients and the amounts of vitamins they contain.

The back of a package will say: Percentage of U. S. recommended daily allowances (U.S. RDA):

Protein	20%
Vitamin A	10%
Vitamin C	2% and so on.

These ingredients are always listed in order of their quantity, the largest amount being listed first. In the spiritual realm, there are also RDA's (Recommended Daily Allowances) which are essential for spiritual growth and maturity of Christian character. Without these, a believer will be malnourished spiritually. They are, in order of importance:

1. Love for God (Luke 10:27), which will result in . . .
2. Daily prayer (1 Thessalonians 5:17), and . . .
3. Daily Bible reading (John 5:39), which will conclude in . . .
4. Departing from iniquity (Psalm 119:11), and . . .
5. Love for your fellow man (1 John 3:14-18).

All of these great faith and life builders can be found in the package of God's Holy Word. Make sure today that you get all the nourishment you need. And if you should ever feel the need for a pick-me-up, don't reach for a cup of coffee and a roll: take a bite of one of God's RDA's and get a real life!

You Don't Cry Alone

"Thou hast turned for me my mourning into dancing: thou hast put off my sack-cloth, and girded me with gladness." Psalm 30:11

Diane Bringgold
Author

Has anyone ever told you, while you were suffering from grief or regret, "Well, you'll just have to make the best of it?" When you're beset with grief, that's cold comfort, isn't it? And it's not very good advice because your main problem is that you *can't* handle the situation. "Laugh, and the whole world laughs with you; cry, and you cry alone," says the old saying. So you keep on trying to bear the burden of grief yourself, without success.

In this scripture, God offers real comfort for suffering. God doesn't point you back to yourself and tell you just to grin and bear it. He declares here that He can turn mourning to dancing, put off the garments of sorrow and replace them with "glad rags," if you'll just stop trying to "be strong" and instead hand your sorrow over to Him.

When my husband and children were killed and I was badly burned in an airplane crash in the California mountains, I at first hid myself, hoping not to be rescued. I didn't know how it would be possible for me to bear the grief. I wanted to die there, but God would not take my life. Finally, my heart simply cried out to Him that He would have to carry the grief, because I could not. At that moment, the burden began to slip from my shoulders. I never picked it up again.

No, when you cry, you don't cry alone. "Surely He hath borne our griefs and carried our sorrows" (Isaiah 53:4). Jesus is right beside you when you weep, waiting to dry every tear. No matter how great the burden of anguish, He can take it and exchange it for joy. If you're hurting right now, ask Jesus to take your burden and give you His gladness this very day.

Living Out Our Faith

"The blind receive their sight, and the lame walk, the lepers are cleansed, and the deaf hear, the dead are raised up, and the poor have the gospel preached to them."
Matthew 11:5

Dr. Fred Ladenius
Editor/Evangelist

Two disciples of John the Baptist stood before Jesus asking on behalf of the imprisoned John if Jesus was indeed the Messiah they were looking for. I can imagine that by the time the Savior had neared the end of this catalogue of mighty miracles, the disciples were probably already hurrying excitedly for the door to bring John the answer of Jesus.

But wait! Jesus had something else to say: "the gospel is preached to the poor." Notice that Jesus spoke first about the miracles He had performed, then about the gospel. In my church, and perhaps in yours, too, we took it for granted for a long time that the miracles of Jesus were always a consequence of faith in the gospel message. But in the New Testament accounts, many times Jesus came first with miracles. Then people were willing to listen to what He had to say.

In the European churches where I preach, I always precede my message with a prayer to God for at least one miracle that can be obviously witnessed by all. As God brings wonderful healings and signs, an openness is created in the hearts of those hearing the Word.

Just so, in the place God has given for you to share His life and message, people will be more interested in the things you do than in what you say. You, too, can be a vessel of His love and healing power wherever you are. You can, by your prayer and living influence, bless others in your home, place of business, school, or church.

Lord Jesus, we pray that we might be demonstrators as well as sharers of your gospel. We ask You to show us just what You would have us do for glory, wherever we find ourselves this day. In Jesus' name, Amen.

Start Dreaming

"Now unto Him that is able to do exceeding abundantly above all that we ask or think, according to the power that worketh in us . . ."
Ephesians 3:20

Paul D. Zink
Pastor/Author

Has God given you any ideas or dreams that are just lying on the shelf of your mind, never coming to pass? Well, I've got some exciting news for you! As long as they're in line with the Word of God, those dreams are tangibles, and not intangibles: they can come true, and this scripture is the proof of it. If you can ask or think it, God can do it, and even more, as long as it's in His will.

All of my ministry rests on the belief that there's no task or ministry too big for God. Dr. Cho of Korea is a good example of this. In March of 1979, over 81,000 people were attending his church. So many times we put limits on God when there aren't any. The only "limits" He has are our lack of vision and imagination.

Satan is the thief who comes in with discouragement and negative thinking to steal and kill and destroy your dreams. His biggest trick is to try to make us inferior. But Jesus came to give us life abundantly, and that abundance means "more than we could ever possibly use."

I believe the greatest ministries are yet to be. The greatest books are yet to be written. The greatest dreams you have are yet to become realities. The Holy Spirit within us can empower us to make them real. And He's speaking to your heart, saying, "Hey, you do have that ability." The devil is trying to steal it from you. But if you'll hold onto it, there's no way he can do it!

You're a child of the kingdom. You're God's best. He's put you where you are, to will and to do His good pleasure. He's made you responsible to be diligent to dream and to accomplish that godly heart's desire He gave you. Start to make that dream a reality today.

Closet Christians

"For I am not ashamed of the gospel of Christ: for it is the power of God unto salvation to every one that believeth; to the Jew first, and also to the Greek."

Romans 1:16

Donny Gatlyn
Singer

There are just too many closet Christians in the world today. They're like suits that have been to the cleaners and had all the spots and stains taken out. Maybe they've been Spirit-filled, too, so they've got cellophane wrapped around them just to keep them clean. They look great, they're beautifully pressed and smell all fresh and new. But nobody ever sees them, and they're doing nobody any good. They're just hanging out there, keeping out of trouble, waiting for the big wedding banquet to begin when all the struggle's over.

Now, I don't mean to sound condemning, but Jesus did say, "Whoever therefore shall be ashamed of Me and of My words . . . of him shall the Son of man be ashamed, when He cometh in the glory of His Father with the holy angels" (Mark 8:38). I don't want to be in the company of those Jesus is ashamed of, do you?

How in the world can we, who've got the world's best-dressed souls, be ashamed to tell people where we got them? What's the matter with so many of us? Are we afraid we're going to get smirched with mud or have tomatoes thrown at us if we get out there and share the good news? So what if we do! There are souls out there, going to hell. The time is getting short. It's better to get a little dirty and see a soul saved!

The next time you're on a supermarket line, or at the bank, or at work, or talking to an unsaved neighbor or friend, take that Jesus suit out of the closet and put it on display. Maybe God will have you give it away. Are you willing to do that for Him?

Don't Second-Guess God!

"Call unto Me, and I will answer thee, and show thee great and might things, which thou knowest not."
Jeremiah 33:3

Archie Dennis
Evangelist/Singer

Never try to second-guess the Lord: He's in touch with details in your life that you cannot possibly know ahead of time. Let me tell you about some "little surprises" He's had in store for me.

Back in 1972, while still unmarried, I asked the Lord to let me set eyes on my future wife. And that year, everywhere I went, I looked with expectancy, asking the Lord each time I met a likely lady, "Is she the one?"

In September, I was invited to dinner, and one of the guests was a young, attractive widow. I knew she was a woman of quality, but when I found that she had four children, I started raising objections to the Lord: "Oh, no Lord, you wouldn't do this to me!" Time and time again, I entreated Him: "Lord, I feel that she's the one, but what about the children?" And the Lord answered, "I can take that which is not and cause it to become. You are saying that the children are not yours but I can make them yours."

That was over three years ago, and God has done just that. The children have been adopted; they all now have my name, along with my dear wife. So God certainly showed me great and mighty things that I'd overlooked. Thank God I sought His aid!

After you have entrusted a problem to the Lord, be ready for an answer that might be much different from the one you'd at first expect. Putting the situation into His hands really means that you are making *Him* the Master of it. Are you willing today to let Him be Lord of the unclear issues in your life? Perhaps it's time to seek the answer from Him and accept a surprise if you must!

Go Forward!

"And the Lord said unto Moses, Wherefore criest thou unto me? Speak unto the children of Israel, that they go forward."   Exodus 14:15

Benson Idahosa
African Evangelist

Have you ever been afraid?

When God spoke this command to Moses, it must have been with some sadness, realizing just how frightened His people were. The Pharoah and his soldiers were racing toward them and the Red Sea was blocking escape.

Instead of remembering the great works God had performed to deliver them, including the plagues He allowed to fall upon the Egyptians in order to show His mighty power—the children of Israel began complaining.

Then in the midst of their fears, when the children of Israel had given up on God, He spoke to Moses to lift his rod over the sea, and as he did the waters parted.

In our pressurized society, it is very easy to turn around and see, as the children of Israel did, all of our problems about to overtake us with no way of escape. But as David wrote in Psalm 46:1, "God is our refuge and strength, a very present help in trouble." He is forever intervening on the behalf of His children to deliver us from those that seek to overcome us; our enemies, failures and circumstances . . . He is bigger than all of them!

He tells us in Jeremiah 33:3 to "Call unto me, and I will answer thee, and show thee great and mighty things, which thou knowest not."

Today, as in the day of Moses, God is speaking to His people to "go forward." He will part your "Red Seas" for you and lead you to the "promise land" of His purpose and fulfillment for your life.

We Are His Hands

"Verily, verily, I say unto you, He that believeth on Me, the works that I do shall he do also; and greater works than these shall he do; because I go unto my Father." John 14:12

Tim Bagwell
Pastor/Evangelist

We have been commissioned not just to be blessed, but to be a blessing to others. My feeling as a pastor and evangelist is that when God brings somebody to His home, into His body, that He's not brought us there just to receive. He has also given us the power through the Holy Spirit to do the exploits that Jesus did.

Because He ascended into the heavens, we took His place in the physical realm on the earth. When His physical body returned to the right hand of the Father, He left us, to be filled with His Spirit, that the sicknesses could still be healed, the bondages still be broken, the confusions still be calmed, the heartaches still be mended.

Instead of His physical hands touching those in need, now our hands touch them. Our voices cry out in prayer. Our legs do the walking. Our eyes do the seeing of the needs. But His Spirit still does the work.

He says, "You believe in Me—what I did, you can do!" I believe this to be a definite decree to us to take the limits off of God, and off of our own lives. We are His temples, His vessels, His people, and all things are possible in our lives. The healings, deliverances, and miracles of the Bible are not just things recorded in historical pages, but they have been given to us to show us what we can do.

So as you read through the Gospels, recognize that anything you see the Lord do, any power you see Him manifest, including resurrection, healing, loosing the captive, ministering to the broken hearted and confused mind, He has given you the right to do! And once you know that it's yours to do, you may do it at once—starting now!

Warriors For Christ

"And from the days of John the Baptist until now the kingdom of heaven suffereth violence, and the violent take it by force."   Matthew 11:12

George Otis
Author/Lecturer

Today as never before, the warrior spirit is needed among Christian believers, to wrest ground from the enemy. Make no mistake about it: we are in a battle, wrestling against "principalities and powers, against the rulers of the darkness of this world, against spiritual wickedness in high places" (Ephesians 6:12). While our weapons are not fleshly ones like guns and swords, the willingness to get into the thick of spiritual warfare is stressed by Jesus' words.

The Greek here indicates that the kind of people Jesus is speaking of are forceful, determined, tenacious, the sort of people who desire to lay hold on the kingdom of God so much that nothing will discourage them. The walk of faith in Jesus Christ is not passive, but active—God is accomplishing His will on earth in large measure through what we will reach out for and make happen.

Recently, I had a part in founding a radio station in Lebanon, which I sincerely feel will fulfill a Bible prophecy found in Isaiah 29:17-18. This passage speaks of something coming out of Lebanon which will awaken the nation of Israel. Today that radio station is beaming the Word of God throughout Israel. It was built literally under fire, with artillery shells exploding all around. But the gospel message is going out, and God promises that it will bear a harvest.

You have within you the same determined spirit Jesus spoke of, waiting for release. Think of the power of God that may be released right where you live, if you begin to exercise the God-given spiritual authority that is yours. Resist Satan today and he will flee from you. Don't hang back—pick up the Sword of the Spirit, and win ground for God.

Your Part In Life

> *"I sought the Lord, and He heard me, and delivered me from all my fears."*
> Psalm 34:4

David Zimmerman
Actor

As an actor, I played many different parts over the years. The one part I didn't know how to play was myself. I was living an image of myself. I couldn't get down to where my true emotions were. I was afraid to find out who I was. I portrayed the people from day to day that I thought I ought to be.

But God made me and molded me to be a unique individual, and after I met Him, he began to show me who I was. My wife Sherry experienced some very serious medical problems, with much suffering. And somehow as I stood by her side and endured with her, my own real emotions began to come to the surface. I cared so much about what was happening to her that it took me beyond myself. Soon it dawned on me that God wanted to show me that I could be a real person, so I began to ask Him to show me my true self. The more I asked Him, the more He showed me.

Then, as the Lord brought Sherry through and gave her courage, my fear left, because I could see that through it all, God was sovereign, totally in control of our lives. That meant that both Sherry and I could rest in what God was doing in our lives. I knew that I no longer needed to be self-conscious, because in God's hands, there was nothing to fear.

God is shaping and transforming your life right now. He knows all of your fears, and He wants to tell you that they are groundless if you belong to Him. You're free to trust Him, love Him, obey Him, and be all He desires for you to be. Ask Him this minute to help you repent of that sin or fear in your life, and fill you with boldness and peace.

You Are Being Watched

"For I think that God hath set forth us the apostles last, as it were appointed to death: for we are made a spectacle unto the world, and to angels, and to men."

1 Corinthians 4:9

Sherry Zimmerman
Actress

Everything we do or say in this world is being witnessed by either men or angels! That's right, that's what this verse says. The word translated here as "spectacle" means "theater" in the original Greek. The Apostle Paul is saying in this verse that our lives are always on display to someone, and this should affect how we behave.

Have you ever had to give a speech or act in a play? Do you remember how careful you were to know your lines well? Can you remember how concerned you were about standing and moving properly? Why did you make such careful preparations? Because you knew that there was an audience out there before which you had to appear. And you knew you wouldn't be able to do a good job without rehearsal.

Do you think your life might change in anyway if you could always see an audience around you of men and angels watching your every move? Are there some things you now do that you'd cut out of your life? Are there some places you now go that you'd begin to avoid? Would you perhaps guard your tongue a little more carefully? Perhaps God through the words of Paul purposely painted this "scene" just so we'd begin to take the way we live more seriously.

Notice what kind of scene we're called upon to play. It's a death scene. Our life is meant to be one of death to self so we can be poured out for others as we become alive to Christ.

You have a part to play for God right where you are. No one else can take your place. No one else can be the witness for Christ that you can. How are you going to play that part, knowing the great audience that surrounds you? Jesus says: "Play it by the direction of My Word, from the heart."

The Eternal Seed

"Being born again, not of corruptible seed, but of incorruptible, by the Word of God which liveth and abideth forever." 1 Peter 1:23

Pat Shaughnessy
Pastor/Conference Speaker

Not many living things have the durability of plant seeds. The seed of corn and some flowers has carried the germ of life in it for hundreds of centuries: seed has been found in the pyramids of Egypt that can still reproduce if it's planted.

But in the passage of time, all material things become subject to decay and corruption. When we as individuals are born into this world, in a sense, we have already begun to die. But as we who believe in Christ, experience our new, or second birth, a seed is sown in us that will never perish: and that seed is the living and abiding Word of God!

That lively seed pulsating within us is our strength and our light. Regardless of all the things around us that seem to be falling apart, that part of our being which God has sown in us through His Word will stand firm and safe.

Now, if I had believed while involved in a serious explosion at an airport that God was mad at me, or had stopped loving me, or had discarded me, I would have reacted negatively, getting discouraged or depressed. But I knew that nothing happens to me without God's knowing it, that all things work together for my good because I'm His child, and that His living Word in me was turning that death-type event into life for my spirit.

You will always react to the stimuli of life according to what you believe. You may perceive some things as good, some as bad. But because God loves you and cares for you, each experience can become "fertilizer" for that eternal seed. Be an open furrow for the Lord's cultivator today.

The Shield And The Prize

"After these things the word of the Lord came unto Abram in a vision, saying, Fear not, Abram: I am thy shield, and thy exceeding great reward." Genesis 15:1

Sylvester Blue
Singing Evangelist

In the preceding chapter, the king of Sodom had offered Abram all the spoil that the king had taken from a battle. But Abram had refused it, saying that he would not accept even a shoelace, lest the king say that he had made Abram rich. For Abram knew that his real riches lay in knowing the Lord Most High, possessor of heaven and earth.

So not long after that, the Lord Himself appeared to Abram and offered something far better than any earthly king could: the Lord gave Abram Himself. Imagine, the Lord of hosts, becoming Abram's shield, his protection, his security, standing between Abram and all his foes. God Almighty here became Abram's exceeding great reward, his supply, his sufficiency, his all in all.

Oh, just to be filled with God! Since we found this verse, my wife and I have learned just to pray for God to give us Himself. We don't have to be worried about money or material things or security, but just to be filled with the presence of God every moment of our lives. We've found that in Him, all our needs are met, for being within us, He knows just what they are, just as they happen to us. And the joy He's given us, no man can take away. For His joy is within us along with His own presence, which has come to abide.

Paul said, "If God be for us, who can be against us?" (Romans 8:31). And if God is in us, there is nothing greater to possess. Ask God this day to make you aware of the shield and protector you have in Him, and the reward of the exceeding joy of all that is yours by His indwelling presence.

Stand For Righteousness

"I can do all things through Christ which strengtheneth me."
Philippians 4:13

Judy Mamou
Evangelist

We Christians can affect our world far more than we do, if we'll just take this verse and run with it. For example, all over America, believers are disgusted with the fare being produced by the worldly entertainment industry. Yet, we're not doing the things we can to stop the spread of filth and corruption in the media. Let me share with you what God is able to accomplish when we take Him at His Word.

A major television network recently produced a feature length motion picture dramatizing an incestuous relationship between a mother and son. It was scheduled to be aired in just a few weeks. Many Christians in Texas where I live, got upset about it. Some merely said, "Isn't it terrible? But there's nothing we can do about it but pray." Brother or sister in the Lord, this simply isn't true! You *can* influence what is shown on the networks in *your* locale! Others told us, "Nothing will happen if you get involved." They were wrong.

In spite of ridicule and huge odds, a few of us who were concerned organized a write-in campaign directed at the local station. Then we followed it up with a mass demonstration. When we arrived 300 strong to picket the station and hold a pray-in, the station manager began to listen. God took control of the situation, and the program was stricken from the schedule.

God is not only trying to inspire us in our personal lives. He wants to stir us up to be instruments of change in the world around us. If I and a handful of people can do things like this, so can you. Ask God right now to show you what part you might play in helping to make your town, state, and nation a fit place to live.

Delighting In God

"Delight thyself also in the Lord; and He shall give thee the desires of thine heart."   *Psalm 37:4*

Nancy Harmon
Music Artist

Usually you hear a lot more teaching about the second half of this verse than you do the first. But if the joy and gladness that you take in the Lord doesn't outweigh all your other heart's desires, you're going to end up missing both the joy and the things you want. But what is it, really, to delight yourself in the Lord? I think that once you know that, the main heart's desire you'll have will to be always rejoicing in Him!

How does something become delightful to you? A dictionary will tell you that something that delights is attractive, desirable, and draws you in so you can enjoy it. In 1 Peter 1:8, it is written of the early believers who loved the Lord so much that they rejoiced "with joy unspeakable and full of glory." Why? Perhaps it's because great joy is at the center of the heart of God. "The joy of the Lord is your strength" (Nehemiah 8:10), means that we become strong as we share in the joy that the Lord Himself possesses. "The Lord thy God in the midst of thee is mighty," says Zephaniah 3:17. "He will save, He will *rejoice* over thee with joy; He will rest in His love, He will *joy* over thee with *singing*." The Hebrew word translated "rejoice" means "to jump up and down," and the "singing" in the verse means "loud singing."

So first, God has joy in Himself, so much so that He's pictured as jumping up and down and singing at the top of His voice. Second, He's so joyous to be near and to know. He's the lover of our souls, the Lily of the Valley, the Bright and Morning Star, the Fairest of Ten Thousand, and "in His presence is fullness of joy" (Psalm 16:11).

There's nothing greater you could want than to be in the presence of the Lord Himself. If you haven't been feeling close to Him, make it your sole heart's desire right now to seek and find Him!

Child-Like Faith

"Ask, and it shall be given you; seek, and ye shall find; knock, and it shall be opened unto you."

Matthew 7:7

Dr. Barry Thomas
Pastor (Originator of First Athens Congress on World Missions)

A great way to learn about faith is to watch a child. I have never seen one of these little ones worrying over where he or she will get his next meal or where he will lay his head to sleep. In children I see an unquestioning trust. The same trust God wants His children to have in Him to love and care for them.

God does not expect or want His children to be burdened down by concern. In Matthew 7:7 Jesus instructs believers to ask, seek, and knock at God's heart for their needs. God promises to respond and more than meet those needs.

I believe today that the reason there is still so much poverty, depression, and lack of abundant living in the world and lives of many Christians is because too many people do not exercise their privilege to ask, seek, and knock at God's heart for their wants and desires. They do not take the promises of the Bible literally.

It was a great revelation to me when I realized how much God loved me to have allowed Christ to die for my sins, and an even greater one when I realized that I had been given the same inheritance as Christ. I have no reason to question such love. Nor can I doubt God's ability to meet my needs, knowing that by His power Jesus Christ was raised from the dead.

In the Lord's Prayer, Jesus instructed believers to pray in specifics; "give us this day our daily bread." Praying in specifics means bringing our individual needs both small and large to the Lord. This prevents us from holding on to any problem, while assuring us of God's peace that "passes all understanding" (Philippians 4:7).

Start practicing child-like faith now. Whatever your need is, give it to the Lord in prayer and believe that His answer is on the way.

Stick With God!

"And let us not be weary in well doing: for in due season, we shall reap, if we faint not."   Galatians 6:9

Royal Beaird
Owner/Director,
Professional Softball Team

It means a lot not to be a quitter. This verse is telling you to hang in there with the Lord on your side, for if you do, you are going to achieve and conquer and end up victorious.

Your life may be full of problems. Well, the Lord never said He'd take away your problems. In fact, He allows challenges to come into your life so you can stand strong in Him and watch Him see you through. God doesn't take away the mountains in front of you, but He acts as your lead guide: all you've got to do is hold onto the rope. "Come on," He says, "I'm leading the way."

Some people have called softball a sport born in a cow pasture. Being a rancher or a farmer is hard work. There are a lot of rocks, trees, and rough places that need to be cleared out before a piece of land is fit for agriculture or softball. But what may start out looking like a negative in your life, God can turn into His own playing field, as He works out His perfect purpose. That problem you're struggling with may turn into one of your greatest blessings once it's wrestled into the dirt.

You'll never get strong enough for hard labor for the Lord by doing just light work. The Lord wants to get you ready for great spiritual work, and He's just using troubles to get you in shape.

If you stick with God and don't run from the problems He puts in your way, you will reap. The crop? The fruit of the Spirit, the joy of accomplishment of good deeds and great things for Him. Give it your best, never get discouraged. Never run away, and you'll never lose, with Jesus by your side.

Catcher In The Kingdom

"Therefore, my beloved brethren, be ye steadfast, unmovable, always abounding in the work of the Lord, forasmuch as ye know that your labor is not in vain in the Lord." 1 Corinthians 15:58

Eileen Francabandera
Professional Softball Catcher

Being a Christian isn't just a momentary thing, it's a lifelong continuous dedication to the Lord. It means learning to be faithful and steadfast no matter what. And that's only possible when you know in your heart that God is working through every situation you ever go through in life.

Perhaps being a softball catcher makes this a little easier for me to understand. Catching isn't one of the glamour positions on a ball team. The catcher's mask and mit and protective pads have sometimes been called "the tools of ignorance" by taunting fans and sports writers. They're unwieldly and not very attractive, but they're very necessary to the catcher's job. A catcher has to be steadfast and unmovable, standing firm when fast balls and curves come whirling in, catching foul tips, and especially when blocking home plate when an opposing player comes crashing in spikes high trying to score!

Catchers don't get to run a lot in their position. They only chase foul balls and bunts no one else can reach and aren't known to be very speedy around the base paths. But from that lowly stance, almost kneeling, a catcher becomes the hub of the team on the field, directing the defense, settling the pitcher, calling the pitches. Though he seldom does the spectacular, the ball game can't be won without him.

Maybe you're a "catcher" in the Kingdom of God: reliable, faithful, staunch, and strong. You will then know that though you're going through problems, a heavenly reward will be given for your dedication. If you're not a "catcher," perhaps you need to "catch" some of that hardy spirit, to stand firm and strong, until your final "out!"

The Hub And Pivot Of Life

*"Seek ye first the king-
dom of God, and His righteousness; and all these things
shall be added unto you."*
Matthew 6:33

Jerry A. Jones
Pastor

The whole of Christian life on a daily basis turns around this one verse: Christ the center, Christ the hub, Christ the pivot on which all of my life turns. My personal, family, and physical needs, and financial matters are taken care of. Everything is automatic if I do this one thing Jesus said for me to do. That is, seek first, not second or fourth, but first the kingdom of God.

What is God's kingdom? In Luke, it says that "the kingdom of God is within you." So Christ within me is in essence God's kingdom. As I make Him King and Lord and Master within myself, then He fills up the whole of me, making my decisions, directing my life, moving and motivating me. I do nothing outside of His will, at my own impulse.

Why do I need to seek His righteousness? Because I have none of my own—all mine is but filthy rags. If I'm put beside Jesus, I stink. Righteousness is nothing more than rightness with God. So to be right with Him, I must put Him first in my life.

We must develop the habit of always going to Jesus first. If we have a problem, let it be Jesus before the human advisor. If sickness, go to Jesus before the doctor or the pill. If puzzled by the meaning of God's Word, to Jesus before the commentary. He must be our source, our total source.

The Lord hasn't made walking with Him difficult; it's as simple as just seeking Him first, always. Today, see if you can remember this: whenever any occurrence takes place that causes you to hesitate, ask Jesus about it; and watch Him settle this issue.

The Growing Token

". . . Christ in you, the hope of glory."
Colossians 1:27

Louis Paul Lehman
Pastor/Stage Director

What happened to us when we met Jesus Christ? So many of us have the idea that when we were born again that we were "us made over again." But what really happened was that we were invaded by God.

The man-made religions of the world teach that they will improve men, enhance their experience in life, or teach something of value, if their indoctrination is applied systematically. But what Christ brings to our lives is not a system or a body of teaching, but Himself. Being born again in Christ did not result in you becoming a better you, or me becoming a better me, but in Christ's entering into us, exchanging His life for ours, and abiding. It is not Christ *with* us, but *in* us that is the hope of glory.

Had we any hope of glory before He gave us His life to share? No, merely a few short hours on this earth, lived painfully or pleasantly, only to crumble into dust and ashes, at most remembered by plaques and ruins that tarnish and collapse. The world can but remember with anguished longing "the glory that *was* Greece, and the grandeur that *was* Rome," knowing at heart that the same fate awaits today's futile attempts at greatness.

But Christ's life in us becomes a growing token of the perfection of Jesus' incorruptible life, that will be fully manifested in us when we see Him as He is. And in this life, we shine out with His glory even now, as we realize that, because He lives in us, "as He is, so are we *in this world*" (1 John 4:17). Let Him shine through you today.

Forgiveness

"And forgive us our debts, as we forgive our debtors." Matthew 6:12

Ray Peterson
Singer

Did you ever wonder how much potentially productive time is wasted in this world by people while they criticize and think bitter and angry thoughts about others? Perhaps enough to build whole civilizations, to restore millions of broken relationships, perhaps enough to have won the world for Christ many times over.

Did you ever notice how much time babies and small children spend squalling and grumbling and getting angry when things don't go their way? God is telling us in this verse to grow up! Oh, but how we hate to hear that sometimes. So we go about judging others, and that feels pretty good. But soon something comes along to pop our bubble of self-esteem, and then we start judging ourselves. Whew! Isn't there any end?

Yes! I know I'm not perfect, and never can be here on this sinful earth. But it's so marvelous when I realize that God is with us here, always forgiving us as we stumble along, growing in Him, seeking to learn new life. And He wants us to learn to forgive, too, so we won't waste our lives troubling over problems in others and ourselves that we can't change. Only God can change that brother or sister you've got the bad eye on. Only God can change *you*.

Instead of bitterness, forgiveness is always available, and we should constantly praise God for it. How much less time and anguish it takes to forgive and to be forgiven than it does to eat your insides out with rage.

Lord, I've been so busy being angry at myself and others. Teach me to forgive and forget quickly and get on with your good business!

Jesus Is Boss

"I am the Vine, ye are the branches: he that abideth in Me, and I in him, the same bringeth forth much fruit: for without me, ye can do nothing." John 15:15

Zig Ziglar
Author/Motivational Speaker

Sometimes in my human weakness, I'm tempted to rely on my own human strength more than on the Lord. This verse reminds me that on my own, there's not really anything of value that I can do. But relying on the strength of the Lord, and letting Him operate through me, there's nothing I cannot do, because it's not me doing it, but the Lord.

Not long after being born again, while speaking one night in Los Angeles, I soon felt like I had the audience in the palm of my hand. "Ziglar, you've got em," I gloated to myself. A minute later I preened some more: "Boy, you're really on target today!"

Just then the Lord confused my tongue! Suddenly I was stating things in reverse: instead of saying, "He was going to town," it came out, "He town going to was!" I steadied myself, but a few seconds later, it happened again. Then it dawned on me what was happening: I was taking the glory for what God was really doing! So while speaking, I said a silent prayer: "Lord, I'm terribly sorry. It's You who're making this talk, please take control again, and I'll never again get confused about who's doing what!" Then He took charge again, with all the skill at His disposal.

Some Hollywood stars make much of having made a motion picture under the direction of a famous director. But as a Christian, you have the privilege of being under the direction of the Creator of the Universe. It's exciting, knowing that He'll be listening in on every word, and make Himself a part of every action in your day.

So give Him the glory, and expect Him to do His best in you today!

Looking Ahead With Joy

". . . we confidently and joyfully look forward to actually becoming all that God has had in mind for us to be."
Romans 5:2 (LB)

Jeanne Johnson
Singer

I know that the Lord can see into my future, He knows what's ahead for me and He knows all the potential that's in my life. I know that in Him, all I can find is happiness, and that makes me excited to find out what He has in store.

I didn't always have that confidence. Several years ago when my husband's business transferred him to Charlotte, I had reason to wonder what God was doing. I'd been singing for over eight years with the Speer family! "There goes my career," I thought.

As I was flying in from the West Coast to join my husband, I gave it up to the Lord. I hardly knew about PTL at that time, and thought, "What can I ever do in North Carolina?" But God gave me a peace that stilled my questioning mind even though I didn't have the answer.

Since then, PTL has been the means of God's opening areas in my life and more singing than I could have ever imagined then. Who'd have thought I'd be ministering to so many people so often?

The Lord has things for us to do that we can't even imagine, or dream about. If we could only see through His eyes, we'd realize how much we have to look forward to. I know we won't be perfected until we see Jesus face to face, but how wonderful it is to let Him direct our life here and now! What a comfort we can have if we face even things we don't understand with this joyful attitude.

You Are His!

". . . I have redeemed thee, I have called thee by thy name; thou art mine."
Isaiah 43:1

Sister Raphael
Nun

How I love the Old Testament! Throughout its pages the gospel is beautifully expressed both prophetically and in the multi-formed interaction between God and people. The verse above, taken from it, is the epitome of God's call for me; that He has chosen me so I belong to Him personally, for His service.

I was just a young girl growing up when the Lord made me realize that the values of the world were empty; that He had His eye on me; that He knew me intimately and that He wanted me to follow Him into the darkness of faith. Upon entering into the monastery, I began to see the uniqueness of my calling and that of each child of God.

After breakfast each morning, the sisters talk over everything and anything sharing about our prayer lives. We discover that each of us has our own way of talking to God; no two of us approach God the same way.

It is the same way with living out God's call on our lives in daily practice. As we interact together from day to day we are learning that each of us expresses God's nature in his or her own particular way. As the Body of Christ, each of us has an irreplaceable part of His wonderful, infinitely varied personality.

You as a child of God are shining in this world's darkness with a unique part of His vast light. There is no good thing in you or me that He doesn't put there with His great love. But He has chosen to need you, and you alone, to bring to the world a part of Him no one else can bring. Be fully yourself, as He has given Himself to be *you*.

The Most Important Thing

*"The fruit of the right-
eous is a tree of life; and he
that winneth souls is wise."*
Proverbs 11:30

Cecil Todd
*Director, Revival Fires
Ministry*

The only thing important enough to bring Jesus all the way from heaven to this earth; to drive Him up and down Palestine: to prostrate Him in Gethsemane; and to nail Him to the cross; was to seek and save the lost. If that was the most important thing to Him, it ought to be our most pressing business, too, as His disciples.

Because someone cared enough to show Christ to you; eternal life is yours today. You are the fruit on that tree of life that God is growing in eternity. You are on your way to heaven, not on your own merits, but because you've got a stem of faith that's attached to God.

Now God is telling you to be wise enough to go out and win souls yourself. Paul, considered even by worldly men to be one of the most brilliant men of his time, spent his life trying to win souls. The Bible is full of examples of men and women who gave everything to introduce Jesus to others.

If you've ever won a soul to Christ, you know that God gives you wisdom as you share Him with others. Scripture comes to life in a new way as the Holy Spirit works through your mind and lips to reach others' hearts. And God's wisdom of the heart becomes yours as you feel the love and concern of Jesus for lost souls in need.

If you would be like Jesus, you point all that you do in the direction for which He came. Let His mind become your mind. Let His heart become your heart. Let Him live all of His life through you by reaching out to touch lost souls and turn them into sons of God for His glory. Ask God to let you share Christ with someone today.

A Life Of Praise

"The Lord is my strength and my shield; my heart trusted in Him, and I am helped: therefore my heart greatly rejoiceth; and with my song will I praise Him . . ."

Psalm 28:7

Terry and Wanda White
Music Artists

A couple of years ago, Wanda and I were touring in Ireland. Wanda had just had an operation, and one particular night, she didn't want to go to the church and minister.

She asked me, "Can I stay in tonight?" "Well," I answered, "yes, if you've talked with the Lord and that's what He wants you to do." She said, "I'd better go and pray."

So she asked the Lord about it, and felt Him saying: "No, you don't have to sing for those people at the church, but will you sing for me?" "Lord, I guess I'm willing," said Wanda, "but you know my throat's bad, I'm tired, I'm not sure I can get through." Then she picked up her Bible, and the Lord led her to Psalm 28. She knew then that the Lord was going to enable her to sing. She was a blessing that night, and the Lord's been blessing us through that scripture ever since.

You know, this isn't just a verse for singers. You have a God-given way of expressing yourself that's yours alone. Perhaps you're a housewife, or a businessman, or a student, or a secretary. Maybe God's called you to a trade or a craft, or even to a pulpit! Whatever it is, it can be a praise to Him.

There may be times when you seem to run out of energy or face opposition and discouragement. But you know, it doesn't take any energy to trust God. It just takes an act of your will, asking Him to help you, and see you through.

The Lord is ready today to take that load off your shoulders. He's willing to share the burden with you. Are you ready and willing to accept His help and to be faithful in that responsibility He's given you? Trust Him, and turn your life into praise for Him today.

Not By Bread Alone

"And Jesus answered him, saying, It is written, That man shall not live by bread alone, but by every word of God."   Luke 4:4

Dr. Benjamin Smith
Pastor

Man, as a being with the threefold nature of body, soul, and spirit, also has three hungers which need to be fed if he is to enjoy the abundant life Jesus has offered. Man's body needs to be clothed, fed, and sheltered. His soul's emotional needs must be met through love, friendship, and companionship with other men. And his spirit, or innermost being, must be fed, too. God has designed the spirit of man to be fed and satisfied only by His Holy Word.

The key to abundant life in Christ lies, in fact, in feasting upon the word of God. For it is only in being nourished in our spirit that we are equipped with the wisdom, the faith, and the boldness we need to properly pursue and receive what God has for our bodies and souls.

Just as our bodies require certain nutrients in the form of vitamins, minerals, and proteins to function well; and our souls need the right kind of human contact to keep us emotionally healthy, our spirits need the word of God in order to follow the leading of His Spirit with clear perception and power.

In feeding our spirits with the word of God, we are tending to the only appetite we possess which will survive and be satisfied eternally. For no matter how much we partake of the things of the world, our satisfaction is only temporal; but in partaking of the word of God, we are satisfied and strengthened eternally in building up the inner, spiritual man who will enjoy fellowship with God forever.

Just as you would never willfully neglect your physical or emotional health, never neglect to tend to the inner man, who matters most to God. Have you properly fed your spirit upon the word of God today?

Stand And Shine!

"Arise, shine; for thy light is come, and the glory of the Lord is risen upon thee. For behold, the darkness shall cover the earth . . . but the Lord shall arise upon thee . . ."   Isaiah 60:1-2

David Clark
Missionary

At this hour in history, we as Christians can arise and shine out for Christ as never before in spite of the darkness of sin, insecurity and political unrest that surrounds us. For the light we carry is the glory of the Lord, which He is spreading all across the world by His Holy Spirit's power.

It is so easy for us to give Satan more credit than he's due in a world like ours today. We ought always to realize that nothing we see around us is a surprise to God. How could we even know darkness at all if there were not light in the world to reveal its nature? In these verses God tells us plainly that He has chosen for us *not* to succumb to the darkness, but to stand up and be the light in it. It is in the greatest darkness that light illumines the things it shines on most plainly.

The courage we need to shine out with the light of Christ can be ours because it is His power and glory that are lighting up the world. We need not struggle to do God's will on our own. We can rest with confidence in His Almighty power even while we work for Him.

I thought I had clear direction from God about the task He had for me on the mission field, but I didn't understand at first that I couldn't make it happen. The doing and timing of God's work was His business; and I had to learn to be His instrument.

After it seemed that I had failed, God opened up the work, and I simply walked into the place in it He'd prepared for me.

God does not want you walking and working in darkness. Let Him light your way and do His will through you. Stand and shine.

Giants on The Run

"The Lord is my light and my salvation: whom shall I fear? . ."   Psalm 27:1

Jerry Houser
Actor

Sometimes, when your eyes get fixed on the problems that sur- round you instead of the Lord, life can be like one of those old-time monster movies. You know, the kind where tiny spiders have been fed some radioactive potion that turns them into giants?

Problems have a way of seeming large enough to begin with, but when you've fed them with fear and anxiety, they really look immense. Before long, they start dimming out the light of the Lord, and you feel trapped alone with those problems, as if in a long, dark hallway with no doors.

When I've been in that state, scurrying around, bumping from one side of the wall to the other, struggling to get out, I've just had to stand still and remember that my best Friend is the biggest kid on the block! Because once I've stopped long enough to look straight ahead, the Lord's always been there to put the giants to flight.

Sometimes, as we grow in the Christian life, we imagine that our view of things is becoming much grander because we know a lot more Scripture and teaching in our heads than at first. We begin to think that the light of our own understanding will lead us along the path.

Or that when we get into trouble, what we *know* about God will save us.

But no! The Lord Himself is our light and our salvation. When we get that firmly in mind, we can laugh in the face of our problems and fears.

What kind of "movie" will you be in today? Keep your eyes on Jesus and no matter what happens, it won't be a scary one!

Be Alive—Believe!

"... whosoever shall say unto this mountain, Be thou removed, and be thou cast into the seas; and shall not doubt ... he shall have whatsoever he saith."

Mark 11:23

Carl Ortiz
Bible Teacher

My son was born with a broken collarbone, which the doctors discovered when he was less than a week old. He was in great discomfort, and according to the doctors, faced months of the same in allowing the bones to set and heal. But in that hospital, the Lord led me to lay hands on his little body and command in Jesus name those bones to go into place. Right then I heard crackling noises, and that day the doctors verified a complete healing.

We named him Anthony Mark, Once Veinte Y Tres, Veinte Y Quatro, which means in English, Mark 11:23,24. Some people might say, "Oh, what great faith!" But no, it was just that in a childlike way I did what God told me to do. My other baby was born with crossed eyes. Again I spoke to them and commanded them to be straight. In this case, they did not turn straight right away. But I kept saying by faith that they were. Over a year later, I noticed one day that they had indeed become straight! God gave me the thing that I said.

Do you remember how easy it was as a child to believe in Santa Claus? You really believed he would bring those presents, and they came. Being born again brings to your spirit a rebirth of that childlike innocence. God plants faith in you as a seed. You must let your doubt die for that seed to bring forth fruit.

My friend, don't just read these words. Allow them to penetrate your bones; God's word goes deeper than x-rays, to the marrow. Believe what God says and simply act on it. To believe equals to be alive!

Get To Know Him

"That I may know Him, and the power of His resurrection, and the fellowship of His sufferings, being made conformable unto His death;"
Philippians 3:10

Milton Bourgeois
Composer of "Rise And Be Healed"

In the third chapter of Philippians Paul listed all the accomplishments of his life before he met Jesus. He was born an Israelite, was circumcised the eighth day, was a Pharisee of the Pharisees, his "righteousness" according to the law was blameless. What a strange conclusion he reached. Paul counted all these things as "loss," that he might win Christ—"that he might know Him and the power of His resurrection, and the fellowship of His sufferings, being made conformable to His death."

What a day in which we live! We have been privileged to witness the mighty power of God as He poured out His Spirit upon all flesh. We have seen blinded eyes opened, the lame walk, cancers healed, financial miracles, deliverances, and families restored. We have sat under the greatest preaching and teaching. We've learned the doctrine and theology. We're so involved in the Church and all its activities. And yet, how well do we really know Him in that personal, intimate way?

I have awakened many times in my life to feel an overwhelming hunger in my spirit to know Him in a deeper, more fuller way than I had ever known Him before. It's as if like nothing else in the world mattered but finding Him that day, and getting to know Him in a greater way. He is the Source of everything we need—everything! And yet, how little time we spend communing with Jesus everyday.

The Bible says that we shall seek Him and shall find Him WHEN we seek Him with all our heart. Pray that above all else, as we go about ministering in His Kingdom, we will come to know Him as never before.

God Works It Out

"And we know that all things work together for good to them that love God, to them who are the called according to His purpose." Romans 8:28

Bill Warren
Singer

How God could bring any good out of the plight of a Bible school student locked in a jail cell for 34 traffic tickets was a scary mystery to me. My bad habit of driving too fast had earned me a berth with two rapists and an attempted murderer who liked to call himself Mephistopheles, a Greek name for the devil.

This last guy was a jailhouse hero, a kind of spiritual con man who practically ran the place and who knew more scripture than some ministers. He had a field day making fun of me, and for a while I wondered whether I was going to last out my 40 days. He tried to snare me in all kinds of debates about God much to the delight of the other prisoners. Though I wasn't his equal in arguing, I started to share the love of Jesus with him, as simply and as directly as I knew how.

Well, the Holy Spirit began to move on him, and to my great amazement, he fell down on his knees one day and accepted Christ. After he got saved, he started leading other prisoners to the Lord. Soon the whole jail was alive with revival!

I'd sheepishly told him, "The devil made me do it," when the judge sentenced me. That was wrong and a lie. Actually, it was God who had the master plan, even in that nutty situation.

No, I haven't tried to repeat that performance, praise God! But it shows the lengths God will go to get glory, even when we ball things up. Please, don't do what I did. But do have confidence in the Lord's ability to straighten things out, no matter where you find yourself.

Seeking With A Whole Heart

"And ye shall seek Me, and find Me, when ye shall search for Me with all your heart." Jeremiah 29:13

Carl Gustafson
Pastor/Teacher

The top priority in the life of a child of God is learning to seek the Lord with a whole heart. God desires so much for us to seek Him that He is willing to go to any extreme to bring us to the position where He has our full and undivided attention.

In this passage, God had taken Israel for 70 years into captivity in Babylon in order that they might be ready at last to seek His face. This has become an important theme in my life because at times I have gotten so wrapped up in service and "busy for the Lord" that I have neglected to find time for the Lord Himself.

But God in His love engineers circumstances that make it necessary for me to trust Him. In the flesh, I'll do anything rather than trust the Lord. There's a good deal of programming in me that makes me want to do things my own way and to trust myself. So if He sees that happening, God will throw into my path a need or challenge or pressure situation simply to reveal Himself as the solution of it. Then once again, when I've come to the end of my own ability to deal with the problem, He takes control and works everything out to His satisfaction. And I learn how utterly dependent I am upon Him.

That problem or seemingly insurmountable situation that may be troubling you today: could it be that God is using it to try to get you to give up trying to accomplish a solution by yourself? God loves you today. He is pursuing you, doing everything at His mighty disposal to bring you to a meeting place with Him where He will give you freely all that you're struggling for on your own. But why wait? Seek Him with your whole heart—right now.

Out Of The River

"And the priests that bear the ark of the covenant of the Lord stood firm on dry ground in the midst of Jordan, and all the Israelites passed over on dry ground, until all the people were passed clean over Jordan." Joshua 3:17

Lee Robbins
Singer/Evangelist

A few years ago, I was in a deep, dark spiritual valley. My life was really shattered through grief. And my mother wrote me a letter, saying, "I know you're hurting, and you think there's no end to this valley." She went on to share about the scriptures, how by faith the priests stepped on the water and she said, "Son, most people think that's the great story of faith."

"But actually," she concluded, "the great faith in this story is that those priests stood on the bottom of the river Jordan and without looking on the walls of death on either hand, refused to look at the circumstances. They kept their eyes on the far bank, on Joshua, waiting for him to say, 'Come on up out of the river.'

"You're at the bottom of the river, Lee. The devil wants you to look at the walls of circumstances. He's saying, 'Lee Robbins, you're never going to get out of this one. God cannot bring you through.' Son, you just keep your eyes off those walls and keep your eyes on Jesus on the other side. And when your valley is done, not one day too late, Jesus will tell you, 'Come on out of that river,' and you'll have your Canaan." And God did that for me.

So what God did for the children of Israel and those priests, God has done for Lee Robbins and will do for anybody if they'll ignore the circumstances and keep their eyes on Jesus and believe that He's going to bring them out of that valley.

Speak, Mediate, And Do!

"This book of the law shall not depart out of thy mouth; but thou shalt meditate therein . . . to do according to all that is written therein: for then thou shalt make thy way prosperous, and then thou shalt have good success."   Joshua 1:8

Marilyn Hickey
Voice of Life for Laymen

Bookstores and magazine racks today are filled with material on "how to." "How to Be Successful," "How to Be a Millionaire," "How to Improve Your Marriage," and on and on.

The greatest "How To" book of all time is the Bible. It tells us how to *come* into harmony with others by being in harmony with God. It tells how to *overcome* the forces that hinder us from being victorious in life. And the Bible tells us how to *become* what and who God created us to be.

Joshua 1:8 give God's three-fold formula for discovering a prosperous life and success.

We are to *speak* God's Word . . . to use it in our everyday conversation. As the Sword of the Spirit, it is our weapon against Satan whose power is broken by the spoken Word of God.

Secondly, we are to *meditate* on God's word day and night. Psalm 119:105 describes the word as a "lamp" and "light" to help us find our way in this life. As we meditate on scripture, our decision-making becomes more illuminated by God's wisdom dwelling in us.

After we have spoken and meditated on God's principles and commandments, we are instructed to *do* what they say. Advice heard, but unheeded, is useless. Jesus says in John 14:21, "He that hath my commandments and keepeth them, he it is that loveth me . . . and I will love him and manifest myself to him."

For a prosperous life and success, start practicing the three-fold formula of speaking, meditating and doing what God's word says.

Blind But Seeing

"I will bring the blind by a way that they knew not; I will lead them in paths that they have not known: I will make darkness light before them, and crooked things straight." Isaiah 42:16a

Kim Wickes
Singer/Minister

I have been blind since I was three years old. I was born in Korea, and lost my sight in a bomb explosion. The Lord began to lead me and has continued to lead me, from Korea, where my poverty-stricken father tried to drown me; to an orphanage for the blind; to a dedicated Christian family in America, who adopted me.

God led me through the drastic adjustments of a new culture, new language, and new parents. He led me through college, through a bachelor's and a master's degree in music, through course work for a doctorate, and on to a Fullbright Scholarship in Music in Vienna, Austria.

Now, as a blind singer and head of a ministry, I often get into circumstances where there are no human predecessors to whom I can go for advice. I get discouraged at times, and the only thing I know is to go to God's Word. God has promised He'd never leave me or forsake me, and He's always brought people into my life who've been instrumental in leading me. He even led me to a Korean reporter who was able to discover that my father was still alive. And through the U.S. Ambassador to Korea, I was able to visit with my father!

If God has been able through such a complex whirl of situations to lead a poor, blind little girl, from near-death to adulthood in an active ministry, He will surely lead you through all those dark and difficult areas of life where you are unsure or fearful. Yes, there may be times of confusion and discouragement in your life. But when they come, just remind the Lord of His promises: "Lord, You said You wouldn't leave me. I'm yours, and you must help me, or I'll never get through. Be with me now, and lighten my way to Your perfect will."

Harmony with God's Will

"Likewise the Spirit also helpeth our infirmities: for we know not what we should pray for as we ought: but the Spirit itself maketh intercession for us with groanings which cannot be uttered."
Romans 8:26

David Du Plessis
"Mr. Pentecost"

Most of the time, God does not give us the privilege of knowing what He has in store for our lives in the immediate future. As a result, we often do not know exactly what we should pray for, and we very easily slip into giving the Lord instructions about what we want Him to do, without really knowing His will.

Therefore, one of the greatest blessings in my life has been the gift of being able to pray to God in tongues, or with the Spirit, even after I have prayed with my understanding. When I have done this, you see, I have put myself in touch with several vital things which the Holy Spirit is doing.

First, according to this verse, He is interceding for me, putting into operation God's power on my behalf. Second, according to verse 27, He is doing this while the Father is searching my heart, according to the will of God. When I am praying in a heavenly language, the Spirit is praying through me, and He as God knows the end from the beginning, so He can request perfectly the best that God desires for my life.

This is how speaking in tongues edifies, or builds us up, in our walk with God. For when we have thus been placed in harmony with the perfect will of God, we can rest assured that, according to verse 28, *all* things that then follow, even things we don't understand, will work together for our good.

So, never think only of verse 28 alone, but allow God to minister to your weakness and lack of knowledge by praying always to Him in the Holy Spirit. Then you can move confidently into all events that may befall you, knowing you are in His perfect will.

Run Right Back

*"Seek ye first the king-
dom of God, and His righteousness: and all these things
shall be added unto you."*
Matthew 6:33

Connie Smith Haynes
Former Country Singer

Whenever things get confusing, it's great to know that you can always go back and seek the Lord to help you to know what to do. You know how it is: you're walking along with fair weather all around you, feeling comfortable and at ease, all blue skies and soft grass. You're feeling pretty good about yourself, making some plans for the future, without the Lord on your mind, because you don't see how anything could go wrong.

But wait a minute! What are those crows doing in that corn patch? And how did that hole get worked into that barbed wire? And where'd the hogs go to that used to be in that pen? And what are those heavy hoofsteps clippity-clopping up behind you? Uh, oh! Time to get ahold of the Lord again.

If only we'd learn to seek Him *first*, before we got into all that trouble! When I got saved, I was confused—I'd always lived my life so rationally, according to my feelings and my own understanding, and I didn't know how to serve the Lord. So when I got myself into a mess, I'd just have to chuck it all again and go back to praising Him and falling in love with Him all over. Then He'd put all the pieces back together again.

Maybe you're a little like me—maybe you don't always keep things together and put the Lord in the center where He belongs. Yes, He is a lot easier to find if you keep Him in sight. But don't forget: if you seek Him with a whole heart, you'll *always* find Him. So try to keep Him in view—but if He ever gets out of sight, run for Him right quick!

"Oughts" Becoming "Wants"

". . . I am come that they might have life, and that they might have it more abundantly."   John 10:10

Rev. Bruce Larson
Author

Jesus didn't come to make religious people. The roots of the word *religion* mean "to bind back or tie down." Becoming religious is beginning to live a specific way by rigid rules. Jesus didn't come to bind us to a system of regulations. He came to set us free, that we might be fulfilled to love God, our neighbors, and ourselves.

The word translated *life* in this verse is ZOE in the Greek, which implies a quality of life that's so full that it can't be contained. It's heaped up and running over. This is what Jesus came to bring us. The purpose of this life is not "being good." As long as you've got to prove you're good, you're wasting this great spiritual inheritance of life. Real maturity in Christ is not to never sin, but to know what to do with sin if you fall into it (confess it immediately and get forgiveness) and to major in loving people. I believe the unforgivable sin is to say, "I don't need forgiveness; I'm okay." The focus of a Christian's life isn't "not being bad."

The difference between religion and ZOE is going from the "oughts" to the "wants." The people who reached you for Christ didn't say, "you ought to do better and love God. You ought to straighten out." They said, "Do you want Jesus?" And you said, "Yes," and received Him.

Religious people couldn't stand Jesus. He was setting people free, and they were saying, "No, no! We have to keep them under control!" And if we're not careful, we can make the gospel a religion, too.

Have you lost that joy of freedom in Christ. Has your life gotten wrapped up in the "oughts?" Do you want to get back that freedom and joy you once had? Jesus wants to give it to you. It's a free gift, and it's yours. If you "want" it, accept it, right now. And live free in Christ!

Remolding

"Don't let the world around you squeeze you into its own mold, but let God re-mold your minds from within . . ." Romans 12:2
(Phillips Amplified)

Don Osgood
Business Executive

One of the heaviest pressures that people in business experience is feeling forced to take tight hold of the reins of their careers. The business world tries to squeeze people into its mold, to get them racing after success, persuading them that they must always know intimately all of the steps from the present to age 80.

But the Lord is saying in this verse, "You don't need to know all of that! You need to be released from the pressures of living up to everybody's expectations and look to Me to direct your career."

This was a great relief to me. I'm not supposed to direct my life as much as I thought. God loves me right where I am, unconditionally, not for what I'm going to be!

God is telling me to realize that the tremendous fact of relationship with Him is much greater than the power of achievement. Achievement is really a hollow thing, impersonal, and unsharing if it only includes me. I'm not to follow that and let the world press me into its mold. Jesus Christ has got to become my career counselor. True maturity is living for others, listening to the Lord and entering into His plans, which are wiser than mine.

It's not difficult, even as a Christian, to get pushed back into that mold. That's why Paul is warning us here to watch ourselves and not let it happen. Today, you're probably going to face, in one form or another, a lot of pressure to take control of your life. Be on guard, resist this shoving, and let Jesus have full control.

His Child

"But now thus saith the Lord that created thee, O Jacob, and He that formed thee, O Israel; Fear not: for I have redeemed thee, I have called thee by thy name; thou art Mine."   Isaiah 43:1

Joan Osgood
Housewife

This verse became especially important to me when I was facing difficult problems relating with my teenage sons. As concerned as I was with all of the details of my children's lives, it meant a great deal to me that God hadn't forgotten about me, either!

Just look at how personal this verse is! The Lord knows us so well, because He created us Himself. He formed us, gave us the shape and stature and personality which make us unique individuals. And He has gone so much farther than just making us and placing us in this world: He has bought us with His Son's blood, called us by our own names, and made us His own.

When we consider the intimacy with which we know our children, we can only marvel at the greater depth of God's concern for us. As a mother, I can understand His desire to be a part of the inner thoughts and longings of His children.

The first impulse of a mother whose child has awakened at night terrified by thunder is to rush to that child, to hold it close, and tell it, "Now, don't be afraid." She tells the child comforting words: "It's all right, Mommy is here." In this verse God would say to us, whatever the terrors that surround us, "Don't be afraid, you're my child, and I'll work it all out for your good."

That problem that has caused you tears, that fear that threatens to paralyze your spirit, that sin that has marred your fellowship with God: in each of these things, the Lord will lift you into His arms, and help you, if you will seek Him. Don't be afraid, but right now, receive His embrace, and let Him remake you in His love.

Stop The Erosion In America

"This is the stone which was set at nought of you builders, which is become the head of the corner."

Acts 4:11

Moseley Collins
Law Student

Peter, speaking in his sermon on the day of Pentecost, was referring to Jesus, the Chief Cornerstone rejected by the nation of Israel. And I believe in my heart that this rejection is happening again in our United States today.

We began with a public faith in God, as evidenced by the motto still inscribed on the entrances to the halls of Congress: "In God We Trust." The Mayflower compact began "In the Name of God, Amen." All through our history, until the Supreme Court began chipping away at its foundations in the late 1940's, this public faith in God was maintained. When our Constitution was written, every session began with prayer. George Washington, in his farewell address to the American people said, "Two supports uphold this great nation: morality and religion. Let us not think that we may weaken either one and survive as a nation."

Yet in 1962, prayer left our public schools; in 1963, Bible reading was forbidden; in 1977, Bible clubs were excluded from state college campuses; in 1978 in California, it became illegal to display a cross on any civic building or holiday occasion.

So when America was built, the cornerstone was laid, though not in everyone's having a personal relationship with Jesus, at least in a common respect for God. Now, false builders have come in and tried to pull that cornerstone out. We must not allow this to happen.

We must begin to seek counsel from God about our nation's course. We must stop looking to man alone for the answer to today's serious political issues. We as Christians must seek with all our hearts to know the mind of God and found our lives only on Jesus, our Rock.

Christian Character Building

"Blessed is the man that walketh not in the counsel of the ungodly, nor standeth in the way of sinners, nor sitteth in the seat of the scornful."
Psalm 1:1

Reginald Elliott
Educator

The character you demonstrate as a Christian is even more important than the words you say. Personally, the Lord has had to teach me a lot about character because, when I met him five yeas ago, I didn't have any.

It was hard for a guy who'd been living for pleasure and "old number one" to get down on his knees and scrub the floor of a dust-cluttered basement. But this was to be my classroom at the D. C. Street Academy, and the Lord told me to clean it up before I taught anything. My class of high school dropouts pitched in and together, we started learning about responsibility. As the Lord taught me, I taught them to be on time and to develop good working habits.

During the character-building time, I told the Lord, "I want to grow but not get chastened much." He replied, "Then son, do My will!" Step by step, I began to discover His will. I learned my job was to trust and His job was to do. I didn't need to develop *my* character; I had to take on His.

As God worked His character into me, many lives around me were changed. The Lord saved and baptized many students and teachers in the Holy Spirit and lifted me from that basement to Director of Education of the Academy.

No matter what your position in life, God has given it to you as your responsibility. Words alone won't make the difference-what Jesus does through you *will*. So give yourself totally to Him, walk uprightly, and He'll give you the character to fulfill His purpose in your life.

You've Got To Serve Somebody

"The thief cometh not, but for to steal, and to kill, and to destroy: I am come that they might have life, and that they might have it more abundantly." John 10:10

Richard Roberts
Music Artist

To me, the whole gospel is rolled up in this one verse. On one side, all the forces of evil are arrayed, to destroy your life, to steal from you, to kill you. On the other side of the line, are all the forces of good, with God at their head offering abundant life.

God made us all free moral agents. If He hadn't given us the power of choice, we'd be just like the animals. God did give us the choice of which side of the line we would take: the side of God, who is good, or the devil, who is evil. A well known rock singer, newly converted to Jesus, has a song out called "You've Got to Serve Somebody." In it, he says, "It may be the devil, or it may be the Lord, but you've got to serve *somebody*."

Jesus was continually drawing that line in His preaching: "He that is not with Me is against Me; and he that gathereth not with Me scattereth abroad." There's no way around it. Jesus never compromised that message.

The devil is totally bad. There's no good in him. He tries to make his side of the line look appealing. But one thing is certain. No matter what you may be tempted to do, if it's not according to the commandments of God, it'll either steal from you, or hurt you, or kill you. God is totally good. Anything you do that follows His will is going to result in blessing, joy, and fullness of life.

There's never any middle ground. There won't be any for you today. You can't have a foot in both sides. Either Jesus will have all of you or none of you. The devil will either have all or none of you. What's your choice going to be: death and destruction, or life abundant?

Put Your Past To Rest

"For I am not ashamed of the gospel of Christ: for it is the power of God unto salvation to every one that believeth: to the Jew first; and also to the Greek."

Romans 1:16

Sandy Musser
Counselor

How wonderful it is of God to center our lives in a gospel that frees us from all shame! All of the past has been removed from His mind, and it need hinder us no longer from being all He intends for us to be.

God has given me a ministry to young mothers who've given up children for adoption. I was such a mother myself. For a long time, I concealed this part of my past because of the guilt and shame I felt within and that was heaped upon me by condemning people from without. But the good news of Jesus Christ to me was that He had forgiven me, cleansed me, made me His own, and emptied my conscience of reproach. Now I can share with others about a great God who will accept them and say to them, just as He said to me, "Go your way, and sin no more!"

Who could be ashamed of such good news? It doesn't matter to God that you may only have stammering lips to share the message of Jesus. He isn't displeased with any attempt to tell His saving power. For just as He's taken the shame from our life's past, He's taken it from our present. We don't need to apologize for who we are now. We can stand, pure and righteous, kings and priests unto Him.

And God has taken the shame from our future, too. Isaiah 54:4 says: "Fear not: for thou shalt not be ashamed . . . for thou shalt not be put to shame: for thou shalt forget the reproach of thy youth." If you belong to Jesus Christ, never allow anyone to hold your past against you. And if you haven't yet put your past to rest in Him, bow you head and do so right now.

The Clear Path

"Trust in the Lord with all thine heart; and lean not unto thine own understanding. In all thy ways acknowledge Him, and He shall direct thy path." Proverbs 3:5-6

Annie Davis
Housewife

Every person's life contains a myriad of possible directions. How do you choose which way to go, as life becomes more complex from day to day? Feelings change constantly; judgment is often affected by sickness or lack of rest. Can they be reliable as guides? Is our understanding of events full enough to make really informed decisions?

As I was growing up in my teenage years, this scripture became especially important to me. There were times of hard decisions then, about school, career, boyfriends, and getting along in my family. I started relying on the Lord's guidance seriously at age 13, when I learned about it in a Sunday school lesson.

Gods wants to make our path clear and straight. He wants us to accept the fact that He has all the information and wisdom necessary to lead us in the way that will be best. Since He has all that we need, He's worthy to be trusted with *all* our heart! When we're relying totally upon Him, He makes things so much easier. But at other times we try to trust ourselves, and we say, "Oh, I know what God's will is, I'll just go ahead with my plans." So we don't ask God but step off on our own. We may not know it at first, but we've just put our trust back onto ourselves! Soon life begins to seem like a struggle, and we finally come back to God and ask Him for help again.

Have you ever done this, and when you've returned to the Lord heard Him gently say, "Child, are you on your own way again? Remember, I'm still sitting on the throne. Put your faith back in me and rest." And have you then answered Him, "Yes, Lord, I know I don't always understand Your ways, but I'll follow. I want to be in Your will, always."

New Mercy This Day

". . . Weeping may endure for a night but joy cometh in the morning."
Psalm 30:5

Michael Shaw
Evangelist

Sometimes, we may go to bed at night weeping about the problems, trials, and tribulations we experience, thinking that our world is at an end. But each morning begins a brand new day in Jesus Christ, which can be filled with joy, no matter what we've been through, or what we face. Yesterday can never be recovered; it's gone forever. But today we can begin again, fresh, excited, and ready to go with the Lord Jesus.

There was an evening in 1969 that brought sadness to my life. My leg was lost then, in an industrial accident. I spent three months in a hospital, losing weight from 185 lbs. down to 80 lbs. When I had recovered sufficiently, I went to a university in Michigan. Just a day after receiving an artificial limb, the Lord enabled me to walk on it during a miracle healing service. I've walked on it ever since without training.

By 1971, I'd gone on to play collegiate baseball for the #1 team in the nation. Even with the artificial limb, the major league Baltimore Orioles sought me as a prospect. I could run and play with the best. Yes, there were tears in my eyes at first following the accident, but at that time, I had no idea of the wonders God would do later on!

And the weeping you may go through, with all your trials and problems, may be comforted with this thought: just as your sins are forgiven and placed under the blood of the Lamb and forgotten, your yesterdays need to be placed beneath the blood and forgotten, with all their hardships. Every day is a new grace period for you, for which to say, "Thank you, Jesus, for another day in which I might win souls. And this day's going to be better than yesterday, because you've given me another chance to be, and to have joy in you!"

Big Things For God

> "Jesus answered, Neither hath this man sinned, nor his parents: but that the works of God should be made manifest in him."
>
> John 9:3

Elsa Brown
Housewife

Since He made me only 3'8" tall, God hasn't given me too many big things to do for Him. But He's given me a lot of little things! I have a rare bone disease that's only supposed to occur when both parents carry it in their family. As many generations back as I've traced, there's no sign of it on either side. It's made me very tiny, so that God might, I like to think, do some beautiful small works through me.

So many people rush through life not seeing much of what God put in the world. But a person who walks beside me gets introduced to such things as fragrant flowers, beautiful stones, fascinating insect life, moss, and leaves. A person walking with me has to walk slowly, so I get to point out all of these wonders, while we take the time to really breathe the fresh air and watch the shapes of passing clouds. I help people care, too, because it's not too often that they have the opportunity to be considerate of an adult as small as I am.

For me, my size has never been a handicap. I've always been eager to discover how many things I can do with the size I have. The Lord says, "Thou hast been faithful in a very little, have thou authority over ten cities." When you think of it, to rule over much is just to rule over a lot of little things!

God's probably made you bigger than I am. But perhaps you're not satisfied with the body or shape He's given you. Think about this: Is there anything about the way He's made you that makes you able to serve God in an extra special way? You're like no one else in the world, and God has things for you to do that no one else can. Can you turn your eyes today towards Him and let Him show you His perfect plan for you alone?

Nothing Can Defeat You

"I can do all things through Christ which stengtheneth me."
Philippians 4:13

Bob Brown
Vocational Counselor
for the Blind

Most people are surprised to discover that I don't have any use of my left arm and leg, because they can watch me do almost anything as well and as quickly as an ordinary person. When people find out that I have what they think of as a "handicap," they usually ask me how I can so skillfully cope with the many things in life that require skill and dexterity.

My answer is, "Through Jesus Christ!" He has just never let me feel hindered from full participation in life. What is a "handicap" anyway? I would suppose that to a bird, all human beings seem handicapped because we're unable to flap our arms and soar into the air at any time. To a cheetah, we must seem handicapped because we can't run 75 miles an hour. A very graceful dancer complained once that she could never dance as well as she liked because she was "just too clumsy!"

God never asks us personally to do anything we can't do. He's a whole lot smarter than that. When Paul wrote the words to this verse, he was imprisoned in Rome. God didn't give him leave to go, so Paul didn't walk through that prison's stone walls. But what powerful letters he wrote from that confinement. We're only responsible to God to obey Him in all He asks us to do. And He has never failed to give me the strength I've needed to do His will, when I've been willing to do it.

Have you ever found yourself making excuses to avoid launching out into God's purpose for your life? Have you let imagined inadequacies hold you back from full obedience to Him? He'll let nothing defeat you, if you're willing to let Him use all of you, just as you are, all day today!

We All Need Love

"He that loveth not knoweth not God; for God is love."   1 John 4:8

Jan Opperman
Sprint Car Driver

"What the world needs now is love, sweet love." That was part of a song written in the Peace and Love hippie days. That time of drugs, rock music and "free love" snared a lot of people in my generation, myself included. What got us into it? We thought that through drugs, music and sex we were going to find love.

We got turned off by religion, that said, "You can't do this; you can't do that." But love never turned anybody off. People flock to love, even a little bit of it, like dried out desert rats to an oasis. Any chemical, booze,"joint," or idea that seems to give a likely hope of love will attract followers. We all need love.

Well, that's how I got into it. How did I get out of it? By finding the love I was looking for in a follower of Jesus Christ. He was a guy whose eyes shined out with the love I knew my whole generation had been groping for, but somehow missed. He didn't condemn me, He didn't tell me a bunch of do's and don'ts. I said to Him, "All you need to do is smoke a little dope, and you'll be right on." I went to his house the next day to turn him on to some grass. Instead, he turned me on to Jesus. He didn't put me down, but he did say, "Jan, one of us is wrong." Then he told me about Jesus. He didn't even look like a hippie, he looked like a redneck. But what made me willing to listen to him was that love.

You and I have got to keep this question in mind: what are we projecting to this world around us that's starving for love? Are we beaming out condemnation? The world has enough of that. Or are we shining with the love of Jesus? People are only going to see God's love if we show it in action. If you've got it, let it shine today.

How To Quit Worrying

*"Don't worry about any-
thing; instead, pray about everything; tell God your needs,
and don't forget to thank Him
for His answers."*
Philippians 4:6 (LB)

J. T. Williams
Land Developer

Worry isn't something to be sympathized within a Christian. It's a form of disobedience to God's Word. This scripture says "Don't worry." Jesus said, "Don't worry." Worry is a sin that's difficult to overcome, because it's so common. Yes, almost respectable. Yet, it can be licked, and praying instead of worrying is the answer.

Until about five years ago, I worried a lot. I'd had an ulcer since 1960 and was on tranquilizers that a doctor had prescribed for me to take for the rest of my life. My life and business were successful by worldly standards, but that ulcer kept being aggravated by worry. And it was something I was told I'd just have to live with.

But when I got really serious about reading the Word, this verse started to make sense to me. So everytime I'd get tempted to worry, I'd start praying. Real peace started to fill me more and more. Within a month, I told my wife I was going to leave the tranquilizers at home because my ulcer wasn't acting up anymore. I took them out of my pocket and haven't touched them since.

Since then I've been through times of financial reverse and business struggles, but God's peace beyond all understanding has always stayed with me. You see, I never stopped praying and thanking God in advance for His answers.

That's how I quit worrying. Now you try it. Every time that worry tries to trouble you, recognize it for what it is: just not believing that God has things in control. Then start praying instead. Talk it over with God. Thank Him for the answer He's going to bring. Just keep praying, and God will bury your worrying. Start today.

What Is Your Strength?

"The Lord is my strength and song, and is become my salvation."   Psalm 118:4

Fred Wiegand
Heritage School Student

I don't have the strength of a muscle man. And my best singing is "Jesus Loves Me," which I do with a Donald Duck voice. But the strength I've got and the song I sing, I got from Jesus.

I wasn't a strong student in school. During my first few grades in school, they called me a "slow learner." But my parents knew the Lord and started praying for me. Over the years, my grades went from F's to D's to B's, and my last two years in high school, I was on the honor roll!

The Lord really made me grateful for everything He did in my life. So in school, on the football field, or at work, He made me just love to praise His name and to pray for people's needs. I guess I never thought much about being afraid to share Jesus with everyone around me. In football huddles or classrooms, or on the way home from school, there was just no place that wasn't right for a prayer or a song.

It's amazing how people will react to you, if you just let Jesus be Himself in you in everyday situations. Sometimes they think it's funny at first, but one thing people sense is that it's real. People who didn't know the Lord came and asked me to pray for them about problems, and after awhile, they would want to come to know the Lord.

Just think, if you've got Jesus, you've got the strength of the Holy Spirit, and a song deep down in your heart. And best of all, you have the message of salvation, to share with everyone you meet! I hope that excites you as much as it does me. 'Cause that excitement is going to draw others to Jesus! I hope it happens in your life today.

Make Stress Work For You

"Be careful for nothing; but in everything by prayer and supplication with thanksgiving let your requests be made known unto God."
Philippians 4:6

Robert Swenson
Operatic Tenor

Grand opera has become very popular today, especially in America. Talented voices are emerging from all parts of this country, and competition has become intense for operatic roles, even in small companies. Pressure such as this can almost be guaranteed to produce anxiety and tension.

Relaxation and a sense of inner peace are essential factors in a successful singing performance. Tightness and constriction keep the body from expressing free musical tone. So it is necessary for a singer to find some way to deal with all of these varied pressures.

Just so in the spiritual life, our walk and warfare can be complex and trying. As "the whole world lieth in wickedness"(1 John 5:19), we are surrounded by a bewildering onslaught of corruption, greed, lust, and all the other sinful drives that motivate a sinful world's attempts at finding happiness.

Some people have asked me, "How can a Christian sing on the operatic stage?" But is the back-room drama of business, education, or middle-American home life anymore conducive to Christian living? No, in every area of human life, there is the stress of our battle with the enemy.

And as in singing, anxiety and tension, which result when we lose our sense of assurance of God's protecting power, can cripple our ability to walk successfully from day to day.

The twofold discipline that will combat these weakening forces is spelled out in this verse. First, refuse to allow anxiety to take hold of you. Second, seek God in prayer, place youself in the center of His will, and believe that He, not the circumstances, will decide the outcome. When stress approaches today, drive it out with faith in God!

Thoughts From The Moon

"I will lift up mine eyes unto the hills, from whence cometh my help. My help cometh from the Lord, which made heaven and earth."
Psalm 121:1-2

Col. James Irwin
Former Astronaut

After I returned to earth from the moon, I was amazed to find out how many people all around the world had prayed for me. Right here, I want to thank you. I was aware of that while standing there on the moon.

The hours I spent on the moon were the most thrilling of my life. Not because I was there, but because I could feel the presence of God. On the strange surface of the moon, so very far from "home," there were many new challenges to meet. Help from God was always immediate. He was there because of your prayers.

This Psalm conveys to me the thought that, as far as it was possible for the writer's eye to see, the help of God could be found. The psalmist couldn't imagine heights far beyond the lofty mountains, but he knew God as the Creator of everything, great and small. We can see a lot farther now, with telescopes and electronic instruments that probe the depths of the universe. We have soared far beyond the highest mountain on earth, and seen the globe floating silent in space. But this only increases our wonder at the extent of God's power, and our confidence in His ability to be a present help to us wherever we are.

You probably will never stand, as I did, on the moon. But there may be times when you see yourself or a loved one just as distant from the helping hand of God. But no matter where you are, or no matter how far away that person is for whom you seek God's aid, the Lord is never more than a quiet bow of the head away. He was with me on the moon. He is with you this moment. Reach out to Him and find His help for that need.

Sales, Not Management

"Trust in the Lord with all thine heart; and lean not unto thine own understanding. In all thy ways acknowledge Him, and He shall direct thy paths."   Proverbs 3:5-6

Mary Irwin
Author

We're not in the management department of God's business. We're in sales. We mistakenly think sometimes that it's our job to understand everything that happens to us and to make and execute God's decisions for Him. God says, "Don't do that, because you have to lean on My understanding and not your own."

We don't always like to do this because it hurts our pride. We like to think of ourselves as being knowledgeable and self-sufficient. We can pretty well manage our own affairs, thank you! So when God tells us that our understanding is not very reliable, we may feel insulted.

But you see, our humanness has placed upon our eyes a set of blinders. If only because we're finite creatures, our ability to be perfect judges of what's right for us is limited. In spite of our pride, we're constantly confronting unexpected events and surprises that throw all our plans out of whack. How many ulcers grow from life's unpredictability? Then we're further limited by the veil that sin places over our eyes. Spiritually, we've been blinded by sin, the Bible says. We need guidance, just as a newly blinded person needs guidance. When we meet God, we receive a new set of eyes. But like a blind person needs training with a guide dog, we need to be trained by a thorough understanding of God's Word and close contact with Him to walk rightly.

God wants you to be satisfied with spreading the message of His love to all the people around you. If you'll keep busy in the "sales" department of His kingdom and trust Him with all the management, you'll find real fulfillment in life. Start trusting Him wholly today. Step down from the Boss's chair. It's too big for you, isn't it?

The Blessing of Receiving

". . . It is more blessed to give than to receive."

Acts 20:35

Dr. Gary D. Smith
Business Consultant

The blessing of giving is certainly great, but it cannot be obtained unless a giver manages to get his gift into the hands of a willing receiver. Many good gifts of God *and* brethren in Christ never get to produce blessing simply because people refuse to receive them.

Why should this be? Receiving a gift is a blessing, too, isn't it? Why do we refuse to accept so much of what God has for us?

Perhaps it's because outside of Christ, there is really no such thing as a gift. What I mean is that without the love of God in his heart, every giver really expects a return for his gift. This turns the gift into a loan that puts the receiver under obligation. "You owe me a favor," is an expression all too common in the world.

Also, freely receiving a gift doesn't come naturally to us because we've been trained since we were very small that we have to work for or somehow merit everything we get. When someone offers us something for nothing, we naturally get suspicious of their motives: "What did I do to get that, and what does he want from me?"

God is more good and loving than we can sometimes believe. He desires to bless us continually, to "freely give us all things" (Romans 8:32). This is how God Himself is blessed! In dying on the cross, Jesus gave us healing, deliverance, sanctification, salvation, joy, victory, power, and authority—all for no money and for none of our labor. Jesus paid the whole price for all these things.

There is nothing you can add to what God's done. But you can bless Him today by receiving what He has for you with a joyful, thankful heart.

Broken Bones of Doubt

"And when they saw Him, some worshipped Him: but some doubted."
Matthew 28:17

Bob Houlihan
Missionary

If the Bible were merely the words of men, this passage would certainly never have been included. For here, after all of Jesus' miracles, even after His resurrection from the dead, scripture reports that some disciples doubted, right there at the Mount of Ascension.

I thank God for the truthfulness of the Bible, for it leaves room in God's love for someone like you and me. The word "doubt" used here doesn't mean unbelief in the Greek, but rather confusion or perplexity. Certainly, a number of the disciples must have been confused there at the dawn of the church, wondering what it all meant. I, along with Thomas, would have had questions and fears about the present and future. But the love of Jesus didn't cast Thomas off, and He won't cast you and me off, either.

When a broken bone has been set and healed, it will never be shattered again at the spot where the first break took place. The calcium that mends that bone forms a bond far more durable than the bone itself was before. Similarly, God can turn our confusion into spiritual strength, if we'll hold onto God in faith. We can come through a puzzling experience strengthened as never before by the "calcium" of assurance God Himself gives us.

Thomas, though he was confused, was later to carry the gospel the farthest of all the disciples, all the way to India. Don't let the accuser persuade you that your confusions and unanswered questions are sin. Dare to ask and keep on asking God for answers. When you get them, you'll be unbreakably strong where you once felt weak.

What Would Jesus Do?

"Thou wilt keep him in perfect peace whose mind is stayed on Thee: because he trusteth in Thee." Isaiah 26:3

John French
Actor/Playwright

Without guidelines to live by, it's easy to be cast adrift in life. Even outside of Christ, human beings must find standards against which to measure their actions. For some, traditions serve as guides; for others, personal example provides the touchstone: "What would old Mr. Moneybags do?" Of course, no such buoy or beacon that the world has to offer can guide a soul into a perfect peace, because none are high enough or accurate enough to surmount man's sinful weaknesses.

But in staying our minds on Jesus, we can know that perfect peace. Using the perfection of His life as an example will always prove successful, for Jesus' life was the perfect adaptation of humanity to this present world.

This was the first scripture verse I ever learned. My newness is Christ, while joyous and liberating, left me in a state of some perplexity. All of my life's former experience was no longer applicable to life in the kingdom of God. I had to learn to live all over again, but didn't know how. Then, through this verse I learned to fix my mind on Christ by asking myself before I made any move: "What would Jesus do?" This was difficult at first; I wasn't trained to think like Jesus. But as I began to know His Word and follow His example, my mind began to change its whole orientation, until it became disciplined to thinking the thoughts of Christ.

I urge you to consider, in every circumstance of your life, *What would Jesus do?* Remarkable clarity will be added to your vision; you will know the right thing to do, and have faith to do it. Fear and confusion will disappear, leaving peace and contentment.

"No Ground"

"Give no ground, foot-hold or opportunity to the devil." Ephesians 4:27 (Amplified)

Rev. Ev Carter Spencer
Evangelist

What did Paul mean in that verse in his letter to the Ephesians? What "ground" was he referring to?

The answer, of course, is *any* area of our life. This includes our thoughts, attitudes, emotions, desires, wills, and feelings. Neither should we give "ground" morally, physically, socially, academically, financially, or circumstantially.

As Jesus told his disciples in John 14:30, "The prince (Satan) of the world is coming, and he has no claim on Me—there is nothing in Me that belongs to him, therefore he has no power over Me." We as Christians with Christ Jesus living in our hearts have the same authority over Satan, and the only way the devil can take "ground" from us is to give it to him by stepping out of God's will.

Our best defense is God's Holy Word. In Colossians 1:13 (Amp.) we read, "The Father has delivered and drawn us to Himself out of the control and domination of darkness and has transferred us into the kingdom of the Son of His love." If we are out of the control of darkness as that verse tells us, we are completely out of Satan's power. How? By being delivered out of the devil's grasp, and into the loving arms of Jesus by God the Father.

If by our own choice, by our own free will, you have given ground to Satan through doubt or fear, right now turn these things over to Jesus through prayer. Only then can you rebuke Satan and exercise your authority as a believer in Christ Jesus over him.

Give every area of your life to Jesus today. Then you can say with God-given force, "NO GROUND, DEVIL!"

The World Is God's

"The Earth is the Lord's, and the fullness thereof; the world, and they that dwell therein." Psalm 24:1

Stephen Nielson
Pianist

The world we live in does *not* belong to Satan. Yes, the scripture does say that "the whole world lieth in wickedness." But Satan is here as an usurper, occupying territory he does not own, awaiting the end of the period of his activity, decreed by the Earth's true Owner, Almighty God.

A failture to understand this has caused many Christians to cringe in unnecessary fear and confusion and to spend more time observing in terror the works of the devil than in worship and glorification of the Lord. It has also caused some Christians to withdraw from the beauty and wonder of the creation God has given to His children to enjoy as rightful heirs, resulting in an impoverishment of their lives that He never intended.

Satan's presence in the world is like what we might see on the screen at an horror movie: it can frighten us, but it need not have any control over us. The eternal reality we must never lose sight of is God's controlling hand in every detail of His creation. We need to occupy our thoughts, not with Satan's deceptions, but with the greatness of Jesus' Lordship and the certainty of His rule.

As a musician, this has meant for me a freedom to explore all forms of musical expression and to help others in the Body of Christ to expand their horizons of worship and praise to God.

For you, I hope this means that you will be able to move with new courage and boldness into this world; become a discoverer, and enjoyer, a ruler of all that God has given you as a son and heir.

He Is Strong

". . . Greater is He that is in you than he that is in the world."   1 John 4:4

Bill Ashpaugh
Former Mr. Indiana

This is a verse you can stand on for strength. When people come to me and share their problems, I tell them to stand on 1 John 4:4. It says that we are God's kids, we are overcomers, and greater is He that is the problem solver than he that caused the problem. So no matter what the devil does to you, you can still be a winner because God said you could.

As you can imagine, this meant a lot to me when I was suffering from what was supposed to be incurable cancer. What the devil had done in my body was supposed to kill me. But believing this verse, I just wouldn't give up. God drove that cancer out of me and made me a champion.

In my view, God is a very strong person. Jesus Christ was a he-man, not a weakling, even when He was stretched out on the cross. Jesus was a robust person, who walked many miles and lived under all kinds of conditions. The Bible says that Jesus as a boy "waxed strong in spirit" (Luke 2:40), and to be a carpenter's boy, He had to be strong.

Strength is knowing that you are God's child, just as much one as Jesus was. You're the head and not the tail. You're a winner and not a loser.

It takes a real man (a real woman, too!) to get turned on for Jesus Christ. Have you got what it takes to be the kind of person God can use? This verse says you do, because you've got the strongest person in the universe in you. So praise God today and flex those muscles.

Seeing God's Purposes

"And we know that all things work together for good to them that love God, to them who are the called according to His purpose." Romans 8:28

Rhea Zakich
Creator of the "Ungame"

God's sense of purpose for our lives transcends all of our own loftiest ambitions and endeavors. Sometimes it takes the stripping away of a lifetime's dreams to show us how wonderfully the Lord can use us for His glory.

A serious throat ailment seemed to put an end to what had been for me a life of high purpose. Facing the prospect of remaining mute for the rest of my life after surgery, I was cast down near despair.

Every meaningful activity of my life had centered upon my ability to speak: teaching and singing in the church, mothering, working, and raising support for the disadvantaged of the inner city ghetto. I could not imagine having purpose in a life as a mute.

During a period of three speechless months, I wrestled with God, accusing, enraged, beyond tears of frustration, trying to bargain, finally releasing all of my feelings, and coming to rest in a powerful sense of His peace and love. After this struggle, it no longer mattered to me that I might have to face a life without speech. I eagerly anticipated the new future He had prepared for me.

All negativity, anger, and fear now gone, the wellsprings of creativity locked within me began to pour forth. I thought of many ways to express myself: music, art, writing. And before regaining my speech, I began to contemplate the problems of human communication. Out of this meditation came the concept of the "Ungame," a non-competitive, game-like group activity which has been used to help thousands express and explore their feelings and emotions and open up relationships with others.

Have you discovered God's true purpose for your life? Ask Him to reveal it to you right now. You, too, just might be surprised!

Learning To Rest In God

"For promotion cometh neither from the east, nor from the west, nor from the south. But God is the judge: He putteth down one, and setteth up another."
                Psalm 75:6-7

Ruthe White
Communicator to Women

Learning to live the Christian life means entering a whole new dimension of existence, rather like trying to swim for the first time. The first thing a swimmer needs to master is floating. This is because unless a person develops faith in the ability of water to bear him up, he can never relax while swimming. Most of his energy will be expended trying to keep his head out of the water by thrashing around with his arms and legs. The more he struggles, the more he will be drawn down into the water.

Similarly, the essence of many believers' walk with God is frantic effort and struggle. They strive mightily to retain God's favor or try with joyless works to maintain a "good Christian" status. Rather than becoming free to be themselves and express God's unique plan for their lives, they attempt to create out of their own will what they believe God desires. The result is exhaustion, discouragement, and a leaden sense of emotional and spiritual inferiority.

God hasn't designed any of us for failure but for a new kind of life. If He has made a perfect plan for our lives, then it is His responsibility to carry out that plan. At a certain point in my life, I knew God wanted me to begin writing books, but my background gave me no reason to expect success. So I had to become totally dependent upon the Lord for advancement. It was then that I realized that, like the swimmer, I had simply to rest in Him and be borne by the current of His Spirit.

I hope you will pray with me today, "Now, Lord, I lay myself upon Your promises, and repose in rest. You carry me where You want me to go." This will mean the difference between frustration and fulfillment, between struggling and trust, between failure and success.

The Love Of God

"For God so loved the world, that He gave His only begotten Son, that whosoever believeth in Him should not perish, but have everlasting life."   John 3:16

Crying Wind
Author

My four children are such a blessing. They teach me so much about God's love. To think that God would trust me as a mother with the lives of four human beings! I'd read this verse hundreds of times, but it didn't really hit home to me until I had my own first born child.

I held him in my arms and loved him so much. I just wept for joy because he was such a great, great treasure. And then I thought: God had only one son and gave Him up because He loved us so much! I love my own son with all the love I've got. But with just my human love, I wouldn't have sacrificed my son for the entire world. Mine was selfish love; were I God, I'd never have given Jesus up.

To think that God gave His *only* Son. Now, I had four children, but God wasn't going to have more. Jesus was the only one. I realized at that moment, when I held my own son so close, how much God loves us: that He loved His own Son even more, that He gave Jesus for me, so that I could live, my son could live, and my other children could have eternal life!

"As arrows are in the hand of a mighty man; so are children of the youth" (Psalm 127:4). If this is true of us as human parents, how much more is it of God! His Son's life was of such infinite worth! How I thank my heavenly Father that today His Son Jesus is risen from the dead, the Arrow of His right hand once again!

And what a Son was Jesus, Who was willing in childlike faith to abandon Himself to the will of His Father. How much we need to learn from Him, and receive as children all of the eternal life He has for us in His great plan.

Light For Dark Places

"The Lord is my light and my salvation; whom shall I fear? The Lord is the strength of my life; of whom shall I be afraid?" Psalm 27:1

Greg Lippman
Construction Worker

Just last November, I was buried alive under tons of rock and dirt for over 1½ hours. The sides caved in on a deep trench where I had been laying sewer pipes, and quite suddenly, complete darkness surrounded me, along with a weight of soil so heavy that I was instantly rendered immobile.

The words of this verse slowly crossed my mind. I'd read them often before, but now, there was no light indeed for me nor any strength other than the presence of the Lord Himself. "Your faith is going to be tested," a quiet voice said: "You'll soon know whether all this is real or not." I was only conscious for a few minutes, perhaps 15 at the most. During that time, no profound religious experience occurred, but a deep peace reigned over those moments, leaving me free from worry or panic.

A series of miracles were required to save my life, both while I was underground and during the lengthy recuperation period that followed. But no miracle was greater than that sense of calm and trust that preserved me from fear on the verge of death.

Someday, if Jesus doesn't return first, you too will have to face death. Right now, you may be facing circumstances or challenges along a road that seems dark, in a place where all your strength cannot prevail. Remember that the Lord, and He alone, is all the light and power you need. The powers of life and death are all in His control. Rest in His strength, and His light will be your peace.

Christ In The Workaday World

"For the good that I would, I do not: but the evil which I would not, that I do."
Romans 7:19

Walter Armbruster
Author/Ad Executive

There are easier things in the world than being a Christian in business, "Oh, tell him I'm out of town," you could say to your secretary when that unwanted call is burning the line. It would be so simple—it would also be a lie.

Expense accounts, press releases, audits, making deals with people who don't hold the same principles you do . . . Some businessmen say, "You can't take God to work. All that's fine for Sunday, but you'll never survive in business." But friend, if you're a Christian doing business, Jesus had better be there.

Paul shows in this verse that he understood the kind of battle that can rage between strong ambition for success in business, and strong desire for success as a Christian—when they strive side by side in one person. I don't think this verse is the confession of an unbeliever; I think it's the experience of all of us as we fight the devil and our self-nature in our walk with God.

That's why Jesus has to be there. How otherwise could I lift up my associates and love my competitors? I need for Jesus to take control. When I enter that conference room in the morning, I swallow hard and say. "Here goes, Lord. Stay with me!" And I keep in touch with Him like that, all day.

Keep talking to God. He ought to be in the bathroom, the kitchen, the car, the office, everywhere. Actually, He *is* always there; we just treat Him like He isn't. If you get into the habit of remembering that He's there, and being thankful, and letting Him know that, He might start talking back to you. You might start listening and doing what He says, and things will sure go better and better!

The Beauty Of Salvation

"For God so loved the world, that He gave His only begotten Son, that whosoever believeth on Him should not perish, but have everlasting life." John 3:16

Dave Boyer
Christian Singer

I like to read John 3:16 and substitute my name for "whosoever." Knowing God sent His Son to die for me and grant me forgiveness for my sin is almost too good to be true. But praise God, it is true!

One of my favorite songs is "Calvary Covered It All," by Mrs. Walter G. Taylor. It explains what John 3:16 means to me:

> "Far deeper than all that the world can impart
> Was the message that came to my heart
> How that Jesus alone for my sin did atone
> And Calvary covers it all
>
> Calvary covers it all,
> My past with its sin and stain;
> My guilt and despair
> Jesus took on Him there,
> And Calvary covers it all.
>
> How blessed the thought,
> that my soul by Him bought,
> Shall be His in the glory on high.
> Where with gladness song
> I'll be one of the throng,
> And Calvary covers it all.
>
> Calvary covers it all,
> My past with its sin and stain;
> My guilt and despair
> Jesus took on Him there,
> And Calvary covers it all.

Every time I sing this song the beauty of my salvation comes back to me. Jesus loves me and He loves you. Let's never forget to return that love.

Overcoming The Past

"Brethren, I count not myself to have apprehended: but this I do, forgetting those things which are before, I press toward the mark for the prize of the high calling of Jesus Christ."
Philippians 3:13-14

Dr. Richard Dobbins
Psychologist/Author

Perhaps one of the greatest hurdles a new Christian has to scale is overcoming their past-the guilt of their sin.

In this writing to the Philippians, Paul is speaking from experience as he tells his brothers in Philippi how important putting their past behind them really is. Paul himself, before his dramatic conversion on the road to Damascus, was described in the Book of Acts as a "wild man, going everywhere to devastate the believers . . . eager to destroy every Christian."

If Paul had allowed guilt over his past to dictate his life after his conversion, he would have been hindered from doing the great work he did in the early church. His acceptance of Jesus Christ included full pardon of his past. Paul acknowledged God's total forgiveness of his sins and lived in the liberation of freedom from guilt.

Every born-again believer has the right to live in that same freedom; however, to continue in that freedom and receive the great things God has in store, Jesus explicitly explains the importance of turning away from the past. He says in Luke 9:62, "No man having put his hand to the plough, and looking back, is fit for the kingdom of God."

With that knowledge, and the assurance of 2 Timothy 1:12, "for I know whom I have believed, and am persuaded that He is able to keep that which I have committed unto Him against that day," we can, as Paul, put our past behind us and go forth to do the things that God would have us to do for His glory. In this, we will reach "the mark of the prize of the high calling of Jesus Christ."

No Room For Bitterness

"Looking diligently lest any man fail of the grace of God; lest any root of bitterness springing up trouble you, and thereby many be defiled."
Hebrews 12:15

Al Palmquist
Police Officer/Youth Worker

Allowing bitterness to get a hold of you is like taking poison. I've had considerable opportunity as a cop to fight bitterness. Accusations fly all around a police department: the department's on the take, the mayor is on the take, nothing's getting done. But nobody seems to know how to make it any better.

Stay sweet. Don't get bitter. Because if you're bitter, you're going to destroy yourself before you harm those you're bitter against. Psalm 23:5 says: "Thou preparest a table before me in the presence of mine enemies." What's referred to here is the activity of the shepherd as he goes ahead of the sheep into the pasture, digging out the poisonous plants that might be harmful to the sheep and cause them to transmit disease to one another.

How does bitterness spring up? Parents can sow it in their children through lack of love, a bad example, broken promises, and no discipline. Every kid wants to respect his parents, so a kid who is wronged may hold it in for a long time, but one day, just like a bottle of fermenting liquid with a cork on it, he'll explode.

The same thing can happen with employers and employees, wives and husbands. That inner rage will find its way out, given time. The way to avoid causing bitterness is to humble yourself if you've wronged someone, go and say, "I'm sorry. I was wrong. Will you please forgive me?" Don't nourish bitterness in your heart. If you're guilty of it, ask forgiveness of the person you've held anything against.

Is the Lord speaking to your heart right now about any bitterness you may have been harboring? Don't delay, get it out of your heart, root it out, and let God seal up the hurt with His love today.

Salt And Light

"Ye are the salt of the earth . . . Ye are the light of the world . . ."
                    Matthew 5:13-14

David Lewis
Bible Teacher

When Jesus compared us as His followers to salt and light, He was crediting us with possession of tremendous power to influence our world. Before refrigeration, salt was used throughout the world as a preservative. And in a world where, for most people, sundown was the end of the day, light could at times be a scarce and precious luxury.

Jesus was saying that to a world decaying from sin and death, groping in the darkness of fear and confusion, we would be the only sustaining and illuminating force. We would be holding in the balance, with God-given spiritual authority and the power to "bind and loose" (Matthew 16:19), the fate of humanity.

Now as Christians, we're not putting the devil out of business. Only God is strong enough to finish that job. Salt doesn't prevent decay, but it does slow it down. Likewise, light that shines on obstacles in its path will always cast shadows. There will be moral and spiritual darkness in this world until God recreates the earth and heavens in which His righteousness will shine unhindered. But until the Church is drawn from the world by the rapture, we are retarding the rate of wickedness and sin.

This gives each of us a weight of responsibility to be salt and light wherever God has chosen to "scatter" us. We are to influence the world around us, by our lives, our prayers, and the exercise of our spiritual authority. Jesus has told us not to hide our light and not to let our saltiness lose its savor. Consider right now what you can do to influence for good the home and community you live in.

Greater Is He!

"Ye are of God, little children, and have overcome them: because greater is He that is in you than he that is in the world."   1 John 4:4

Justus Du Plessis
Administrator

How much we need to become conscious of the indwelling presence of Christ which is ours as believers in Him. So often we are overcome by circumstances or victims of bodily illness because we have not acted in awareness of the power that is ours because of His life within us.

What sort of power? First, the power to be quickened in our bodies, according to Romans 8:11. For as the resurrected life of Jesus Christ is incorruptible, the power of that life can restore us from sickness or disease.

Second, the power to meet circumstances of all kinds fearlessly and victoriously; for if Jesus could not be defeated, and He lives forever as Lord of all within us, we may be unconquerable, too. Third, Jesus' living presence in us enables us to be the same blessing to others as He was, to see ourselves as His extensions in doing His work in the world.

When is this power available to us? Notice that this verse is written in present tense: this power is ours in the now. Indeed, "As He is, so are we—*in this world*" (1 John 4:17). This is not just a theological concept or theory, but an accomplished fact.

The world today is not searching for another "ism" or way of life, but for the resurrected Christ. I believe His personal return to this world is imminent, but He can already be met now in us who love Him. Will someone meet Him in you today?

On The Offensive

"For I am not ashamed of the gospel of Christ: for it is the power of God unto salvation to every one that believeth; to the Jew first, and also to the Greek."

Romans 1:16

Ben Armstrong
Exec. Dir., Nat. Relig. Broadcasters Assoc.

This is the correct stance of the born-again believer: not to be ashamed, but to be proud of what God has done for him. He stands on the Word of God, backed up by the power of the strongest entity in existence, the news of the finished work of Jesus Christ.

Historically, Christians as a whole have stood fearfully. Perhaps we've felt that because something has happened to us individually. When our lives have changed for Christ, the whole world seems to stand against us. The catacombs, monasteries, the Middle Ages were instances when Christians retreated from society.

But something new has happened in this electronic age. As we have wedded the gospel message with the power of modern media, we have changed from a defensive position to an offensive thrust face-to-face with the world. Organizations like PTL are making individual believers aware of the fact that they stand with the greatest power in the world, the power of God unto salvation.

In the field of theology, and in our seminaries, we spend three or four years learning to defend ourselves, with hardly any time spent learning about how to aggressively communicate the gospel using modern media's twin miracles of radio and television. But the gospel doesn't need to be defended; it's an explosive force that cannot be contained. Paul realized that the gospel would be "foolishness" to the unsaved world. That's why he pushed out strongly and took ground for God effectively.

Under the leadership God has raised up in these last days, the "minority" of Christians is turning into a majority. You can take your stand today, knowing that you're going to win, if you're on the Almighty's side.

Step Into God's Unknown

"Remember ye not the former things, neither consider the things of old. Behold, I will do a new thing; now it shall spring forth; shall ye not know it?"   Isaiah 43:18-19

Hazel Slaughter
Singer

Certain verses ought to be constant prophecies for our lives. This is one of them, for it's telling us that God is continually doing something new in us and with us.

There are times when we lose heart, because we can only see the future as an extension of what has already happened to us. We tend to think that we're limited by past accomplishments or present abilities. But God is saying to us right now that these things shouldn't even be a consideration as we move ahead for Him.

We traveled for quite awhile with the Gaithers, and when that time was over, I feared for a while that the Lord was going to put us on a shelf. But no, He began doing a new thing in our lives as opportunities arose in the television medium. God expanded and changed our ministry radically, so that we could reach new audiences, and grow in new directions musically.

Try confronting any fears like these that you may have with this scripture. God has given us total freedom from the past! Whatever failures you may have suffered, whatever mistakes you may have made, whatever false starts, whatever sins might have plagued you, *God is doing something utterly new in your life*, which you can get on with, if you'll ask Him just to show you what it is.

Can you believe this outstanding truth of God today? To do so, you'll have to put some things behind you: old excuses, worn-out anxieties, moth-eaten might-have-beens. And you'll have to fix your eyes straight ahead at Jesus and accept His free gifts of "I can's," "all possible's," "crowns of life," and "well dones!" Believe God, and fare forward!

Rooted In God

"Every plant, which My heavenly Father hath not planted shall be rooted up."
Matthew 15:13

Henry Slaughter
Music Artist

Everything in life that ever really lasts has its start in God. The life of a person who has not experienced new birth in Christ, while it may seem to have temporary value, is void and empty, because it does not have roots in God.

And in the life of a Christian, everything that God is not the author of is nothing. This is a stern verse, because it leaves no middle ground. Whatever plans, works, dreams, wishes, or accomplishments God has not sown in us will not survive.

Once we look past its toughness, though, this verse offers us great encouragement. For if God Himself *is* the author of something in our lives, it cannot fail, it will stand for eternity, along with Him.

So often we get into difficulty because we plot and scheme and try to plant things that we think are good, in God's interest. And as believers, we wrestle with things that the enemy tries to plant in us. But one day, we will know complete redemption, and a heaven free from all these strange plants. They will be destroyed, but all that God has planted will remain.

So we need to learn to listen to the voice of God, and to discern His Spirit's movement in us as He tends to our growth. We need to humbly acknowledge that He is the sower who goes out to sow, and that He alone can give the growth. We are at best prepared ground, broken and fertile for His use.

Lord, tend us completely today. Let no weeds or strange growths take root in us today. Nourish in us only fruit that will remain. Amen.

Are You Prepared To Live?

"... I am come that they might have life, and that they might have it more abundantly." John 10:10

James Sustar
Bible Teacher

Jesus spent very little time teaching men how to die; He taught them how to live. If a person knows how to live, he will automatically know how to die. We who are pastors and teachers have spent a great deal more time than Jesus did preparing people to face the hereafter or the rapture. Perhaps in so doing we've contributed to a desire that's all too easy to arouse—that of a longing to escape the daily realities of doing the will of God.

Don't misunderstand me: we ought to desire above all things to see Jesus, to "love His appearing" (2 Timothy 4:8). But Jesus also urged us in the Gospel of Luke's parable of the talents to *"occupy* until I come" (Luke 19:13). Put into modern English, this means that we are to "keep busy" while we wait for Him.

Let me ask you a serious question: in case you don't meet Jesus in the next twenty years, what are you going to do with those years? Are we as a church prepared to *live* for Jesus a productive, overcoming, reigning life? Scripture seems to indicate that His coming will be sudden and surprising, and that believers will be taken in the midst of daily activities, "in such an hour as ye think not" (Matthew 24:44).

The abundant life Jesus has given us is not only for eternity, after we die, nor is it only in material goods we might desire. It is life, here and now, characterized by abundant fruit of the Spirit and joy in walking from day to day with Jesus.

Jesus Himself was prepared for His earthly ministry and His heavenly throne by the ordinary life He lived in Nazareth. He "learned obedience" (Hebrews 5:8) in His daily walk, and His future glory was prefaced, as ours also has to be, in the nitty-gritty of life.

Led By His Spirit

"For as many as are led by the Spirit of God, they are the sons of God." Romans 8:14

Dr. Robert McDonald
Psychiatrist

When Adam sinned, he lost his relationship to God as a son. "God is a Spirit" (John 4:24), and He created man with a capacity to relate to Him personally, through placing in man a spirit. The death that Adam experienced with the Fall was the death of his spirit: when his spirit died, he lost his capacity to fellowship with God.

When Jesus arose from the dead, He brought through His finished work "many *sons* unto glory" (Hebrews 2:10). In other words, Jesus made it possible for the spirits of all those who believe in Him to be made alive that they might again be *sons* of God and enjoy relationship with Him.

The scripture above tells us a particular characteristic of the sons of God: they are *led* by God's Spirit. To enjoy sonship with God means to be led by Him.

I wasn't always aware of this necessity to be led by God's Spirit. Though saved and Spirit-filled, I walked for the most part according to my own judgment, using what some call "sanctified common sense" to direct my actions. But then I realized that I couldn't be led by *God's* Spirit unless I watched what He was doing and listened to Him in close, personal contact. So I began to pray in the Spirit to God and take time to listen for His answer. Then I obeyed His orders from moment to moment.

Get in touch with God first thing in the morning. By faith put your whole will into His hands. Pray to Him in tongues and with your understanding, then quiet your mind and listen to what *He* has to say. You'll soon learn to know His voice and appreciate the wise and wonderful way He orders your day.

Power For Today

"I can do all things through Christ which strengtheneth me."
Philippians 4:13

Carole Carlson
Wife/Authoress

How do people carry on their lives without Christ? America's huge hospital population, statistics on heart disease, ulcers, and mental illness all show our inadequacy without Christ to meet what life throws at us.

Not all of America's teachings about self-sufficiency and human potential can hide the futility of trying to live without Jesus. "Without Me, ye can do nothing," Jesus said (John 15:5). How many times do we take the credit for the blessing that God bestows? And how many even little things can we do better with the Lord's help!

The short verse above has often been used to illustrate the vastness of the power that is ours through Jesus Christ. But I believe it's saying that each and every act we can do is only performable because Jesus is giving us strength to do it. Very often a "little" problem is all that's needed to throw me. It's then that I know how totally dependent I am upon Christ.

In the major tragedy of our family's life, when our son was killed in an airplane crash seven years ago, this verse was a constant source of comfort and sustaining power. But through that experience its truth became more and more real to me for the everyday and ordinary events of my life, too.

Only Jesus can supply the power you will need today. Right now you have no way of knowing whether the day will bring grave challenges or just routine tasks your way. But I pray that you will remember to cast not just some, but *all* your cares upon Christ. And may you so feel His presence that in *all* things you do, you sense His loving and enabling power.

God's Addition

"But seek ye first the kingdom of God and his righteousness; and all these things shall be added unto you."
                            Matthew 6:33

Don Wilkerson
Director: Teen Challenge

When I was a teenager in high school, I'd watch a lot of kids go off after classes to hang out and fool around. My father was a pastor, and I had started preaching, too. But sometimes, there was a part of me, not God's part, that wondered whether I wasn't missing something out there in the world. I had to count the cost of following Jesus.

You see, I wanted to be popular and well liked, to wear flashy clothes, and to be part of an exciting crowd. And sometimes I'd get discouraged with following the Lord. One day, I was witnessing to another young man, and he said, "You know, I feel sorry for you. You can't do anything." That really hurt.

God had dropped the above scripture into my heart two years before and at times like this, I would run over to the church and get onto the altar and talk it out with Him. "Lord," I'd say, "you know my needs. You said there would be a payday. I'm just going to keep putting you first and trust you to do all that you said."

You know, it sometimes seems like you have to give up a lot to serve God at first. But each thing you seem to lose is really a gift: an opportunity for God to give you what He wants for your life.

God has brought me more excitement, joy, and fellowship than I could ever tell you. For God in His love not only prepares us to die—He prepares us to live. He cares about your needs *now*. He will meet that hunger in your heart *now*, if you'll dare to put Him first, just as He did for that young boy with a heartache long ago.

The Creative Word

"In the beginning was the Word, and the Word was with God, and the Word was God." John 1:1

Karen Mains
Author

Four years ago, my father had an attack of encephalitis which damaged the hemisphere in his brain that controls the language functions. As he cannot speak, he is medically called an aphasic. I have thought much since then about what happens to human beings when they are deprived of words.

My father's condition presents to me an analogy of the lack of communication that exists between much of the Church and their heavenly Father. He is not aphasic, rather it's we who have been damaged and diseased in spirit by sin so that we cannot receive the message of the Word who was in the beginning and is always communicative. And from our lips the word of faith, by which the Living Word called all things into origin, falls haltingly, garbled, or not at all.

Yet that same creative utterance is still absolutely alive and at work in our world today. We as the Church must bring ourselves before Him and ask, "Why aren't we hearing the Word as it comes into our lives? And why are we not speaking that Word ourselves, creatively to heal, love, save, and build up as You did? Will You heal our stony ears and loosen our knotted tongues so that we can hear You clearly and speak Your power into being where we are?"

You and I, dear brother or sister, will then receive His Word to create within us the new being He is conforming into His image. And as our hearts and minds are renewed, Jesus' words will effectively flow from our lips to help Him begin in others the new creation He is already working in us.

Trials Are Not Forever

*"Now it came to pass
. . ."*   Ruth 1:1

Thurlow Spurr
PTL Club Music Director

Here's a phrase that's used over and over again in both the Old and New Testaments. I like things that come to pass. My whole philosophy as a Christian is that all things come to pass. God has a plan for my life, and now that I've surrendered to it, those things that are a part of it are coming to pass.

Very often in the Bible, there's a condition for good things to come to pass. God says, "If you will, I will." Whosoever shall call upon the name of the Lord . . . If My people . . . But if we will, the beautiful thing is that God always keeps His promise, as we meet His conditions.

That's the first part, that's easy for me to like. The second part is a different type of thing that also has to come to pass. The Bible says that the trials of this life are not forever. There are things that have to come through our lives that can be unpleasant. They are for our perfecting, for teaching patience, and learning how to relate to one another in order to release Christ in us. Then they pass.

Very often I'll find myself thinking, "This is the most horrible thing that I've ever experienced! How am I ever going to survive this?" But I've come to know that things come—in order to pass! On the other side is the victory and the blessing and the revelation of why in God's will that thing came to pass.

Why did you "miss" that opportunity? God had a plan for you! Why did that adversity come? Why did it seem like God wasn't there? He had a perfect plan. Wherever you are, He's not going to leave you there. That circumstance is going to last just as long as it has to. Then it'll pass. Let it do its work. You'll learn something that'll become a lesson that you can then "pass on" to someone else.

Accomplishing His Purpose

"Being confident of this very thing, that He which hath begun a good work in you will perform it until the day of Jesus Christ."
Philippians 1:6

Dr. David Kithcart
Lt. Col., U.S. Army, Ret.

When Jesus begins a good work, it will be completed, and nothing will stop it. If the Lord expects us to be good workmen, He'd be setting a poor example if He couldn't finish a job Himself. He started out in my life by giving me a high calling in the military service. I wanted to be the best officer possible. Now I'm retired from the army, but in full-time evangelistic service for the Lord. And the vision now is even brighter, broader, with the horizons even more inviting.

I know Jesus is going to finish the work. It could have stopped at almost any moment when I was in Vietnam. There was always a chance of being cut down by the enemy, but somehow inside of me there was a force greater than the threatening forces outside. One time, as my pursuers came closer and closer, my body wanted to give way and faint. I got very shaky, and my mind was flashing messages that I was going to be shot down on the streets of Vietnam. Deep inside of me, however, by the power of the Spirit, I had a peace. It was the confidence that a good work had been started in me, and it was not my time to leave this world. My adversaries suddenly wheeled and turned away. I don't know what they saw, perhaps an angel, but they turned away. God spared my life for a purpose, and I know He'll continue it until the day He comes to take me away.

You can be confident right now that the work He's begun in you will be finished. All circumstances, all stresses of life, all perplexities and difficulties, will not deter Him. He will use them all as the tools to perfectly shape your life as He sees fit. Keep that in mind at all times and continually say, "Lord, use this experience to mold and make me Your own. Finish me, Lord, for Your glory!"

The Real Thing

"For by grace are ye saved through faith; and that not of yourselves: it is the gift of God: Not of works, lest any man should boast."
Ephesians 2:8-9

Jerry Davis
Christian Businessman

I thought I was a Christian. After all, I went to a Christian school, was president of the youth group, and even traveled with the school's music group as part of a quartet. As we went from place to place all summer, I gave a testimony consisting of made-up facts about how I got to be a Christian. Others wrote it up for me, and I recited it, not really knowing what it meant.

It was a testimony that I spoke but hadn't experienced for myself. As a result, I had a hole in my life, with me always. I didn't know what it was or that everyone without God had it. There was so much "Christian" involvement in my life that I couldn't let my aunts or uncles or father know it wasn't for real. They didn't know I was playing a game, but after a while there was no hiding it from myself. In secret I was still doing the things I knew a Christian shouldn't do, just like unsaved people.

But during another summer, I went away to a Christian camp as a part of the staff, supposedly a Christian. One night Dr. Bernard Ram spoke on the verse above, and for the first time I heard what it really meant. Though I'd said it in front of thousands of people night after night, I accepted the Lord right then, 15 years after everyone thought I had.

Take a look at those words again. Salvation is the gift of God. It's not given because of works, or Christian upbringing, or friends who know the Lord, or praying parents. Have you been relying on anything else but Jesus Christ and His shed blood to save you? You may think you're saved, but are you sure of the firmness of your foundation? If you are, praise the Lord. If you're not, look to the Lord and receive Jesus as your Savior right now.

Stand Strong For God

"What shall we then say to these things? If God be for us, who can be against us?"
Romans 8:31

Joy Roulier
Heritage School Student

No matter what we face in our lives, no matter who stands against us, we know that we can stand strong in the Word of God—because Jesus is for us!

Lots of people are manipulated by what people think of them, and by what other people want. I was a people pleaser, wanting to be liked and athletic and successful. And I did achieve all those things, but they just didn't satisfy. Meeting Jesus Christ turned my life around. From that moment on, what people thought began to mean less and less. The only thing really important was what my Lord thought of me. That's what we should think as Christians: is God pleased with me? We're not here to please men, we're here to please our heavenly Father!

The Lord told me when I met Him, "Joy, you're going to have to stand up for Me. You're going to face persecution and misunderstanding. But none of these things will stand against you if you will concern yourself first with pleasing Me." In time, people's jeers and taunts turned to respect, and like Jesus did as a youth, I "found favor with God and man." God turned around that great fear I had of not being accepted. If I was accepted by Him, I belonged, in the eyes of the only person who really mattered.

If you'll stand strong in God, and "Let your light so shine before men," He promises that they will finally "glorify your Father which is in heaven" (Matthew 5:16). No one can stand against God Almighty. And as people look past you, and see Him, they will stand amazed at what He does through you, and come to find Him through your witness.

A Promise For Your Thoughts

"Finally, brethren, whatsoever things are true . . . just . . . lovely . . . of a good report; if there be any virtue, and if there be any praise, think on these things."

Philippians 4:8

Jerry Bernard
Pastor/TV Host

In our day of media saturation in the form of books, magazines, movies, television, and radio, we are constantly bombarded by the opinions and outlook of the world. Most of the information reveals the blatant disregard of God and His laws and principles.

Though we see the devastating impact of what the world considers newsworthy and entertaining, many Christians continue to be willful viewers, listeners and buyers of what the media offers. Like lethal radiation, this information penetrates into our thoughts, eventually deforming and disintegrating our moral and spiritual fiber.

The relevancy of Philippians 4:8 to the Christian life today is immeasurable. It tells us how we are to think and what our thoughts should dwell on. Daily, we are assailed with the negatives of the world. If we read the newspapers, the bulk of their content virtually offers nothing positive or uplifting. The same goes for today's television and movies. As we absorb this information, we begin to live according to its influence. We become negative, depressed, and sick.

The Lord does not want His children to be removed from the world (John 17:15) but while remaining in the world, He does not want them to lose the strength of their Christian witness (Matthew 5:13). Apostle Paul's instruction to all Christians is to establish their Christian witness by strengthening their thought life upon things that are true, just, pure, lovely, and of a good report.

If you do think on such things and act as you think, Paul assures you of the promise that "the God of peace shall be with you" (Philippians 4:9). That's what I call a "promise for your thoughts."

Magnifying Jesus

"He must increase, but I must decrease."   John 3:30

Jack Conner
Musician

As John the Baptist spoke these words, he recognized the end of his ministry of preparation for the Christ: The Lord Himself had arrived. The office of Old Testament prophecy was finished. The nation of Israel as the exclusive repository of God's action was over. From this time on, Jesus was growing, and is still growing, ever brighter until the perfect day.

Once we have met Jesus, this is the realization that the Holy Spirit burns into the deepest part of our hearts. A death blow has been dealt to our self-life and personal ambition. We know that if we are to grow at all, Jesus must be magnified in us.

How contrary to the desires of the flesh is this statement. How easy it would be to read into John's words a note of sadness that his day was done. But not so: the verse that precedes this tells us that John's joy was fulfilled. As new creatures in Christ, our joy will be also to see Him increase.

And who should we rather see glorified, once we have known His beauty and His love? Can our eyes, dimmed by the limits of time, imagine greater things than He has in store for us? Can our plans or ambitions aspire higher than His, who will someday make a new heaven and a new earth? Will we ever hope to be lovelier in spirit and body than the Bright and Morning Star?

Let us worship and bow down before Him, when the flesh would rise up and assert its selfishness and confusion. Let all that we are fall away before the light of His love and grace. He *must* increase: joyfully allow Him to let His greatness dwarf you, this day.

You Can Love!

"And hope maketh not ashamed; because the love of God is shed abroad in our hearts by the Holy Ghost which is given unto us."
Romans 5:5

Dr. Alan Holderness
Pediatric Orthopedic Surgeon

God commands us to love one another. But how do we get that love into our lives? I knew that I was supposed to love my wife as Christ loved the Church. But the more I tried to love her that way, the more I realized that I couldn't love her as Christ does with my own love. But I didn't know how to get that divine love into my heart.

So I really wrestled with that problem. I thought, "Well, I'll read about it." So I pored over books on families and relationships, trying to find the answers by studying the way a medical man does. It didn't work. Janet and I were finally led to a gathering in California dealing with the psychological aspects of personality. As we shared and were counseled, we came to see that a lot of damage had taken place in our emotions before we met the Lord at age 36. We knew that God's Word had something to say about healing the emotions, but we didn't know where to find it.

At that point, Janet and I were in a motel room crying out to the Lord, and He gave us the scripture above. The answer came right out at us: the love of God that we wanted in our relationship had to come from the Holy Spirit working in us. It wasn't something we could manufacture, He had to produce it in us. What a relief this was, not to have to create this love! It was ours in Him as a free gift, for the asking.

Only God can give you the love that you need to make you the kind of person He wants. Yes, God does command *you* to love others, but not with your own love. You must receive *His* love that He has for others, as a free gift imparted through the Holy Spirit. If God's kind of love has been hard for you to attain, abandon the struggle right now, ask Him for that love, and receive it as a gift of His grace.

In The Same Way . . .

*"As ye have therefore re-
ceived Christ, so walk ye in
Him."* Colossians 2:6

Jane Haile
Bible Teacher

When we met the Lord Jesus and accepted Him as personal Saviour, we came with the attitude expressed so well in an old hymn: "Nothing in my hands I bring; only to Thy cross I cling." With nothing of our own to offer Him, we received forgiveness and salvation and Jesus Himself as gifts freely offered through His love.

Now, the Apostle Paul says, we should walk in Christ *in the same way*—that is, without the notion that we possess any merit great enough to earn His favor, and without the fear that He may reject us for our shortcomings.

When we received Christ, we became part of the *finished* work He did on our behalf at Calvary. There is nothing we can add to it or take from it. We often stumble as Christians because we imagine that we are required to build a bridge from here to eternity on our own works. Then we lose our boldness in approaching God because we don't believe our works are good enough to please Him. "Behold, I stand at the door and knock," Jesus says (Rev. 3:20). We usually speak these words only to sinners, but they were in fact intended for hearers who were already Christians. Jesus is still standing at the door of your heart, seeking admission in an even newer and fresher way than you have ever known before.

Do you still have fears, needs, and guilts, however small, that have not been resolved between you and God? Each morning, lift up to Him boldly all that is in your heart, and ask Him each day to take your life as fully as He did when you and He first met. Then walk daily in the newness of life Jesus continually offers as your own.

Reach Out To God

"Ask, and it shall be given you; seek, and ye shall find; knock, and it shall be opened unto you."

Matthew 7:7

Carl F. De Moon
Businessman/Teacher/Speaker

There is such a sweet assurance of God's love and care in this verse. Our part in receiving His blessings is so simple: all we need do is ask, seek, and knock, until His answer or gift or opening surely comes. Much as we might be willing to do much more, to try to earn these blessings, this is all the Lord requires.

Jesus said that a father would not give a stone to his son when he asked for a loaf of bread or a serpent when he asked for a fish. All of us who are parents can understand this level of love. If a parent lavishes love in this way upon his child, should we expect less from the incomprehensible love of our heavenly Father?

My daughter was born with Down's syndrome, more commonly known as mongolism. I'm certain that God answers prayer just as freely as I've told you because I asked Him to heal her, and He did. And here I was an agnostic when I first reached out to Him. This tremendous healing changed my life. I sought Him in Massachusetts through the intercession of Father Ralph DeOreo. I had heard that he prayed for the sick. In his presence, I knocked on God's door and asked Him to forgive me. I told Him that if He healed my daughter, I would go back to Him and the Church after so many years away. And God in His infinite love touched her. We saw her physical features change before our very eyes!

If you have even the tiniest faith, like a grain of mustard seed, and you are willing to seek God and ask Him as a loving Father to meet your need, He will certainly answer you. Have you hesitated, wondering if you should approach Him? Do so right now. He understands, He cares, and He is waiting to meet you this very moment.

Seeing God At Work

"Trust in the Lord with all thine heart; and lean not unto thine own understanding. In all thy ways acknowledge Him, and He shall direct thy paths."   Proverbs 3:5-6

Clyde C. Downing
Attorney

There are simply no areas of our lives in which God is not at work. God is concerned in these verses that we not be blind to His influence. So often we leave God out of situations that we don't think are "spiritual." But in so doing, we miss out on the wisdom and peace that could be ours if only we'd remain open to His direction at all times.

It wasn't until I was baptized in the Holy Spirit in my late 80's, that I began to learn this. Then, after having practiced law for over 60 years, I started drawing on the Holy Spirit's power in business matters, with wonderful results.

One of the companies of which I'd been a long time director had been bogged down for over 20 years with a certain problem. The board just could not agree unanimously on a proposal that would settle the issue. The Lord directed me to go on a fast for a few days. After that, I sat down, under the anointing of the Holy Spirit, and wrote out the solution the Lord gave me.

The next day the board got together at my house. They all said they sensed something strange as they entered the door. We sat down, I read the proposal, and they all tried to jump up at once to accept it. You see, the Lord knew the answer all the time; He just wanted us to recognize Who the real director of the business was.

Whatever your business happens to be, from digging oil wells to changing diapers, it really belongs to the Lord, just as much as your Sunday pew-sitting time. Get God into the middle of everything that concerns you today. You just might find out that He's more concerned about how it goes than you are and has better answers than yours.

God Wants To Bless You

"And all things, what-soever ye shall ask in prayer, believing, ye shall receive."
Matthew 21:22

Steve Teague
Singer

Before you read on any further, stop and take another look at the verse above. What an exciting promise! Could God really mean it, that when you and I became children of God, we received such tremendous power? Whatever we ask Him, believing, we'll receive? That's what I really call being a real son and heir to God!

Let me think now: what do I really want from God? Wow! With this kind of power at my disposal, I'd better give that question some serious thought. Something that would do harm to others? I wouldn't want anything like that. Something that would be a blessing, to make the world better and lift Jesus higher! That's my heart's desire.

"Lord, give me a voice that I'll be able to use to bless people in song!" That was a prayer I prayed once, and God answered it miraculously. When I started singing after that prayer, sounds came out of my mouth like none I'd ever uttered before. That desire of my heart to bless others was right in His will, and that's why it was so easy to believe He'd give it to me.

How many things that could be ours we don't receive from the Lord just because we forget that He'll give them if we'd just ask Him! Have you ever been in love? Do you remember how delighted you were to get that special present for the one you loved? Well, God is in love with you, and He never makes a mistake when He gives a gift.

Do you dare today to really think hard about what you want from the Lord? Why do you want it? Who is it going to bless? Can you step out and believe Him for it? If you will think daily about what you want God to give you—and about what He wants you to give Him—you will enter into a dimension of joy and blessing in your life that you've never imagined before. He wants it for you: reach out to Him now.

Put God First!

"In everything you do, put God first, and He will direct you and crown your efforts with success."
Proverbs 3:6 (LB)

Rev. Kenny Foreman
Pastor/Author

Insecurity is built into the hearts of people who build their lives around individuals or things that can be taken away. But a life that's built around Jesus Christ, the Holy Spirit, and God the Father has total security. After putting God first, mercy and goodness will always become by-products of such a life (Psalm 3:6).

I've been told that 1/10 of life consists of what happens to us and 9/10 is how we respond to what happens to us. But if God is directing our lives and we've put Him first in all things, we don't have to react to situations—we can always *act*, the way Jesus would have us to act in response to them. Jesus never *reacted* to situations. He said, "I only do the things which please My Father. I only speak the things I hear My Father speak." That's why Jesus never had to react to a situation. His being in such close touch with the Father made Him able to know how He was going to act in all circumstances.

If we put God first, God will certainly give us the desires of our hearts, because His wisdom will inform our desires. We will be able to see life from His point of view, to think His thoughts, to allow Him to use our minds, to speak His words, to love other people through our hearts. Directed by the Lord, every day will turn into a good day, as we watch Him work all things out for our good.

Does all this sound too good to be true? It's not! But have you ever really tried putting God first in everything you experience? Do I really mean everything? Yes, everything! He's either trustworthy in everything or not to be trusted at all. Why don't you try trusting Him with a whole heart today? Then you'll know for sure how true this verse is!

Pressing Ahead

" . . . I am bringing all my energies to bear on this one thing: Forgetting the past and looking forward to what lies ahead, I strain to reach the end of the race . . ."
Philippians 3:13-14 (LB)

Mike Ditka
Asst. Coach, Dallas Cowboys

A professional football player has got to be good at forgetting the past. If an end drops a pass, or a lineman misses a block or tackle, he'd better not spend any time dwelling on his failure. The next play is called very quickly, and if a player has his mind on the play before, he'll get left in the dust.

It's the play that's happening that's important. The challenge that lies right before you is all you really have to deal with. You can't change the past; thinking about the far future will only distract you from what's at hand. Remember your goal, but live in the present.

To me, that's the whole essence of the Christian life. If you live in the past, you're bound to live in fear. You'll remember too many sins and mistakes, and what good will it do you to dwell on them? You can walk away from the past and look to the future with hope. God has given us the power in Jesus to obey His commandments and reach for the eternal prize: the fullness of our salvation in Christ.

It's as you concentrate on living out your salvation from moment to moment that you'll draw nearer to that goal of fullness. Sure, your past was sinful; mine was, too. And I've made my share of mistakes as a Christian. But I'm not going to bother reviewing all of them until the game's over.

There'll be a time later to look over the "game films" of your life. And I think that even then, as you review them with Jesus, you'll have the joy of hearing the Coach say, "Well done." Today concentrate on making the plays right. If you muff one, forget it. Remember, you've got another chance ahead and a sure win to look forward to.

Abiding In The Secret Place

"He that dwelleth in the secret place of the Most High shall abide under the shadow of the Almighty." Psalm 91:1

Andrew Culverwell
Singer/Songwriter

There is no safer place to be than in the very center of God's will. For the dignitaries and the wealthy of this world, luxurious and well-protected dwellings are reserved in the exclusive neighborhoods of large cities. But our Lord has kept for all His people a secret place in which they may abide, regardless of their earthly station in life or place of residence. For our true home is in His very presence, where we find fullness of joy.

"Prone to wander, Lord, I feel it," says an old hymn. With my own wayward nature, I realize such a strong need to keep aware of where I'm standing, and just where God is at all times. Should temptation come, I need to remember that there is a way of escape always available. And this often narrow path inevitably leads into that secret place set apart especially for me in the Lord's presence.

So much unrest exists in the Church because believers move away from these places of calm. God never moves, but we tend to edge our way out of that particular place in Him that is ours alone.

At times, when I am on tour, the flurry of activity can whirl around me and threaten to swallow me up. But did you know that at the center of every whirlpool, spinning furiously around it, is a still place of complete calm? It is here, by God's mercy, that I find shelter.

Does your life often seem dizzying with complexity? Does the world around you seem fearful to face, with its manifold temptations and stresses? Take heart, Beloved of God! There is a place of rest for you, close to the bosom of God, at all times. Right now, ask the Lord to lead you to that place, and to keep you there in joy all through this day.

Being A Friend Of God

"Acquaint now thyself with Him, and be at peace; thereby good shall come unto thee."   Job 22:21

Jessy Dixon
Singer

You will never enter into a really close relationship with another person without working to cultivate their friendship. Common sense tells you that if you neglect to take time for sharing, walking together, and exchanging life with a friend, you will never get to know him very well. You will never come to the point of trust and mutual understanding that brings the peace and assurance of a loving relationship.

Many Christians today are being robbed of a peaceful walk and the good things God has for them because they haven't done their part in getting acquainted with the Lord. Before you can really commit yourself to a person, you've got to know enough about him to consider him worthy of your trust. The place where you can get to know God is in His Word.

The Bible tells us that God is always with us, that He knows everything, that He has all power, that He loves us, that He wants to take care of us, and hundreds of other things that, if we only knew them, would help to give us a portrait of Him as He really is: the Prince of Peace.

God is altogether wonderful! The more we know of Him, the more we will trust Him with, and the more good things we will expect and receive from him.

Has that deep peace been missing from your life? Have you ever felt that there were good things from God's abundance for you that you had not yet received? God wants to take the veil from your eyes and show you who He really is! Get acquainted with Him, dig into His whole Word, and you'll find yourself bathed in His peace and good things.

The Same Till The End

"I am with you alway, even unto the end of the world."   Matthew 28:20

Sister Mary Beatrice
Catholic Nun/Ret. Teacher

Have you ever hurt someone you love very much and upon realizing what you did, been struck with the fear they may not forgive you?

At times, I have felt this way in my relationship with Jesus Christ. I was convinced I could never expect His forgiveness or continued friendship, not after grieving Him like I had. I actually felt I had completely destroyed His love towards me.

Then during my Bible study I read Matthew 28:20 and received the assurance of His steadfast love. Through my experiences I realized our adversary would want me to think Jesus does not love or care for me anymore. It is Satan's highest aim to convince me I am unlovable and unworthy. If he can do that, my own self-condemnation will keep me from calling on the Lord to be my Strength when I am tempted and to be my Saviour when I am afflicted in body or spirit.

Jesus did not put a condition on His promise to always be with you and me by making the stipulation "If you are perfect," or "If you memorize the entire Bible." He simply promises He will always be with us. Though Jesus Christ will never leave me, I know I can choose to leave Him. When I realize I have turned my back on Him in some way whether unintentionally or willfully, I ask His forgiveness and accept His promise of forgiveness and cleansing (1 John 1:9), and to remove my sin from His memory as far as the east is from the west (Psalm 103:12).

It is so precious to know Jesus' love for me is the same yesterday, today and forever (Hebrews 13:8) and He will never leave me.

You From God's View

"In the body of His flesh through death, to present you holy and unblameable and unreproveable in His sight."
Colossians 1:22

Roland H. Buck
Pastor/Author

We as believers enjoy a unique "safety position" in the sight of God. Because we've accepted Jesus, He sees us, through the covering of Jesus' blood, as holy, unblamable, and unreprovable. The accompanying illustration* will help you to understand the meaning of this.

Notice that above and below the covering of Jesus' blood sacrifice, are two points of view: God's and man's. From our human position, we see ourselves, others see us, and Satan sees us, with all the faults and failures which we interpret as sin. But God sees us from *above* the covering. And in place of sin, He sees holiness; in place of fault, blamelessness; instead of failure, perfection.

Many fine Christians have lived in fear that their acceptance with God is based on their spiritual achievement. They fear every day that they will lose fellowship with God or miss His will for them. But God has promised that because of their faith in His covering, they will remain safe throughout the normal course of life!

The faults that people may see in you, or you may see in yourself today just won't be seen by God! He sees you through Christ, as if you were just as perfect as Jesus. And think of this, too: the Holy Spirit is working right now underneath this covering to help make you so much like Jesus that you and others will notice the difference, too!

*Illustration used by permission of the author.

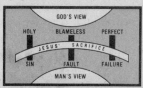

The Healing Of America

"If My people, which are called by My Name, shall humble themselves, and pray, and seek My face, and turn from their wicked ways; then will I hear from heaven, and will forgive their sin, and will heal their land."

2 Chronicles 7:14

Bobbie James
Wife of Governor of Alabama

When I hear the "Battle Hymn of the Republic" or the "Star Spangled Banner," something inside me wells up with tears and supplication that we might allow this fantastic country, America, to go down the drain in the swill of our own sin. As Christians, we need to ask ourselves why we have not held on in the kind of prayer with fervent supplication that changes the heart of God.

This country was an experiment in freedom founded by its fathers upon an inspired Constitution. The strength of that document is the reason we still have a country. Its stability has thus far prevented us from destroying ourselves.

But when God has given birth to something, He will keep His hand upon it until the stench of sin becomes intolerable. Then He must in His holiness turn away. Sin's odor has been allowed to ferment freely in our country today, and we as Christians have not been the salt and the leaven that we must be in order to turn it around. We're at a crossroads, the apex of our history. Which way are we going? And what can we do?

First, we must begin by cleansing our own hearts and lives in our own homes. We have to set our wills to do the will of God rather than our own. That's the great battle. Then we must decide, in spite of all the negative propaganda about America, to be proud of her and affirm the good things about her. Then we must fast, pray, and deny ourselves.

What does this self-denial mean? We must live honestly before the world, not only turning from the gross wickedness around us, but from sin of our own hypocrisy, self-satisfaction, and lack of real involvement. God can heal this land. Will you be a part today of bringing that healing to America?

Give Him Your Fears

"For God hath not given us the spirit of fear; but of power, and of love, and of a sound mind." 2 Timothy 1:7

Reggie Vinson
Recording Artist

Recent headlines proclaimed: "Alice Cooper Hospitalized for Acute Alcoholism." Then Elton John was sidelined by near-insanity for over a year. These two people I worked with in the world of rock music became additions to the casualty list that already included Janis Joplin (dead of a drug overdose); Jimi Hendrix (dead of asphyxiation following drug injection); Elvis Presley (cause of death listed as heart attack, with over a dozen stimulants and depressants detected in post-mortem examination); and many other rock personalities and fans. What drove them into this crazy world, and what killed them? Fear!

Fear is the biggest problem I run into with young people. It starts with having to be like everyone else. Even as a kid, you're made to feel that if you're not "in," you're not going to make it in life. So you go along and get into drugs. Then you're afraid to step out of drugs and really cope, so you roll a joint or snort some cocaine so you can keep cool. The devil is an evil comedian, and this world of fear is his idea of a joke. A lot of laughs, and you laugh your way to hell. I almost did, but God saved me. And when He did, He gave me a sound mind. I know what I'm doing and where I'm going, and there's no need to fear anything or anyone. I tell young people I've been there, and they don't need drugs and sex and popularity, they need Jesus.

If fear plays any part in your life, you're the butt of the devil's joke, too. But you don't have to be. You don't need an escape, either. You need more of Jesus. If you've been looking anywhere else, stop it right now, and receive His power and love, and a sound mind to boot.

The Greatest Decision

*"Seek ye first the king-
dom of God and His right-
eousness; and all these things
shall be added unto you."*
Matthew 6:33

Mayor Lambert C. Mims
Politician/Author

My position as commissioner and mayor of Mobile, Alabama is one
of much decision-making. The importance of some of these decisions is
enormous, as they affect the lives of a quarter of a million people and the
flow of millions of dollars. But personally, the most important decision I
ever made was the decision to trust the Lord Jesus Christ as my own
personal Savior.

From that moment more than 21 years ago, when as a drunken and
defeated young salesman, I met Jesus by the roadside, God began to
work wonders in my life. He opened doors in the business world and in
politics. When I first ran for public office, I'd never been involved in
politics, but I felt the Lord's leading. The political experts didn't give me
the ghost of a chance. It's been my privilege in public life to witness for
the Lord in church meetings and conventions, in airplanes and rescue
missions, in state houses and city halls all across the land.

I had no idea all this would take place that night; everything I had
and will ever have was laid on God's altar. I can look back and recall a
number of occasions when my back was against the wall financially or
politically, and there seemed to be no way out. But God always got me
through. In the 22 years I've known Him, He has always given me just
what I needed. I didn't say everything I wanted. But all I've needed,
He's provided, as I've attempted to put Him first in my life.

To have the kingdom of God, and to be living rightly is to possess
enough. But God has promised to add all the things we need if we'll
pursue His interests as priorities. Have you decided what you're going
to put first today? Let it be Him, and let Him take care of the rest!

Amazing Angels

*"Are they not all minis-
tering spirits, sent forth to
minister for them who shall be
heirs of salvation?"*

Hebrews 1:14

Charles Hunter
Author/Evangelist

God is doing amazing things with angels today! As part of the outpouring of His Holy Spirit, He is letting His Church in on the great dimensions of angelic ministry to the unsaved. Did you know that angels help to draw those outside of Jesus into salvation?

The Lord has chosen to use us as human beings to preach and share the message of the gospel, but God has been revealing that He actually sends out angels to guide unsaved people to the person who will witness to them.

Just the other day on the plane, Frances and I sat down near the front, and it seemed like person after person just passed us by on their way to the back. As the plane filled up, the seat next to us continued to be empty. Suddenly,. a young lady walked by, then turned back and asked, "Is this seat taken?" God had saved that seat for her, and I believe an angel was causing people to pass by. As a result, she got rededicated, baptized in the Holy Spirit, and given a sense of fresh direction for her life from the Lord.

Just coincidence? No, it happens to us all the time, as the Lord's great arms of love are reaching out, to "those who shall be" heirs of salvation. He is accompanying His earthly hosts of witnesses with the hosts of heaven, just to bolster the work. What love and wisdom God has!

Think of the help you have beside you as you share Jesus! Think of the hope you have even for your unsaved loved ones: God's mighty angels are striving to draw them! Resolve today to give an angel a hand by sharing the sweet message of Jesus' love to all whom those soft wings nudge into your path.

Light and The Word

· *"The entrance of Thy words giveth light; it giveth understanding unto the simple."* Psalm 119:130

Frances Hunter
Author/Evangelist

Without God's Word entering into our hearts and spirits, we would never have come into the light of Jesus Christ. You may have thought, like I did, that you were a Christian because you've been making tuna fish sandwiches all your life for church suppers. But when the light-giving power of God's Word touches you, you begin to see that you're in sin and darkness.

Then, God starts to shine that Word deeper and deeper into your being. So many Christians complain about being discouraged, defeated, fearful, or sorrowful, because they have failed to realize that the Word of God will give them light on those areas of their lives, if they'll just let it sink in and start confessing it. When there is light in your path, you're not afraid, are you?

Some people, when they get up in the morning, begin to complain immediately. But you will have what you say, and you need to get God's Word into your heart so you know what you ought to say. "Oh," some say, "but I'm too dumb to understand a lot of the Bible." Well, that's why this verse is so important because God's Word also gives understanding to the simple. God just doesn't save you through the preaching of the Word to let you stumble along. He's given you the Word to impart wisdom to you and to build the mind of Christ into you, so you know how to walk wisely, as Jesus did.

You see, you've got to stop confessing what the devil says. Start right now to line up your life with the Bible. And do you know what'll happen? You'll be amazed to see how well the Bible starts lining up with your life!

The Goal of True Champions

"Let him know, that he which converteth the sinner from the error of his way shall save a soul from death, and shall hide a multitude of sins."
James 5:20

Jeffrey Park
Author/Evangelist

How wonderful if it were said of America that her national pastime was soul-winning! For all the glory we heap upon those among us who are winners in sports or business, cheered today and forgotten tomorrow, how much more is soul-winning the activity of true champions!

What could be more worth striving for than the winning of an eternal soul, a friend for all eternity? No wonder God has placed such value on soul-winning that He has crowned all those who pursue it with the fruit of "a tree of life" and with wisdom (Proverbs 11:30)!

God also promises that soul-winning will "hide a multitude of sins," not only, I believe, the sins of the newly won soul, but those of the soul-winner, too.

By this I don't mean that God has a scoreboard up in Heaven from which He erases so many of our sins if we win a soul. But when we get interested in soul-winning, we forget about ourselves. Every one of us has weaknesses and shortcomings that prevent us from having a winning attitude in life. But if we get out of ourselves and start thinking about others as we win souls, the negativity and discouragement of self-concern will be forgotten. And the sins we so easily get trapped in when we're self-centered will be hidden in the glory and joy of doing God's work and using His power.

This is why God is urging every one of us to labor to win souls for Him. In doing so, we'll find an eternal satisfaction, even as Jesus did. For He saw "the travail of His soul, and was satisfied" (Isaiah 53:11), even facing the cross, in the thousands of souls He knew He was bringing to glory. Let's get on the course He ran today, as true victors by soul-winning.

Separators

"For I am persuaded that neither death, nor life, nor angels . . . shall be able to separate us from the love of God, which is in Christ Jesus our Lord."

Romans 8:38-39

David Meece
Singer/Songwriter

Very few people have ever faced as many of these "separaters" at once as old Noah! It must have seemed to him, especially in the middle of that terrifying deluge, that there was nothing more in all creation that could be thrown his way. Yet the ark remained atop the water safe and sound. Then Noah and his family still had to confront the hard job of waiting until the waters subsided.

After they'd been floating around in the water for weeks on end, I imagine Noah and his family got a little sick of being cooped up in the ark (the animals must have been a mite restless, too). So what Noah finally did to get his family off his back a bit was to let a raven loose to scout the earth. The raven took off and flew around but found no place to land. When he came back to the ark and saw Mrs. Noah nagging at old Noah, he said to himself, "I'm not going back in there," and being a scavenger, he soon found some food and was never seen again.

So Noah let out a dove, and, not being a scavenger, it kept coming back to the ark for food. Noah must have wondered after awhile whether God hadn't forgotten His promises. But one day the dove returned carrying an olive branch, and then Noah knew that all his worrying had been for naught. God had remembered, and He sent Noah out to get things going again.

Sometimes, even after God's taken care of the big things; the little problems we have try to get between us and the Lord. It's amazing how things like impatience and petty annoyance can nag at us, isn't it? That's when we have to remember that nothing can separate us from Jesus' love. Come floods, come fleas, keep that in mind today!

Getting To The Root of The Problem

"So shall My Word be that goeth forth out of My mouth: it shall not return unto Me void, but it shall accomplish that which I please, and it shall prosper in the thing whereto I sent it."

Isaiah 55:11

Thomas Snipes
Professor of Psychology

Having been a psychologist for a number of years, I have found many theoretical explanations of the workings of the human mind, and tried most of them in helping to solve peoples' problems. But the words of mere men have limited value in the depth of their application to the recesses of the human soul. God's Word, however, is able to minister to the whole man, with the fruit of complete success.

Several years ago, I began to realize that there was only one genuine model that could produce real healing in the mind: the Bible's description of the nature of man. All of the models in man-created psychology typically treat the surface behavior of man rather than his real need. A man's problem is not that he has trouble with his wife or children; his problem is his basic sin nature. And until his spirit is changed, altering the surface of his behavior will not result in permanent healing. Another problem will emerge, with which the individual will still be unable to cope.

So my practice became centered in God's Word, not man's. The first question I ask all of my patients, even if they are not Christians is, "What is the state of your relationship with God?" If they will not deal with that issue, I cannot hold out a promise of successful treatment. I believe that all personal problems stem from an area that needs to be dealt with in the spiritual life.

The application of God's Word to the spirit of a man or woman is the answer for any difficulty that might be troubling you today. Are you willing to stop blaming the people and circumstances around you for the things that may be wrong in your life? If you are, and you are willing for God to have His way, your healing will begin.

Beyond And Within

". . . I dwell in the high and holy place, with him also that is of a contrite heart and humble spirit, to revive the spirit of the humble and to revive the hearts of the contrite ones."   Isaiah 57:15

John Erwin
Prison Chaplain

This is the Lord God speaking, the "high and lofty One that inhabiteth eternity, whose name is Holy," as the first part of this verse lets us know. That sounds pretty forbidding, doesn't it? Since I'm down here struggling on earth, not in the forever and ever of eternity, but in the now, I would seem to be shut far away from God's mighty attention, if it weren't for the beautiful reminder of this verse.

Before I met Christ, this is just what the Bible and the things of God meant to me: they were beyond me, and they had no meaning for me, because I knew I couldn't measure up.

But the full truth of the gospel becomes clear in the verse's entirety—that in Jesus Christ, the Ultimate becomes intimate, that God dwells not only in the exalted reaches of eternity, but in the now, and with undeserving people like you and me. For to be contrite merely means to know that we don't measure up to God's standards.

If we can merely admit to God that in our weakness we have need of Him, He has promised that He will revive our spirits and revive our hearts! What a wonderful message of hope!

Do you ever feel that living the Christian life is beyond you? Are you acutely aware of your shortcomings and weaknesses and your failure to meet God's holy standards? I have good news for you: God is ready to dwell in you and to make your broken heart and spirit alive again—now! Bring your need and weakness to Him now and let Him lift you up with His mighty power and gentle love.

Put Your Faith To Work

". . . if ye had faith as a grain of mustard seed, ye might say unto this sycamore tree, Be thou plucked up by the root, and be thou planted in the sea: and it should obey you." Luke 17:6

Ralph McRae
Rodeo Cowboy

You've probably heard it said before that faith in God has to be planted like a seed in order for it to accomplish anything in the world. You may have found however, as I have, that sometimes you have a problem in getting that "seed" of faith out of the "seed packet," (or the Word of God) and into the ground of day-to-day reality where it can bear fruit. You have to find a way to carry that seed to the field and get it sown.

In His wisdom, God has in fact given us a whole staff of servants whose job it is to get God's Word into operation. These servants are the words that come from our lips. The word of faith which we speak is what puts the Word of God into action in our lives.

If you had a staff of household servants in your home, and I were your guest, you might tell me, "Ralph, these servants will attend to all my needs; they'll do anything for me." Yet, I might be at your house all day and never see them do a thing—if you never gave them any orders.

"Ralph," you say, "you sound more like a Bible teacher than a cowboy." Well, maybe so, but I know that on a cattle ranch, a good foreman isn't one who does everything himself, but one who knows how to tell others what to do.

You can get that faith to work today. Don't let those servants of yours become lounge lizards. Confess your faith, get your words into action, and get ready to reap some crops.

God Expands And Preserves

". . . Oh that thou wouldest bless me indeed, and enlarge my coast, and that thy hand might be with me, and that thou wouldst keep me from evil . . ."
1 Chronicles 4:10

Ethel Barrett
Author

This obscure little prayer of a man named Jabez came to my attention at the time in my life when my ministry in writing began suddenly to reach large audiences. Two important ideas stand out in it that should always be kept in mind together as we seek to be used of God: that God should expand our influence for Him, but that He should also preserve us from the many temptations and failings that can accompany our growth in service to Him.

Yes, the first part of this prayer is very attractive. Yes, Lord, bless me, enlarge my usefulness for you! The remainder of verse 10 tells us that the Lord granted Jabez that which he requested. And our love for Jesus should drive us to reach beyond our present boundaries, to win souls for His kingdom, to conquer territory for Him.

But the great wisdom of this prayer is in Jabez's request that the Lord keep him from evil. When the work God had for me began to grow, I faced temptations I hadn't imagined—to pride, to laziness, to jealousy of others, to resting on past laurels. These I didn't always meet successfully, but through such experiences, the Lord taught me that I needed Him to make me grow and to keep me, too.

It's my fervent prayer for you that you abound in every good work to the glory of God. And I hope you'll pray with me that as the Lord prospers your ministry, He will cause you at every moment to depend upon Him wholly as your keeper and shield from evil.

Who's Responsible?

"The thief cometh not but for to steal, and to kill, and to destroy: I am come that they might have life, and that they might have it more abundantly."   John 10:10

Danny Dyer
Christian Disc Jockey

It's important to know who's responsible for what in this world. A lot of troubles and heartaches come along in life that we Christians put up with that we shouldn't. James says that "every good gift and every perfect gift is from above, and cometh down from the Father . . ." (James 1:17). If anything less than good and perfect comes into your life, don't blame God, because He didn't send it. Once you recognize the devil's stealing and killing and destroying nature, it's a lot easier to resist him and enter into victorious living.

Let's get this straight: God's window is open to us, for salvation, for healing, for deliverance. God through Christ bought back the things that Satan got in the Garden of Eden when man gave them to the devil by sinning. So when someone tells me that God sent a tragedy or affliction into their lives, I can't go along with that. God can use that experience to teach something of value or to knock out some prop we're using to stand apart from Him. But don't thank God for the thing itself, because He didn't send it. He's not the thief or the destroyer.

If my daddy said he loved me, for example, and then turned around and broke my leg, "to teach me something," I'd have a real hard time accepting His love. I'd think he had a funny way of showing love.

Any time you try to walk with Christ, the devil is going to try to do you in. But don't blame God when Satan tries. Instead, submit yourself to God and obey Him, and resist the devil. He'll flee! And don't neglect to accept and hold onto the good gifts that God brings your way today!

Following Him

"The Lord is my Shepherd, I shall not want."
Psalm 23:1

Stanley Long
Exec. V.P., Tom Skinner Evang.
Assoc.

Once you become a Christian, you begin to realize that there is a journey between receiving Jesus and the ultimate fulfillment of God's purpose in your life. It's like a pilgrimage taking you in directions and through experiences that you can't see at the beginning. So there is a great deal of comfort and satisfaction in knowing that leading you is not only the God who has redeemed you, but the God who is your Creator, who has made a commitment to present you faultless before the throne of God in exceeding glory!

Yes, the God who supervises the whole universe is the same God who is so concerned about your life that He takes the same role towards you as a faithful shepherd does towards his sheep. Palestinian shepherds always led their sheep by walking in front of them, testing the pasture and water and shelter for their safety. How wonderful to know that our God loves and cares for us so, that He goes before us overlooking each circumstance and guiding us through safely to make sure that we reach our destination according to His plan.

It's also exciting to realize that our walk with God is like an adventure. It's never dull. We never know just where He's going to take us, or how we're going to be tested. But we always have the assurance that He's in charge.

There may be dangers ahead, from snake-like deceptions, luscious-looking paths of desire, verdant-seeming pastures of greed. But the Lord will be right ahead of you, testing each experience and temptation, showing you the way through. Follow Him closely today!

Not Your Own

"For ye are bought with a price: therefore glorify God in your body, and in your spirit, which are God's."

1 Corinthians 6:20

Ben Zickefoose
Gymnastics Instructor

What? You mean I don't belong to myself anymore? That's what this scripture plainly says. The price of the blood of Jesus shed for my salvation bought me, and I can't even claim ownership of the body I'm in or the spirit within me. Therefore, my sole purpose for being here on earth is to bring glory to God.

If there isn't a single part of me that's still my own, then every thing I do with any part of me must be capable of glorifying Him. Since He has taken total possession of me, He must want to enjoy my whole life with me.

So I need to take stock of my talents and abilities and decide how best to invest them so that they can demonstrate Christ's power and love. And the way I glorify Him is to do His will.

Just as young people, when they are obedient to their parents bring honor to their family name, we always bring glory, not to ourselves, but to our heavenly Father, when we do His will. God has given us His name and reputation to uphold.

God owns a great variety of ability in all of us who know Him, doesn't He? He owns gymnasts, cooks, professors, tradesmen, mothers, artists, businessmen, soldiers, children, and preachers, too. His will certainly is broad, isn't it, to contain so many different activities?

Isn't it great to know that you, just as you are, can be a glory to God? That's the good side of not being your own anymore: that God can use all that you are more fully than you ever could have imagined. God, use us for just the purpose that you bought us, today.

All Or Nothing At All

"I know thy works, that thou art neither cold nor hot: I would thou wert cold or hot."
Revelation 3:15

Jana Wacker
Singer

"Are you really willing to die for Jesus?" What a time to confront such a question: on a television show, before a live audience, with nowhere to hide! Though the hostess wasn't asking me, but the audience, I knew the Lord at that moment was sounding out the depths of my own commitment to Him. Tears streamed uncontrollably down my face as I realized with sorrow that I could not answer, "Yes."

Oh yes, I had known the Lord for over ten years and had sung for Him and shared Him with thousands. But it had been an easy road for me. Even before meeting Him, it wasn't difficult for me to float along in an entertainer's life, with natural talent and a glib smile to get me by. But at this moment, with the harsh spotlights showing up each ragged streak of running mascara, I no longer could live a lie. It would have to be all or nothing for Jesus from then on.

Every Christian needs to be asked this question. It's not an easy one to face. It frightened me to think of what might happen if my resolution to follow Jesus were ever put to the test. I believed that my salvation was secure in God's hands. But I also knew that God had given me a job to do wholeheartedly, and there could be no more compromises. As I tremblingly expressed to Christ my willingness to go all the way with Him, He gave me this confidence: that if I'm ever backed against the wall, even if I'm tempted to be a coward, He will give me the grace when I need it to stand for Him.

Have you explored this ultimate question with the Lord? The answer you give will determine whether you will move beyond lukewarmness for Him. Prayerfully consider the depth of your commitment to Christ, right now.

"Working Out" Your Faith

". . . work out your own salvation with fear and trembling. For it is God which worketh in you both to will and to do of His good pleasure." Philippians 2:12-13

Father Bill Sherwood
Evangelist

If you know Jesus, God is constantly working His salvation into you, but you've got to work it out. This became very clear to me some months ago when I had a stroke. During my hospitalization, I claimed my getting well as a miracle from God, but knew that I still had to get up and work it out. Even so, once my soul was saved, I still had work to do to change my far from perfect character and daily walk.

God gave me a quicker recovery than the average stroke victim. In just 12 days, my hospitalization was over, including the cutting of a plug of blood from an artery in my neck. I knew that God wanted me to get completely well, so I determined to learn how to do everything possible to be fully restored. In everything, I tried to meet each challenge as from the Lord, and made a special effort never to give up or be defeated by anything. My hand was completely paralyzed at first. I didn't have the strength in my thumb and forefinger to light a match, but I kept working at it until I could.

Now, I've joined a gymnasium to finish the work. I want to be well and strong even though I'm 90 years old, and with God working in me and through me, my success is guaranteed.

What God told me though this verse, He's telling you right now. No matter what's the state of your health or finances or personal life, God says: "You can count on Me. I saved your soul and spirit, and I'm going to save your body, but you must cooperate. It's not always going to be easy, but I'll be working in you, if you'll start working with Me." Brother or sister, do you believe this? Then don't shrink from taking on that difficult task. God will see you through it, and you'll have the very "good pleasure" of doing His perfect will!

The "Forever" Things

". . . Though our bodies are dying, our inner strength in the Lord is growing every day. . .Yet this short time of distress will result in God's richest blessing upon us forever and ever!"
2 Corinthians 4:16-17 (LB)

Becki Conway
Student

In America, we put a lot of emphasis on our physical selves. We're often super-active and athletic, wrapped up in our outward appearances and the skills our bodies can perform. There's nothing wrong with being healthy and looking as good as possible. But all of this dedication to trying to preserve ourselves physically can make us forget that it's heaven we're really made for and service to God from the heart that should come first in our lives.

I really began to understand this when I lost my leg to cancer two years ago at age 16. I was very athletic then, and still am. But I was caught in a nice kind of trap without knowing it. God's purpose for me was tied together in my mind with my fulfilling my physical potential. I only felt good about myself when my body was tuned just right. But when my leg was gone, I could see that God wanted me to develop inner character and get concerned about others. That's why I'm training to be a recreational therapist. I want to help handicapped people to make the best use of the bodies they have, and to direct their lives outward towards others, rather than concentrating on their handicap.

If there's anything in your life that you feel so attached to that it means more than Jesus Christ, you need to offer it up to Him. You can lose everything else, but to lose Jesus would mean to be without the only reason there is for living. God's priorities are always the "forever" things of winning souls and growing in Him. Re-examine your priorities right now, and if you need to, get them back in line with His.

Take No Thought

"But seek ye first the kingdom of God, and all these things shall be added unto you. Take therefore no thought for the morrow . . ."
Matthew 6:33-34

Delilah Troffer
Highwire Artist/Aerialist

Many people think that the only real worries we circus folks have are the dangers we face under the Big Top. But sometimes as I'm strolling high up there above the sawdust, my mind is wandering back down to earth. For it's the day to day problems I face outside of the circus ring that I struggle with the most. And it's there that these verses mean the most to me.

Since my son was born, I have been very busy because having him to care for as well as another baby just two years old is a lot harder than walking the tightrope. I'm trying to run around cleaning up the house and dashing from one baby to the other, and soon I find that the Lord Jesus is left sitting on the side.

So after a while I get frustrated, and I throw my hands in the air and shout, "Lord, why aren't you helping me, so I have more time to get my house cleaned?" And the Lord keeps answering me very quietly, "Seek ye first the kingdom of God, and worry about the other things tomorrow—first come to Me." So I say, "You're right, Lord, but first let me do my dishes. First let me do this or that."

Finally I said, "Okay, Lord!" And I got back to my old habit of getting up early, before the children, and spending time praying to the Lord and reading the Bible. Now my days are beautiful. My work gets done! Before, I just couldn't get caught up; now, I'm up to date!

Maybe you don't have two babies, but are there other things in your life that have gotten it all tangled up like mine was? I think you already know the answer. You put the Lord first, and then He can set you up on a "high wire" with none of tomorrow's worries down below.

God's Advice Works!

"That your faith might not rest in the wisdom of men, but in the power of God."
1 Corinthians 2:5

Linda Howard
Wife/Mother/Author

Having lost my way to a friend's house in another city, I stopped at a service station to ask for directions. While getting help from the attendant, a local townsman standing nearby joined us and began offering what he considered to be the best way to get to my destination. My question became their disagreement.

As I drove away I was more confused than before I stopped. Pulling off to a phone booth I called my friend who gave me simple and specific directions. Her cheerful voice made me ask myself why I hadn't called her sooner. I knew she would be happy to tell me.

Enroute to her house, I began to think about 1 Corinthians 2:5, "That your faith might not rest in the wisdom of men, but in the power of God." How often we seek the opinions and philosophies of men and ignore the sound and inspired instruction of God that is ours through prayer and reading the Bible.

Philosophies are like the two men at the service station. Each offers *a* best way, but between them they could not agree on *the* best way.

As Christians, we know that Christ is "the way, the truth, and the life" (John 4:6), and He alone knows the best way we should go when we encounter crossroads in our life.

The next time you are lost in a world of decisions, ask God to reveal His wisdom to you. His advice will always work! For "there hath not failed one Word of all His good promises" (1 Kings 8:56).

Forgiven And Restored

"And I will restore to you the years that the locust hath eaten, the cankerworm, and the caterpillar, and the palmerworm, my great army which I sent among you."
Joel 2:25

Jay Robinson
Actor

This promise cuts through one of the worst deceptions Satan tries to foist on new Christians (and old ones as well, if they'll let him). That is that even if you have met the Lord, you're forced to suffer through the rest of your life as a victim of your past. That's a lie, because God can so enrich your new life in Christ that the old one will fade into forgetfulness. How do I know? God brought me back from a lot of locust-eaten years.

In my first movie, "The Robe," back in 1953, I played the role of the merciless Roman emperor Caligula. By the time I'd finished the sequel, "Demetrius and the Gladiators," I'd exalted myself into almost living this role off-screen. I saw myself as the master of the whole world and began to treat everyone around me with arrogance and contempt.

After a while, friends and "hangers-on" started to abandon me. Before long, I was totally abased, reduced to poverty, near starvation, arrested on a drug charge and sent to prison. For ten years I didn't act at all and could only get menial jobs, like cleaning zoo cages, or cooking in "greasy spoons."

It was a long fall down. The devil brought me that route. But notice something in this verse: it says that all of these "worms" and "locusts" were "My (God's) great army." Even with all the devil tried to do to destroy me, God was still in control, humbling me so I could meet Him.

Now all that was lost is being restored: career, marriage, health—it's all new. He did it for me; He can do it for you. Do you have any "bad years" holding you back? Give them up, and ask Him to restore them to you, right now.

Keep Praying!

"Pray without ceasing."
1 Thessalonians 5:17

Pauline Robinson
Housewife

Nothing but unceasing prayer can account for the survival of my marriage and life. Prayer can overcome any obstacle. The many God helped me surmount, included several near-fatal illnesses, poverty, and 18 years of waiting before my husband met Christ.

I'm not the kind of person who can batter down people's doors with Jesus. Love and prayer are the only ways I know to work for Christ. Jay and I met when he was in the hospital. I didn't know he was a famous actor, but his need spoke to me. We went through great deprivation and misery when his life fell apart. But God never gives up, though He may take time to bring about His will.

Fifteen years ago, I was hospitalized in upstate New York, both my lungs and my larynx filled with tuberculosis. My mother came to visit me, bringing my little son. He couldn't come up; I had to call down to him from the balcony. I knew the doctors were giving me practically no hope. My heart was ready to break. I ran to my room and cried out to God, "You've got to heal me of this! I expect it, and whatever I have to do, You're going to cure me." Soon after that, I started having a terrible reaction to the drugs they gave me. As soon as they stopped the drugs, I started getting well very quickly. In six months, I was totally healed. This is one example of the pit from which God drew both Jay and me. But when He lifted us out completely, what a sweet life He gave us to enjoy!

How little difference a short time of pain makes compared with an eternity ahead with Jesus! But while this life lasts, spend it close to Him. Keep your heart in touch with Jesus today. Keep trusting Him, and keep waiting for the joy He's sure to bring.

Purpose In Disappointment

"For none of us liveth to himself, and no man dieth to himself. For whether we live, we live unto the Lord; and whether we die, we die unto the Lord . . ." Romans 14:7-8

Helen Correll
Bible Teacher

Our son was a missionary surgeon to Africa. He spent many years preparing to go to work among the people of Africa. He was only there a short time when he was badly burned and died in a gasoline explosion.

It was a terrible grief and shock to us, and also an anguishing disappointment. "Why," we asked the Lord," should his life have been cut so short after this long preparation for ministry?"

But soon we received this assurance from the Lord: we are His if we live for Him, we're His even if we die for Him. Our life as parents was still a ministry to the Lord, and our son's life was still a ministry to the Lord after he died because of his testimony and life's sacrifice. Many young people consecrated their lives to Christ because they had been so touched by our son's devoted walk with God.

Also, on his gravestone in Africa, there was a testimony placed there by those native people who had never before heard the name of Christ: the verse "For me to live is Christ, to die is gain," inscribed there in the African language. This was a Moslem and pagan area, but many people came to our son's funeral. One African businessman came up to me and said, "When your son died, a million people wept." This was his way of telling us that even then our son's life was telling for Christ.

In every disappointment, God has a purpose. Even tragedy can be multiplied by the Lord into joy for many. Remember today what the sacrifice of Jesus' young life meant to the world. Be willing, through life or death, to minister to Him today.

Picture Tubes And Mansions

"In my Father's house are many mansions: if it were not so, I would have told you. I go to prepare a place for you." John 14:2

Chuck Wheeler
Businessman

Some people feel that science and technology have made it more difficult to believe in heaven and life hereafter, but a revelation the Lord brought through a T.V. antenna has made it easier for me.

My house is built on the shore of Lake Michigan, and one night as I looked out the window at the stars and the moonlight dancing on the waves of the lake, my eye caught sight of part of my T.V. antenna. A thought suddenly occurred to me:

"If a person can stand before a television camera, and their image can be invisibly transmitted to a point such as this, hundreds of miles away, and then be captured by this antenna and transformed by the tube into a picture, even in 'living color.' If man can do this, certainly our God, when our bodies die, can take our spirits invisibly to that place which He calls Heaven and reform that invisible substance into a glorified body."

The findings of science have only expanded our vision of what is possible. Contemplation of the vastness of the universe or the minute intricacies of the subatomic world should only cause us to wonder all the more at the might and grandeur of their Creator. There is no limit to His realm of possibility.

Today, gaze upon the world of nature and on all that man has done in God's world with eyes freshly enlightened by God's Spirit. Pray that He will show you, as never before, His Presence, plan, and purpose in everything you see.

Rest assured that God has that place for you all prepared, and that He has all the means necessary to get you to your new home.

Pick Up The Pieces

"Wherefore lift up the hands which hang down, and the feeble knees."
Hebrews 12:12

Barbara Johnson
Author/Founder, Spatula Ministries

There is no magic place to go when we face insurmountable problems. There is no never-never land "where troubles melt like lemon drops, away above the chimney tops." We may have to just live with some mountains that will not move. But with God's help, we can face the inevitable, and discover that we have greater inner strengths than we ever thought possible.

After the loss of one son in the Vietnam war and another in an accident with a drunk driver, I couldn't imagine another tragedy being more difficult to bear. I didn't know that things like homosexuality happened in Christian families, but they do. When I found out that my youngest son was a homosexual, I was devastated. After someone close to you dies, you can heal, but with something like this, you feel like you're being continually ripped open. Like you've been washed out, run through the wringer, and flung up to hang dripping from the ceiling. The emblem of SPATULA ministries is a rag doll in a wringer, because we help to hold up the hands of mothers at their nerves' end with tragedies, to "peel them off the ceiling," and get them to praise the Lord.

We can never get out lives together after tragedy until we stop looking back; we must "launch out into the deep" with God's promises. We must accept the sovereign hand of God to sort out the possibilities. Let's remember that regardless of the turning of the tides, God alone is the source of our adequacy.

So no matter how deep tragedy has struck, we cannot let our hands hang down in defeat and discouragement. If we will raise our hands and look up and praise the Lord, we will find joy and victory. We must look forward and love and believe God, regardless of the circumstances, to work all for our good, for He always will!

The Hope Of His Appearing

"But I would not have you to be ignorant, brethren, concerning them which are asleep, that ye sorrow not, even as others which have no hope." 1 Thessalonians 4:13

Dr. Thomas Toman
Dentist

Several years ago, the Lord gave me a dream and a vision in which I saw the rapture of the Church meeting Jesus in the air. By God's Spirit, I was allowed a sense of participation in this glorious event; the face of Jesus appeared to me as my body and garments changed. This experience was so strong that Jesus' face seemed to have been imprinted on my retina, and I saw Him, during waking and sleeping hours, for about three months.

Paul must have seen a similar vision in order to write this note of encouragement to the Thessalonian believers so long ago. But God has never given visions to men just for the building up of their private spiritual lives. Paul was given this vision of the rapture in order that God might use it to generate faith in believers down the ages.

At times it seems to us that the Second Coming of Jesus scarcely relates to our daily lives. But notice that Paul had in mind dealing with a very practical situation: the distraction from God's purposes for a Christian's life, that can be brought on by needless sorrowing for lost loved ones. God wants us to know, not only what is in store for us, but also for all those loved ones in Christ who have passed on before us.

Whether we contemplate the past, present, or future, we have something in the promise of Christ's appearing that the world can't give or take away: hope, meaning, direction in life. The world's lot is sorrow; ours is the hope of His glory—for us, and our loved ones in Him.

The Joy Of Surrender

"The Lord hath done great things for us; whereof we are glad." Psalm 126:3

Robert Hill
Author/Publisher

The Lord can do greater things for you than you can ever imagine or plan. But the price of His undertaking on your behalf in a mighty way is your total surrender to Him. The wonderful things God can do, and the joy of seeing Him work wonders in your life are very attractive. But somehow turning over total control of yourself and all of your interests, even to God, seems like an unattractive thought.

Why do we maintain so tightly this grip on all that we think of as *ours*? This question brings to mind a vision of two small children tugging angrily at opposite ends of a toy, both shouting, "*My* toy!" What must the Almighty think when we clutch to ourselves the small portion of His vastness that's nearest us?

What we are really doing in trying to deny His control in our lives is holding to ourselves only a tiny portion of the great inheritance He Himself would generously put into our arms, if we would just let go of the little bit that we think is so dear! We are convinced that to "surrender" means to lose all we have. But in God, surrender means a gaining of all He has!

Has your level of gladness been reduced by a fear of releasing all that you have to God? Now, give whatever you have withheld to Him, and find the true security of receiving all good things from His hand.

The Normal Christian Life

"And these signs shall follow them that believe; In My name shall they cast out devils; they shall speak with new tongues; they shall lay hands on the sick, and they shall recover . . . the Lord working with them . . ."

Mark 16:17-18b,20a

Wayne Stubbs
Singer/Evangelist

If you think this is a description of the ministries of great preachers and evangelists alone, you're wrong. All this activity is supposed to be normal Christian behavior. Do you think I'm being extreme? Well, I thought this passage was a little far out, too, when I first encountered it. The church I was raised in didn't think these things were for today at all! It took God's Word to convince me otherwise.

This was Jesus' great commission to His disciples just before He ascended into heaven. In it, He was telling them what He expected of them after He left. First, they were to preach the gospel. Then, these signs above would follow, not the preachers, but *"them that believe!"* Did you catch that? The same power to work all these miracles would be passed on by the Holy Spirit to all who believed the disciples' preaching. Next, I don't see any time limit on this verse. Jesus didn't say, "just for the first century." As I really absorbed these verses, I realized that all this was for me. I was a believer, and if I would step out and start in faith doing these things, *the Lord would work with me*, to confirm what I did with miraculous signs. Once I started to do what Jesus commanded, He did step in and start to work miracles.

We all need boundaries in life. We need to know what we can and can't do. Many believers, like me, don't fulfill a lot of what God has for them because they don't know that they can.

Well, God's Word says right here that you can! Are you a believer? You may never have a ministry to millions, but right where you are, you can start doing God's will, too. And experience the Lord Himself working with you! If you get a chance, just try it today, and you'll see!

Joy In The Heavens

"I say unto you, that likewise joy shall be in heaven over one sinner that repenteth, more than over ninety and nine just persons, which need no repentance."

Luke 15:7

Willie Murphy
Singer/Evangelist

It's a shame that very often a born-again experience that began with joy in the camp of heaven, ends up to be down in the mouth here on earth. We can imagine from this beautiful scripture the angels and glorified saints shouting and singing and clapping their hands as a sinner comes into the fold. What a thrill it is to think about it!

But then we see that the angels aren't rejoicing so much over the just persons already in the fold. Could that be because, once they get saved, too many Christians lose their joy and settle into a daily rut that doesn't give the heavenly choirs much reason for rejoicing?

You know, a rut is nothing but a grave with both ends kicked out. And that's what life can easily become when we see salvation as nothing but a ticket to heaven. It's too easy to say, "Yeah, I'm on my way to glory," but never to get hold of any of that glory now. Beloved, God never meant that to be.

My salvation years ago at a Kathryn Kuhlman meeting was a joyous experience. And for a while I tried to ride on that high, but soon I came down. Thank God, I then started to get into the Word and began to realize that God had plenty to give me in this life. I started to find scriptures like Psalm 18:2, "The Lord is *my* rock and *my* fortress, and *my* deliverer; *my* God, *my* strength . . . *my* buckler . . . and *my* high tower." Suddenly, while I was looking at all those "mys," I understood that God's promises were for me. My heart lit up, and I said, "My, my, my!"

Now you see, when you get hold of God's Word for yourself, you'll have a whole lot to shout about, too. And when you start *living* in what God has for you, you'll start to know that first joy all over again yourself! And think: you'll have the camp of heaven singing again!

Clinging To Christ's Mind

"Let this mind be in you, which was also in Christ Jesus:"   *Philippians 2:5*

Dr. James E. Kilgore
Author/Counselor

The more you try to grasp what you are, the more of yourself you will find slipping away. Jesus said: "Whosoever shall save his life will lose it" (Luke 8:35). Did it ever occur to you that it is impossible to cling to what you are in this world? All things on this earth that are in bondage to time are going someday to pass away along with time itself. Anything that you might be ambitious for in this life must pass away: "Let it," Jesus is saying.

Understanding this, Jesus did not cling to His own earthly life; instead, He poured it out, giving it freely to and for others. He knew that in letting it go, He was laying hold on eternity.

The way a follower of Christ allows Christ's mind to be in Him is to allow himself to become the source of supply for others in the needs of this life. He gives to others rather than demanding that they give to him. In one of his poems, Robert Browning wrote: "A man's reach should exceed his grasp, or what's a Heaven for?" The way a Christian does this is to give more of himself to other people than he ever has before.

Jesus gave up His rights, His reputation, His possessions, even His temporal standing with His Father in becoming sin for us. He gave up His earthly, physical life, pouring it out for you and me—and rose, never to die again. And in giving Himself up, consider what He gained: not only all power and rule and authority for Himself, but life eternal, and the right to share all these things with you and me!

And He has even given us His own mind, that we might do likewise. Can we do less today than let that mind be in us and do richly what He did?

God's Dwelling Place

"What? Know ye not that your body is the temple of the Holy Ghost . . . therefore glorify God in your body, and in your spirit, which are God's." 1 Corinthians 6:19-20

Hilda Brittain
Bible Teacher

The last fruit of the Spirit mentioned in Galations 5:22 is *temperance*, or self control in our bodies. And in most cases, the last area of our lives that God deals with, after our spirits and souls, is our bodies.

Many of us who love Jesus are quite concerned about our progress in the spiritual side of life, and we forget that God desires us to be Spirit-led in regard to our body care, also. If our bodies are to be presented to Him "as a living sacrifice" (Romans 12:1), we need to seek His guidance as to what we should eat and drink and how we should care for our body. From time to time, some have arisen in the Church and proclaimed that the body is evil. But God's Word places high value on our physical bodies, calling them *temples*, fit to glorify God.

What an honor, to be chosen as a dwelling place for God's Holy Spirit! I have a responsibility to make Him comfortable and happy within me. When a cherished guest visits my home, my greatest desire is to serve him or her the best that I have to offer. I want my guest to be pleased with the pictures on the walls, the furnishings, and the yard around my house.

How much more ought I to inquire of the Lord: "What would you be pleased that I eat and drink? How would you like me to clothe my body? What kind of exercise would you like to enjoy with me?"

Dear brother or sister, make it your aim to please Him in every area of your life! Ask Him today what will make Him most happy with your body. Oh, let Him dwell with perfect pleasure in all of your being.

Happy Landings

"The eternal God is thy refuge, and underneath are the everlasting arms."
Deuteronomy 33:27

Juan Romero
Host, Spanish PTL Club

A few years ago, three fellow-workers and I were flying over Uraguay in a small airplane, and we ran out of gasoline at about 8,000 feet of altitude. We had been sold barely enough gas to reach our destination because the government, fearful of revolutionary uprisings, wanted to limit the possibility of gun smuggling to rebel forces by air.

First one engine died, then 4,000 feet lower, the other sputtered out. As we glided down, the pilot glanced about and quietly said, "Gentlemen, be prepared for anything." As we each prayed to the Lord silently, the pilot searched out a clearing and with great skill guided the plane to the ground. A wheel struck a rock, and some of the luggage fell forward onto our heads, but we were all uninjured and most thankful to be back on the ground. As I was climbing out of the cabin, this scripture suddenly entered my mind. I shared it with my colleagues and together, we thanked the Lord for His sustaining power.

You also can undoubtedly look back upon incidents in your life when God's strong embrace kept you from disaster. Never fail to give Him the thanks He is due for your deliverance. Never say it was merely luck or chance that saved you. For even when you appeared to be falling, you were still upheld by Him. And He was as much your refuge in dangerous times as any fortress could be on solid ground. So He is now, too, as you read this book, and so He will always be.

Wholeness

"When Jesus saw him lie, and knew that he had been now a long time in that case, He saith unto him, Wilt thou be made whole?"   John 5:6

David Crabtree
Pastor/Teacher

Somewhere, some time, we as Christians must decide that we want to reach out to Jesus for wholeness. So many times we find ourselves locked into situations from which we feel there's no way out. We blame our environment, we blame our heredity, we blame our circumstances for our predicament. That's what the lame man in this passage did, while Jesus stood right before him, asking this tremendous question.

The man did not answer "Yes" or "No." He said, "I am like I am because of all these other people." But Jesus did not ask him about the circumstances; He asked him, "Do you want to be made whole?"

If Jesus is in our midst, regardless of our background, our present state, or the "bad breaks" we've had in life, we can be made whole.

In order to do this, we must be willing to get rid of the obstacles in the way of our becoming whole. It's possible to become comfortable in the dependency of emotional or physical helplessness. It's easy to resist change with the attitude, "That's who I am, and I've been this way too long to change now." We need to ask the Lord to strip away these excuses.

Next, we must be ready to face the challenges wholeness will bring to us. The lame man after his healing had to go back to work like other men. We may have to face "giants" of difficulties we never dreamed of.

Jesus stands before you right now, asking you, "Will you be made whole?" Answer "Yes" to Him, with all your heart. He is able to make you whole and keep you whole, if you'll only want Him and trust Him to do so.

The Place Of Quiet Rest

"He that dwelleth in the secret place of the Most High shall abide under the shadow of the Almighty." Psalm 91:1

James Blackwood
Singer

The safety we can know in the presence of God depends upon the place in which the roots of our lives are set. The sun of worldly adversity, and the wind of change can parch and blast the soil of a wrong life foundation, sweeping us away, if we are not grounded in the secret garden God has prepared for us.

"There is a place of quiet rest,
Near to the heart of God,
A place where sin cannot molest,
Near to the heart of God."

So says an old hymn. And where is this place of peace and refreshment where we must be rooted and growing? The Apostle Paul tells us: ". . . in the grace and knowledge of our Lord and Savior Jesus Christ" (2 Peter 3:18). Just as the place of nourishment for a plant or flower lies in the dark and moist soil surrounding its roots, so the source of spiritual life for our faith is in the grace and knowledge of Jesus. This place lies under the shadow of the Almighty, where the hot winds and scorching sun cannot hinder the tender life springing into beauty and fruitfulness.

If we will find that place and abide there, most of the needs within us will be satisfied, too. Protection from without, and nourishment within: together these make up the experience of a peace that passes understanding.

Have you searched for this place of fulfillment? It can only be found in the shelter of God's grace and love in Jesus Christ. Can you make yourself worthy of it? No, but it can be yours by faith, right now, if you ask God to take you there.

Wings Of Worship And Praise

"O come, let us sing unto the Lord: let us make a joyful noise to the rock of our salvation." Psalm 95:1

Dino Kartsonakis
Music Artist

Music and praise to God have gone hand in hand since the beginning of time. Almost a third of the Bible is written in verse, and a good deal of it was written to be sung. Many of the introductions to the Psalms include directions for instrumental accompaniment. If we obeyed all the commands in the Psalms about praising God musically, worship would always be a lively time indeed.

Trumpets, harps, tambourines, stringed instruments (even pianos and electric guitars?), organs and cymbals: sounds like God appreciates a full orchestra! And that's just in the Old Testament. Paul exhorts us in Colossians 3:16 to be "teaching and admonishing one another in psalms and hymns and spiritual songs, singing with grace" in our hearts to the Lord. The Body of Christ is supposed to be a musical!

If you're not actively enjoying and participating in music as a Christian, perhaps you ought to be. Christian music today encompasses the whole range of musical styles and tastes from rock to classical. In a musical fulfillment of Matthew 13:52, Spirit-filled musicians are open today to searching out musical treasures both "new and old." Some of you older folks will be glad to know that a lot of contemporary Jesus-loving music people are starting to discover the old hymns of the church, and you'll be hearing a lot of young artists singing your favorites very soon.

Don't neglect this important *command* of God. God designed music to give your praise and worship wings. Whatever your taste in music, let the Holy Spirit be glorified in your enjoyment and participation in what God's doing musically today.

Patience And Your D

"In your patience possess ye your souls."   Luke 21:19

Debby Kartsonakis
Vocalist/Songwriter

I was only 12 years old when my mother wrote those meaningful words in my diary. The message this verse holds has been dear to me from that day forward.

Reflecting on my teen years, I had so many dreams of what I wanted out of life. I wanted to sing and write songs. I wanted to get married and have children. I wanted to be happy. But sometimes those dreams seemed so far away. There were times I wished I could skip ahead a few years like you skip grades in school. Growing a year at a time just took too long.

I remember feeling depressed and angry wondering why God didn't seem to realize how important it was to me to hurry and grow up so my dreams could come true. My mother would listen as I poured out my anxious adolescent thoughts and tears.

With love and understanding she would assure me that God knew my heart's desires and He knew the best way and time to bring them to pass. She would remind me of Luke 21:19: "In your patience possess ye your souls." Alone in my room I would read that verse and repeat it until its promise turned my discouragement into hope.

James 1:2-3 points out the importance of being joyful in patience. "My brethren, count it all joy when ye fall into divers temptations; knowing this, that the trying of your faith worketh patience." This can change your times of "waiting" into times of expectancy and joy. The joy of the Lord becomes my strength when I practice "counting it all joy."

Be patient in your circumstances and God will fulfill your dreams.

His Desires And Your Talents

"Before I formed thee in the belly I knew thee; and before thou camest forth out of the womb I sanctified thee, and I ordained thee a prophet unto the nations."

Jeremiah 1:5

Ron Hembree
Pastor/Author

When God commissioned Jeremiah to be His spokesman to the children of Israel, Jeremiah tried to convince God he could not do it. God replied to him that even before he was conceived, abilities were placed in him to do what God wanted him to do.

God created in Jeremiah certain propensities, desires, strengths, and ambitions. By choice, Jeremiah could follow or not follow these inclinations. In choosing to follow them, he would find God's purpose for his life and know happiness. But by not choosing them he would be fighting against God's will and only know frustration.

In my years of pastoral counselling I have seen many people disheartened or frustrated with their lives. Often times it is because they have forsaken using their inborn ability or talents to pursue a career in something that they thought would earn more money, prestige, or opportunity.

One young man I counselled wanted to be a baseball player, and he was very talented in that area. But somewhere along the way he had been convinced that if he wanted to serve God, he was supposed to become a doctor or field missionary.

I asked him who had given him his abilities and instilled in him certain desires and interests. God, of course. Today he is a member of a major league baseball team and also captain for the team. He is happy because he has found the place God wants him to be.

You can find happiness and purpose in your life by recognizing the desires God placed in your heart and using the abilities He has given you to pursue those desires and glorify Him through them.

The Greatest Book Of All

"Jesus saith unto him, I am the way, the truth, and the life: no man cometh unto the Father, but by me." John 14:6

Blanca Chiabra
PTL Rep., Costa Rica

There was the answer, striking for all its clarity, on the page of my eldest son's dusty old Bible. I had always been a seeker, trying to find answers in philosophy, meditation, mental science, and many other sources. A non-Christian friend had given me a book which suggested reading the Bible as a source of Spiritual wisdom. The Church I had attended since childhood had not encouraged scripture reading, so I had never examined the life of Jesus for myself. Now, through God's Word, Jesus was speaking, not to a speaker many years ago, but to me.

This Jesus, who had been beside me all my life, was the end of my search. Putting aside all of the other reading matter I'd accumulated, I began to study the scripture thoroughly. I sought out others who had met Christ, and came to know Him personally. Soon afterwards, I felt the desire to be baptized.

When I first met God, a dream came to me, of a pile of trash, on top of which lay open a large, well-used Bible. To me, this meant that all of the other books of the world were, in comparison to God's Word, of no worth, for only the Bible revealed the person of Jesus Christ.

Outside of Jesus Christ, there is no hope of finding eternal meaning. There are many "ways," "truths," and types of "lives" offered in the world today. But none of them will lead to God except the knowledge of Jesus Christ.

Have you been searching for meaning elsewhere than in Jesus? Have you been looking for answers in the wisdom of the world or in your own understanding? Look to Jesus: in Him alone will you find the answer to your every need.

The Place Of Power

*"Again I say unto you,
That if two of you shall agree
on earth as touching any
thing that they shall ask, it
shall be done for them of my
Father which is in heaven."*
Matthew 18:19

Rev. Edwin Louis Cole
Evangelist/Conference Speaker

The place of agreement is the place of power. Disagreement always produces powerlessness. Agreement always produces power.

If in a business deal, the parties involved can strike an agreement, then they have power and authority to accomplish whatever their aim. But until there's agreement, there's neither power nor authority to act.

The Bible says in Romans 5 that our sinful nature is at enmity, or in disagreement with God. Therefore, there can be no power of God in our lives until we begin to agree with Him.

The whole purpose of Christ's coming to die on the cross was to make an agreement: that if we come to Jesus Christ and agree that He's our Savior and receive Him into our lives, the power of God will enter into us. And as long as we agree with God in Christ, the power of God will remain flowing through us.

There are a lot of people who agree that God exists, but they don't agree with His way of new birth. There are others who agree with God to be born again, but haven't agreed with God's way of being filled with the Holy Spirit, speaking in tongues, and expecting miracles.

The way to reverse all that is to agree with God. That's what repentance is, to ask God to forgive you of being disagreeable, and agree by faith with Him that all of His ways are good, and meant for you.

So get into an agreement with God today. Agree with His prophecies, Word, Spirit, and truth. The more you agree with God in every area of your life, the more of Him you'll have. On the job, in your home, or at church, the fringe benefits will be great: righteousness, peace, and joy through the Holy Spirit.

Above and Beyond

"Now unto Him that is able to do exceeding abundantly above all that we ask or think, according to the power that worketh in us . . ."
Ephesians 3:20

Alan Langstaff
Pastor

Our God is a God of abundance so great that He not only provides for our needs, but gives us more than we need in order that we might share with others from our abundance.

While we undoubtedly need faith in approaching God, this verse speaks of God's sovereign desire to give to us even beyond our faith, "above all that we ask or think." We may ask God directly for various things, and we may have thought of things we haven't dared to ask Him for, but neither our asking or thinking limit His ability to give in ways beyond our expectations.

When I went to Disneyland one year, my daughters gave me a little shopping list of things that they wanted me to buy. Well, I was able to find everything on their lists; but when I came home, I also brought a number of goodies they weren't expecting, just for the sheer joy of making them happy.

Out of our heavenly Father's love, we too, can expect the unexpected. Surely He loves us, as His children, far more than we are capable of loving our own offspring.

Let me encourage you never to be afraid to ask God to accomplish things in your life that extend far beyond your imagination. Be ready for His goodness and joyful Father's love to shower down upon you. Expect the gloriously unexpected from Him—today.

God And Politics Do Mix

"Thy Word have I hid in mine heart, that I might not sin against Thee."
Psalm 119:11

Sen. John Nimrod
Illinois State Senator

When you're in public life as a Christian, the Word of God had better be your ruling guide. For a long time, Christians stayed out of politics because it was considered to be a "dirty business." But it's become obvious that government isn't going to become any less corrupt if we stay out of it. If we don't accept our share of responsibility for the functioning of our government, we have only ourselves to blame for the poor quality of the government under which we are living.

In recent years, the government of our nation has turned away from the great principles upon which it was founded. If we are going to see any change in direction back towards government reflecting God's kind of order, we are going to have to elect officials who fear God and have His Word hidden in their hearts. The many temptations to compromise in the political arena can only be resisted by men and women who will stand firmly upon God's Word.

The Bible tells us that we are to be in submission to earthly rulers and authorities. We are not likely to see government that's easy to obey in good conscience unless we're willing to elect, and even to become, the public servants who will serve God's order first.

I don't believe that it would take many such individuals to turn the tide in this country. If people who love God will stand strong in positions of leadership, with personal lives that back up their public stance, millions can be influenced to join them in developing a better nation. God and politics *do* mix. Are you willing to support or become part of that mixture?

Take A Stand For Christ

*"But when they shall
. . . deliver you up, take no
thought beforehand what ye
shall speak . . . but whatsoever shall be given you in
that hour, that speak ye: for it
is not ye that speak, but the
Holy Ghost."*   Mark 18:11

Ingaborg Nimrod
Housewife

My husband and I have shared in many political battles over the
years, and this verse has always given us courage and a reason for
standing. As we've gone before committees and legislative bodies,
we've just said, "Holy Spirit, come in and let me say what will glorify
you."

It's been difficult sometimes, because people in the political world
often don't want to hear what a Christian has to say. But as the Holy
Spirit has led, the Lord has spoken with power through us, and has
worked changes in the government of the district my husband
represents. As we've taken a stand, many other believers have joined
us, strong and decent people. With their influence, the image of political
life is changing, and people are realizing that politics need not be
considered an area in which Christians can't be involved.

When my husband and I were first Spirit-filled, our first impulse
was to leave politics: how could we walk in the Spirit and be part of this
"underhanded game" of politics. But then we realized through this
verse that Jesus had foreseen a place for us. He had not put us through 14
elections to get us ready to be missionaries to Africa! No, all of life
around us would erode if Christians just dropped out of government.

We stayed in politics, and we're trying to get others involved. It's
not enough just to vote for President once every four years. We need to
vote in school board elections, park districts, county commissions, and
state elections, too. We've got to get in there, work for, back with dollars
and time, even become candidates. God's promised us His help. Let's
get out and do it!

Heart Faith

"For with the heart man believeth unto righteousness . . ."
Romans 10:10

Ralph Brittain
Healing Evangelist

The kind of belief that appropriates the things of God to a child of God is *heart* belief, not *head* belief. The mind of man is programmed to deal with facts, in the realm of the five senses. The mind believes only what it can see or imagine without much strain, and it cannot reach into the supernatural. Only the heart can do that.

Your mind will always tell you, "Don't believe it until you see it." The best it can muster is presumption, or mental assent. God says, "Believe it in your heart, and then you'll see it." That's just the opposite of the mind's way of thinking.

The Word of God will produce faith in a believer once it's heard and allowed to move past the mind into the heart. God wants you to read the Word and listen to it and start to base your life upon it.

As believers, we're called to walk *rightly* or righteously before the Lord. This verse is trying to tell us that there is no right way to walk with God that is not grounded in heart belief. You cannot just give lip service or mind service to God. Proverbs 3:5 tells you to "Trust in the Lord with all thine *heart*; and lean not unto thine own *understanding*," or intellectual ability. God is only pleased with what proceeds from your heart.

Have you limited what God can do in your life by believing Him only as far as your limited understanding allows? Right now, ask Him to deepen your faith by founding it upon His Word rather than on your limited five senses. Plant that Word deep in your heart, and it will grow into heart belief for all that God wants for you.

No Help Needed

"Being confident of this very thing, that He which hath begun a good work in you will perform it until the day of Jesus Christ."
Philippians 1:6

Tom Skinner
Evangelist

The scripture is very clear that the Christian life is not my attempt to be like Jesus; rather, it is letting Jesus be Himself in me, living His life through me, without any assistance from me.

Unfortunately, there are many Christians who believe that living the Christian life is carrying around in their pockets a list of rules and regulations: don't touch this, don't do that, don't go there. They get tricked into believing that it is in overcoming sin that they will be made righteous. But the Bible says that it is in *being* righteous that a believer will overcome sin.

This is because the same Christ who saved me will perform the good work that is required of me—based upon my availability to Him rather than my own striving. So this changes the way I pray; instead of asking God to give me more power or strength or love, I accept the fact that this day Jesus Christ *is* my power and love and strength because He, Himself, is *in* me.

So my prayer for today is: "Lord, today you're going to put me in situations which require patience and power and strength. Of myself, I don't have any of those things. But I thank you that this day, you are in me and you will, yourself, be everything that these situations will demand." Now, I can forget trying to be those good things myself. I just go about my day and watch Jesus act victoriously through me.

Be confident today that Jesus, Who started you off, is going to finish the work He has for you. Relax, and let Him take the pressure—He can handle it a lot better than you can!

The Lord Provides

"But my God shall supply all your need according to His riches in glory by Christ Jesus. But now thus saith the Lord that created thee . . . Fear not . . . I have called thee by thy name; thou art Mine."   *Philippians 4:19, Isaiah 43:1*

Bob Lauro
Television Director

Whenever there's been a need in my life or my family's that's been crucial, we've just gone to the Lord and said, "Lord, here's the need," very simply, and He's always provided for it. Sometimes it's been food for the table, the monthly rent or mortgage payment, gas for the car, clothing for the children: whatever it is, we've learned to go first to God.

There have been times when our budget has gotten really tight. There was one rough time in my life when I didn't have a job. But I still did have a wife, three kids, food bills and house and car payments. All I had coming in was an unemployment check, and mathematically, I can't explain how we got by. It humbled me to be in that position, but after a while, I lost all fear because the Lord met each of those needs, one by one, in ways I would never have dreamed of. Money seemed to come out of nowhere, checks from months back I'd forgotten all about, help that we didn't even ask for from relatives. My children's eyes would gleam sometimes, as they watched God provide. One day someone said to me, "Who works to support your family?" I just pointed up to the sky and said, "the Lord!" That was a witness to that man!

And maybe it speaks to you today. Maybe you're anxious about your material needs or in a tight place financially. Let me tell you that if you belong to Jesus Christ, there's no need to fear. He's called you by name. He knew you before you were ever born or even conceived. He's never going to let you go, and He'll never let you down. Can you believe that? I praise Him right now, because I know that as you just put yourself in His hands in childlike trust, He's going to come through for you!

God Can Turn It Around

"And we know that all things work together for good to them that love God, to them who are the called according to His purpose." Romans 8:28

Sen. Roger Jepsen
U.S. Senator/Iowa

From making the decision to run to the final victorious outcome of the election, no amount of sophistication or expertise in political campaign management could have overcome so many obstacles and gotten me into office. It had to be God behind the scenes, working it all out.

At the start of the race, we were 51 percentage points behind our opponent. We had a young, inexperienced campaign staff. Our campaign manager resigned because we refused to sue a newspaper that was carrying on a smear campaign against us. A week before the election, polls showed us 11% behind, yet we won with 52.7% of the vote!

I also vowed not to let the campaign come before God and my family, and announced that I would not campaign on Sundays. The Lord led us to counter an expensive media campaign by our opponent with hundreds of personal appearances in obscure counties. And He spared us from tiredness and sickness to make these trips. We encountered hostility from opponents of our anti-abortion stance, attacks from newspapers, and shortages of funds. But God actually put all of these negatives to work *for* us. Each problem actually became a rallying point, as support built and built to put us over the top. Through it all, my prayer was, "God, use us, don't let us use you." So He did that, and even used all of the opposition's tactics to help us get to Washington!

If God has purposed to accomplish something, and you are called to be part of what He is doing, you cannot fail if you press on with it. It doesn't matter what problems or setbacks come your way, God can use them to help you along the way He's chosen. So get in the center of His will and walk confidently toward your goal. If He is in it, He'll make it happen!

Leave Your Doubts

"But when you ask Him be sure that you really expect Him to tell you, for a doubtful mind will be as unsettled as a wave of the sea, that is driven and tossed by the wind;"
James 1:6-7a (LB)

Eric AuCoin
PTL V.P./Singer

Living with indecision is always a torment for a Christian. Jesus was decisive: when He heard His Father's voice, He was quick to step out and fulfill it. As believers, we're meant to stand and walk boldly on the rock of our faith , not flounder in storms of doubt. But we sometimes lose our certainty of God's will because faith is based in things we can't see; doubt, founded on what is visible around us, often seems more tangible.

At a time when Rosalinde and I were working for another major ministry, God began to "stir our nest," nudging us to leave. We had no clear direction from the Lord, but we asked God in faith to guide us during a visit to the PTL Club, where we were scheduled to be singing guests. After the show, a long, unplanned meeting took place with Jim Bakker. As a result of this, we were offered positions with PTL. We felt an immediate sense of peace and assurance, with a witness in the Spirit that this change was the will of God for us.

But when we returned home, doubt began to set in. New opportunities arose where we were, we started looking for more "solid" signs to cling to and soon were hurled into four months of excruciating indecision. I finally cried desperately to the Lord for a word, and He led me to Luke 6:46: "And why call me, Lord, Lord, and do not the things which I say?" Then I realized that anxiety had taken over because we had asked in faith, and received God's answer, but then wavered instead of moving out with the confirmation He had given us.

Have you felt prompted in your spirit to make a new step for God, but held back, waiting for everything to seem "sure?" Launch out with Jesus into those unknown waters today, in the certainty of faith in Him.

Rise And Be Healed!

"And we know that all things work together for good to them that love God, to them who are the called according to His purpose." Romans 8:28

Rosalinde AuCoin
Music Artist

"Do you really believe My Word?"

The Lord's blunt question jarred me fully awake at 5 AM several months ago. He added: "Yes, you've decided not to sing on the PTL Club today, because your foot is newly broken and you can't walk on it. But do you really believe the words to the song you were going to sing?"

There's healing in the name of Jesus, healing in the touch of Jesus; Rise and be healed in the name of Jesus! I remembered how in the past, the Lord had healed our son of a club foot. And He had healed the nodules on my vocal cords that had left me unable to sing or talk for 18 weeks. The Lord reminded me then of the verse above: how many times in my life, He had taken seemingly bad situations and worked them together for my good and His glory! So I once again reached out in faith and took God at His word.

I woke up my husband Eric, and together we began to agree in prayer for the healing of my foot. And the more we thanked God for it, the more faith welled up in me. Soon, the pain began to leave, and I was able to stand and walk again.

That day, we were able to testify to this miracle on the PTL Club while we ministered. The phones lit up, as many people called up and were also healed through the power of Jesus.

Do you see how beautifully God was able to turn that situation for His glory? Is there anything in your life that might be troubling you right now, that you would like to see Jesus reorder for your good? Place it into His hands right now, believe His word with all your heart and watch Him shift all the pieces into something wonderful.

Save Yourself A Spanking!

"My son, despise not the chastening of the Lord; neither be weary of His correction: for whom the Lord loveth He correcteth . . ."
Proverbs 3:11-12

Donna Jean Scott Young
Commedienne

If and when we need it, there's no way we can avoid getting a spanking from the Lord (even if we're *daughters* rather than *sons* of His)! It's just great to know that if we do get one, it's not for punishment but for correction, to bring to us what's best.

God has some interesting ways and means of bringing us into line, and I think He has a good sense of humor about our sometimes wayward steps.

Jesus knows that my body doesn't really need coffee. I'm a walking percolator of energy as it is, so He's been trying to get me to quit drinking it. But stubborn me wants to keep on giving herself those caffein jolts. So off I went on a morning, not long ago, to McDonald's to get my big cup of coffee. As I was guzzling it down, I thought I heard a little voice say, "Throw that cup away!" We're so foolish sometimes, thinking that God doesn't see when we're doing wrong. But I said, "Oh, that can't be you, Lord," and I took the empty cup with me, so I could run back an hour later for a refill and save 27¢.

Sure enough, when my next caffein fit hit, I made a dash for the fast food counter, but horrors of horrors, I couldn't get a refill. I'd run into Burger King by mistake. Just down the street at McDonald's the coffee machine had caught on fire—no relief there, either!

Well, the Lord showed me that I can get along without coffee; the hardest part was just believing I could give it up. You know, Jesus loves you and He *will* keep working on you until you let go of that thing in your life He doesn't want. Why not save Him a little trouble and you a little spanking and just give it up to Him right now? Remember: if you wouldn't be better off without it, He wouldn't want to take it away!

God Is Agreeable

". . . if two of you shall agree on earth as touching any thing that they shall ask, it shall be done for them of My Father which is in heaven."
Matthew 18:19

Faye Speer
Singer/Speers

For many years, I left my singing career with the Speers to be at home and raise my younger children. While my husband, Brock, traveled, we kept in close touch by letter and telephone, and through our long-distance communication, we learned that what we agreed for together with God could not be hindered by our separation in space and time. God was faithful and would fulfill His promises as our spirits joined over the miles.

The Lord found some unusual ways to teach us agreement. As we talked on the phone about various family problems, we would agree together that when we hung up, we would spend particular times wherever we were praying for the needs. Often we'd find out as we talked that we had both already been praying about a need we hadn't even discussed before. That seemed doubly meaningful.

The children are grown now and I am back singing with the Speers again; and looking back I can see that if we hadn't had the Lord and united prayer to depend upon during that time of separation, things would really have been rough. Life didn't always run smoothly, but we learned to hold onto the promises of God together. And in time, we believe God will meet every need we committed to Him in prayer.

You may have a loved one who lives a long way off. Remember, prayer knows no boundaries. You can touch that loved one through prayer and enjoy a lovely, sweet communion through God's Spirit. God will always agree with you and a friend when you unite together and touch Him in prayer.

Be Strong In God

"But they that wait upon the Lord shall renew their strength; they shall mount up with wings as eagles; they shall run, and not be weary; and they shall walk, and not faint." Isaiah 40:31

Dave Van Every
Owner of King's Gym

Weight training and body building never interested me much before I met the Lord. I was more involved in drugs and good times. I'd dropped out of school and suffered a broken marriage. It took all that to get me to start thinking about God.

But after my wife and I got saved and back together, it dawned on me one day that I felt real good on the inside but looked so bad on the outside. So I started lifting weights with my friend Dave White, who was overweight and trying to get in shape. My wife and I went to a Christian camp, and while praying there, the Lord told me that my ministry was going to be to open up a Christian gymnasium.

Two days later, the owner of a gym approached me and asked me to run his place. This prepared me for the time when I'd open my own gym. Dave White was gaining some valuable experience in the insurance business, and he and I shared this vision of a Christian gymnasium. So when the Lord's time was right, He gave us the right place and has really prospered us.

The Lord has continued to multiply my own strength. Where I was once a physical wreck, my body nearly destroyed by drugs, the Lord has given me new strength. My first official body-building competition is coming up very soon!

God is concerned with how you treat your body, too. Not that He wants everybody to be a Charles Atlas, or even a Dave Van Every. But because He lives in that body, He wants the best for it. He wants you to start doing all you can to have the physical pep and vigor to get you joyfully through every day. I really believe that if you'll pray for that strength and wait on Him, He'll give it to you.

Do You Want What You Need?

"But my God shall supply all your need according to His riches in glory by Christ Jesus."

Philippians 4:19

Dr. Al Wallace
Pastor/Counselor

Some time ago this was said in my hearing: "Not all your wants are needs, and . . . *you may not want all you need.*" Now, there are obvious needs with which we're familiar, and we so often claim this verse for them: healing, a job, another car, a house to be sold—the list could go on and on!

But there is another dimension to be considered in the provision of this promise. It may be true that in God's sight we have a need for something which is not quite as pleasant to consider. Perhaps we need to be disciplined or taught or tested. These are just as much valid needs as the more attractive ones. We might not even be aware of them, but God is. God may be looking at a different set of needs in your life from those things *you* feel you need. In fact, He may reshuffle the priorities of your needs from His eternal perspective.

I'd like to ask you, "What is your need today?" Remember, *you may not want all you need.* Perhaps God is prescribing what is mentioned in Hebrews 10:36: "For ye have *need* of *patience.*" Without it, you'll never make it to glory, for scripture exhorts us to "run the race with patience."

When you have patience, you can put up with aches and pains, struggle and competition. Patience keeps you from being a "drop-out." It's also the key to discerning between your needs and your wants. God will always supply your needs. He may refrain from giving you your wants. God can only work in you as you "hang in there"—right where you find yourself today. So "let patience have her perfect work" (James 1:4), as God supplies *all* your need!

High Places

"The Lord God is my strength, and He will make my feet like hinds' feet, and He will make me to walk upon mine high places."

Habakkuk 3:19

Olinka Zoppe
Trapeze Artist

When your occupation is flying high above the ground on a little trapeze, this is a verse you need to remember! But it has another significance also, a little more "down to earth."

Few situations we face in the Christian life are more precarious than the "high places" we sometimes come to in God. These are the times when perhaps we have been lifted up by hearing deep teaching, or have just emerged victorious from a spiritual battle, benefited from a miracle, or have been mightily used by God.

How easy for the great spiritual feelings that go along with these "highs" to swell into a sort of glamour that begins to turn our heads away from the Lord. We start thinking about how gloriously we are soaring along, how worthy we must be to enjoy the exaltation of God. We start to cheer ourselves and see our names up in spiritual lights flashing alluringly before us: "And now, ladies and gentlemen, in center ring, Christian the Magnificent, performing devastating, devil-defying feats, 100 feet in the air, and no net!"

Then we cast off on our own, thrust ourselves forth in a swirling triple somersault, reach out, and for a moment of panic grasp thin air, with no hand to catch us! Ah, then Jesus' strong hands grasp us by the wrists, and He pulls us into His arms, safe and sure again.

Jesus, help us to remember when all things are going right to give You the glory. It is You who set our feet upon the high places: Keep us when we rise, and catch us when we fall. Let us always rejoice in You, never only in our being lifted up! Amen.

Walking High

"Because He hath set His love upon me, therefore will I deliver him: I will set him on high, because he hath known My name." Psalm 91:14

Tino Zoppe
Circus Aerialist

Being up on a high wire never quite gets routine. I'm in a dangerous profession. Often when I'm up there, this verse is part of my meditation. As you might imagine, fright and the unsteadiness it causes are unwelcome companions. Some people think that my claiming this scripture is rather amusing, but I can assure you its real importance to me is tremendous.

I take these words as God's personal assurance to me that He'll keep me up there. I have security as I'm walking that wire, because it wasn't me that set myself there, but God. So my concentration on doing my job can be very complete, and that helps me avoid accidents.

God also had other reasons for setting me "on high." Apart from the dangers of the high wire, the entertainment business itself offers plenty of dizzying predicaments. But God set me in the midst of a trying show business world to minister to a lot of people who probably would not be reached any other way. The lives of performers can become so entwined with their work that there's often little sense of a need for God. Usually, an opening to share the gospel comes when a personal life starts to break down. When that happens, I can be there to bring Christ to the point of that hurt.

Wherever God has set you, He never forgets you. For when He set His love on you, He set it on whatever circumstance you're in. Even if it seems like He's set you down rather than on high, be assured that in His timing, He'll reach down and pick you up. Someday, He'll come back to get us and take us so high, we'll never come down again! Now won't that be great?

Walking By Faith

"And we know that all things work together for good to them that love God, to them who are the called according to His purpose." Romans 8:28

Larry Orrell
Singer/Evangelist

Maybe you're in the middle of a puzzling time in your life right now. Maybe you're experiencing something that seems fantastically good. Either way, you might be asking yourself, "Lord, why has this (good or bad) thing happened to me?"

So many times, we just don't seem to have a simple answer to grasp. But if the Lord always answered us yes or no, whenever we demanded it of Him, what would be the need for our faith? It's up to us to trust the Lord, to live by faith, no matter what. The Lord can use easy things or difficult things, pleasant things, and unpleasant. He knows exactly what will work to lead us into the best path possible.

In my life, there just hasn't been much unhappiness. None of the credit is due to me. For though I've had plenty of problems, I've had a lot of joy that's kept me from being burdened. A little over a year ago, I was wondering how I was going to get a new album into distribution. My feet never got quite settled enough to explore the problem. I was constantly on the move, travelling around with Rev. Paul Olsen, so it was just a question that had to be left with the Lord. But the Lord brought a man to me, who invested a considerable amount of money into this album. I had been tempted to get discouraged, but I kept believing God. He worked it out when I couldn't.

That fix you're in right now is really His, not yours. If you can't make it work, remember that God isn't hampered by your limitations. He can do limitless things with any kind of situation. And if it's a good fix you're in, He can turn it, not just into something better, but into what's best! Keep being patient. He'll do it!

Pray And Worship In The Spirit

"But the hour cometh, and now is, when the true worshippers shall worship the Father in spirit and in truth . . ."   John 4:23

Roger Vann
Pastor/Evangelist

There is a direct link between worshipping God in the Spirit and walking with Him in the Spirit. At the Jesus People Church, where I'm pastor, we spend a great deal of our worship time singing and praying in the Spirit. This time set apart is essential to build up the "inner man" in each member, and thus the fellowship as a whole.

Let me explain. Every believer who has tasted the living water that Christ gives has in him a "well of water springing up into everlasting life" (John 4:14). This refers to the Holy Spirit. Now, any well needs to be stirred up and cleaned out from time to time to keep it from becoming stagnant. One thing that praying in the Spirit does is to keep a constant flow of fresh "water" moving through our spirits, flushing out the rust and pollution that can get into us from the world.

Second, the believer who prays in the Spirit "edifieth himself" (1 Corinthians 14:4). This means that he is built up, or strengthened in his inner being. It's like keeping your car in good repair. If you want to drive safely, you make sure that all the parts are in working order. What isn't, you replace or rebuild. As we leave our fellowship, we need to be prepared with wisdom and might to meet the world. Worship in the Spirit is that "machine shop" where we can get fresh "oil" and "water," and the "servicing" we need.

How long can you pray, just in English, with your understanding? Five minutes? Ten minutes? An hour, maybe, if you've got a long prayer list? In the Spirit, you can communicate with God at any time, for as long as you want. You need the building up of worship in the Spirit. Don't think it's just for church on Sundays, either. Get into walking and talking in the Spirit today.

Take That Step Of Faith

"For by grace are ye saved through faith; and that not of yourselves: it is the gift of God: Not of works, lest any man should boast."
Ephesians 2: 8-9

Charles Duke
Former Astronaut

This world seems to say, "You've gotta be a good guy, and if you're just a good guy, that's enough." But the Bible says that we all fall short, we've all sinned, and we can't approach God unless we go through the Lord and Savior Jesus Christ.

But He loved us so much, He gave Himself for us, so through His grace, we can by faith approach Him. My feelings of inadequacy are overcome by His love. No, I can never be good enough in myself to measure up to His standards. But God says, "Just believe that I love you like I do. No matter how you stumble, I'm always there to pick you up. I'll be like a Daddy to you. I'll just pick you up and dust you off and send you on your way. You didn't do it just right? That's O.K. Just try again; I'm with you. I just want you to try."

As I stepped out in that assurance of love in my own life, sharing my faith in a nursing home, or with a sick person for the first time, just telling people how much Jesus loved them, He was with me. He didn't demand a big step, just a little one. What a great relief this was to me, after a life of striving and struggling, after having met my goals and not having been happy, to simply belong to God and share the love of Jesus! I can never be perfect in this world. But I can be loved by Jesus.

You were a sinner when God saved you. And like me, there is still some sin in your life. You may gossip or complain now and then, or get mad at your spouse and kids or on the job. But God's love will keep on meeting you if you'll keep on trying. And His love will change you as you let it lift you up. He's a good Dad!

All Encompassing Love

"For God so loved the world, that He gave His only begotten Son, that whosoever believeth in Him should not perish, but have everlasting life."   John 3:16

Dotty Duke
Wife/Speaker

This means to me first of all that God really did love me, and that I'm special. At one point in my life, my self-esteem was very low. I didn't think much of myself. But when I saw this personally, that God cared for me personally enough to give His life for me, it was awesome and life-changing. This fed my hunger for love and self-worth.

To think of it: that His love, which was beyond estimate, all self-giving, reached out to me right where I was. He knew exactly who and what I was, and accepted me unconditionally. I can scarcely tell you how healing this was to me.

Once this had taken place, and I was at rest in Jesus' love for me, I began to hear Him speak to me as His disciple. His message was that now as a follower of His, He was calling me to love others with that same love with which I had been comforted. Romans 15:7 says, "receive ye one another, as Christ also received us to the glory of God." This means that I was to embrace others, and that this extending of God's love would bring glory to Him.

I knew how Christ had loved me, with an everlasting love even to death and beyond. This meant that I also had to love others without reservation, to forgive people who had wronged me, to give sacrificially, expecting nothing in return. This had to begin with my husband, my children, my Church, and individuals all around me, one by one.

None of us could ever do this with purely human love. But God hasn't asked us to do it alone. He has given us His very heart of love in pouring His Holy Spirit into us. As you begin to obey Him, you will find yourself able to love, as the Holy Spirit joins Himself with your obedience and touches others with that love!

Hand Him Your Cares

"Let Him have all your worries and cares, for He is always thinking about you and watching everything that concerns you."
1 Peter 5:7 (LB)

Flo Price
Singer/Composer

My husband is always having to tell me, "Flo, will you let God handle this situation His own way?" I have a tendency to be a sort of "Mother of the World," forever fretting about baby birds falling out of nests, animals trapped in forest fires, and crying children wherever they are. This is fine and commendable, except that I'm constantly telling God how He should work out all of these problems.

So even if I am letting the Lord in on all my worries and cares, I start trying to make sure that everything gets worried into just the answer I want. Then when He has worked things out to His satisfaction, in better fashion that I had insisted upon, I'm glad, but maybe just a little bit disappointed.

Oh, look at all those "I"s in that last paragraph! That's the real problem, isn't it: that I just don't quite want to believe that the Lord is thinking and watching and concerned as much as I am! And so I have to do a super amount of worrying to make up for what I am afraid God's not doing. Do you have a "I" like that bothering you sometimes, too?

Well, your I and my I have to realize something daily: that it's His *eye* that's on the sparrow, and that His love and concern are going to make the difference, not our "I." We have to put our "I"s into His big *eye* and let Him keep watch over them, too.

"My thoughts are not your thoughts, neither are your ways My ways, saith the Lord" (Isaiah 55:8). Can you and I, starting with today alone, place in His hands all our cares—and then, as they arise, all our worries *about* our cares, too? Let's let our "I"s get small and be lost in the center of *Him*!

Be A Living Witness

"Wherefore seeing we also are compassed about with so great a cloud of witnesses, let us lay aside every weight . . ."　Hebrews 12:1

Gary S. Paxton
Singer/Songwriter

Most Bible scholars agree that the "witnesses" in this verse are the host of departed saints up in heaven watching us living ones still striving for God down here. Now, I don't want to argue with that view, but I get another truth from this verse, too—that, as Christians, we should be concerned with the *living* witnesses all around us, too.

Being a Christian means being responsible for other peoples' lives where we live. It may be the guy next to you in the factory where you work. Perhaps it's your son or daughter, maybe your husband or wife. It might be your mom or dad. There's somebody right near you watching what you do or say or what you look like.

There are a lot of do's and don'ts the Bible doesn't give us. It doesn't say "don't smoke" in the Bible. It doesn't say you'll go to the Hot Place for drinking one glass of wine. But before you do anything, you should take some time to think of how that might affect somebody who is looking at you and Jesus.

Like, what if a former alcoholic should walk into your house and find a bottle of booze on a shelf? He might think, "Hey, he's a strong Christian, and he takes a drink—maybe it's o.k. for me, too." See what I mean? I'd rather quit doing that thing than encourage another person to destroy himself by my example.

You can do a lot of neat things as a Christian and not harm anyone. You can be "terminally weird and Godly right" like me if you want. I'm not saying you have to be a conformist. But just don't let any of those "witnesses" around you be witnesses to anything in your life that would make them commit something harmful to them. Please!

That I Might Know Him

"Let not the wise man glory in his wisdom, neither let the mighty man glory in his might, let not the rich man glory in his riches: But let him that glorieth glory in this, that he understandeth and knoweth Me . . ."
Jeremiah 9:23-24

Bobbie Reed
Writer/Conference Speaker

"Getting ahead in life is all a matter of who you know." This rather cynical statement is probably very familiar to you. You may have said it yourself. It's easy, isn't it, to "ooh" and "ah" over the thought or presence of famous and influential personalities. And how quick we are to let other people know if we're friends with an individual who has "clout," because a "big name" has a way of opening doors!

But I'm really challenged by the idea that God says we can know Him. Not that we can just have Him as our personal Savior, but that all our lives, He's given us the right to say, "I am somebody because I know God."

Yes, God is your Savior, He's your Creator, your Lord—but He's also your friend. And if you're going to develop a friendship with Him, you're going to have to take advantage of His beautiful invitation to know Him. You'll really need to treat Him like a friend you love. You'll spend time with Him. You'll talk with Him and share with Him. You'll do things to please Him out of love. You'll expect Him to be a pleasure to you and to give back your love and to take care of you.

The more personal you get with God, the more you'll understand His love. And in knowing His love, as Ephesians 3:19 says, you'll become "filled with all His fullness." If you can come to understand just one small bit of how much God loves you, you'll grow and become more mature in Christ, and love others with that same love, as they need it.

Today, you can tell everyone you meet with delight, "I know Jesus!" And you can say it in your heart, while His joy warms your whole being. Let His name open doors for you, within you, and all around you!

The Greatest Power Of All

"I can do all things through Christ which strengtheneth me."
Philippians 4:13

Mark Buntain
Missionary to India

In my twenty-five years as a missionary to India, the words of Philippians 4:13 have been my constant comfort and confession. By standing on this promise of Christ's strength to help me accomplish all things, I have been able to do things I was told I could never do.

When I first began to talk about going to India, many people tried to talk me out of it. They said it was too hopeless a situation to make any headway, and I should go somewhere else to start a mission.

But I held onto God's promise of Philippians 4:13 and went to Calcutta, India. After arriving, I was faced with obstacles that did look impossible. I was told I would never be able to build a school or hospital. The odds were too great.

This would have been true if I had depended solely on my abilities and energy. But the Lord has built both, and the gospel of Jesus Christ is being made real to the people of Calcutta because our small ministry refused to accept the "impossible," and instead believed with Christ we could do all things.

Since I have learned to place my weaknesses and inabilities in the hands of God and ask for the Lord Jesus to be my total strength, I have never encountered a task too great or dream beyond my reach. The power of the Risen Christ in me and in you is the greatest power of all.

Remember that God and you always make a majority!

The Acceptable Year

"The Spirit of the Lord is upon me, because He hath anointed me to preach the gospel to the poor; He hath sent me to heal the broken-hearted, to preach deliverance to the captives, and the acceptable year of the Lord."
Luke 4:18-19b

John Wesley Fletcher
Evangelist

This is the acceptable year Jesus was preaching about. You can almost smell it in the air. It's about over. I'm convinced in my spirit that we are living in the closing hours of human history.

We've planted, we've watered. We've had the latter rain of God's Spirit rain down on His creation. Now we're living in the great harvest season, the fields are white. And Jesus has given us power to go out in His name and bring into the Body of Christ the product of the planting.

This isn't to take anything away from those great men of faith who blazed trails over the centuries, preaching the gospel of our Lord Jesus. But now as never before, we see the wheat and the chaff separating. Islamics, Hindus, cults of all kinds are lifting themselves up. And all of these are weeds. Only Jesus, the True Vine, and His branches, are meeting human need. None other but Jesus is answering prayer. We could put our hope and faith in anything else, but none of them would make us stand.

No, Jesus alone is answering. He's healing the sick, He's raising the dead, He's putting the broken hearts back together, and freeing the captives, just as He did 2,000 years ago when He spoke these words. But now He's doing it all over the world, through your hands and my hands, millions of the hands of His servants out there gathering His harvest in.

And He's doing another great miracle: He's turning the harvested crop into harvesters, to reap even more. Time is winding down, friends. Get out into that field while you can!

Never Forsaken

"Be strong and of a good courage, fear not, nor be afraid of them: for the Lord thy God, He it is that doth go with thee; He will not fail thee, nor forsake thee."
Deuteronomy 31:6

Shirley Fletcher
Author/Wife

My father used to preach on this verse when I was young. He'd tell how, in 40 years of serving God, the Lord had never failed or forsaken him. When I was 20, I decided to keep an account of my walk with God, and see how this proved true in my own experience. I had little idea at the time of all the "enemies" that I would have to stand courageously against!

In 1965, I was in an automobile accident. My back, pelvis, and ribs were broken, one lung was punctured, and the other one shredded. My heart turned over and moved to the other side of my body. I was five months pregnant and lost the baby. Told I would never walk again, the Lord enabled me to walk in 10 days, come home in five weeks, and be taken out of a body cast in just three months, rather than the six months that had been predicted.

In 1966-67, blood tests showed that I had leukemia. God healed me of that and of lifelong anemia as well. In 1968, a pressure cooker exploded in my face, leaving third degree burns on 30% of my body. My head was swelled as large as a bushel basket. I was scheduled to have plastic surgery but chose not to, and the Lord healed me eight days later. In 1969, my husband died, leaving me with a young daughter. Two years later, after prayer, I met John Wesley Fletcher and was married within a month. We were told that I should have no children because of a blood condition and the effects of the auto wreck. But we believed God, and I gave birth soon in a normal delivery to a healthy son!

Need I say more? In all these things, there *was* no cause to fear, for God *was* there *every* time. And He is always there whenever *you* are tempted to fear. Then reach out to Him, and find courage and help.

The Need For Anointing

". . . I will take of the Spirit which is upon thee, and will put it upon them; and they shall bear the burden of the people with thee . . ."
Numbers 11:17

Dottie Rambo
Gospel Singer

What people need most from those called to preach and minister the Word of God is some impartation of God's Spirit. Here in the wilderness, God was speaking to Moses about appointing elders from all the tribes of Israel to help carry the burden of leadership. It was important to God that these men be not only natural leaders, but that they have the same supernatural endowment to do the work of God that Moses possessed.

The people of God today are crying out for more than just talk or entertainment from those who stand before them in pulpits and behind microphones. Impressive speaking, singing, and instrumental technique may be pleasing to the ear, and makeup and tasteful clothing may caress the eyes. But it is the spirit of a man or woman that needs to be fed, and that can only be done if ministers share, not only letter and musical note, but the Spirit of God, and His power.

Moses was Israel's leader to the promised land not because he was outstanding in all of his personal qualities. He was called "the meekest man on the face of the earth" (see Numbers 12:3). He was slow of speech and advanced in years. But the anointing of God was upon his life for this great task. Paul likewise, shared that "my speech and my preaching was not with enticing words of man's wisdom, but in demonstration of the Spirit and of power."

As a person who is called to minister in music, I ask that you pray that the Spirit of God would rest upon me as I sing. If I could only tell you how much all those who preach or perform for God need your strong intercession! We only stand because you hold us up before God. Ask Him today that ministers of the gospel everywhere would truly feed His flock in the power of the Spirit.

The Secret Of Contentment

"For I can do everything God asks me to do with the help of Christ who gives me the strength and power."
Philippians 4:13

Dr. Michael Campion
Psychologist

What Paul is talking about in this verse is God giving us contentment in where we find ourselves in life and in God. Notice that in the verse that precedes this one, Paul lists among some of the "all things" that he can do: living "on almost nothing or with everything," learning the "secret of contentment in every situation, whether it be a full stomach or hunger, plenty or want" (Philippians 4:12).

As a psychologist, I realize that if many people had real contentment, I'd be out of business! You can call the feelings people have anxiety or depression or anger, but they basically add up to lack of contentment. Verse 13 tells us how to get that contentment. Jesus Christ will give it to us if we do everything that God asks.

It's also interesting to note that verse 11 adds an aspect of learning to this picture: Paul "learned how to get along happily." There's work involved in learning contentment. And in verse 14, Paul doesn't forget to say that he appreciates the help of others, too, when things were rough.

This isn't just a "zap" then, it's a process. I had to learn it myself as my career went through ups and downs. Some psychologists didn't accept me because I was a Christian, and some Christians didn't accept me because I was a psychologist! But I gradually learned to rest in what God was doing in my life by His grace.

You may be faced with doing one of the "all things" Paul mentions in these verses. Paul didn't always have it easy. But he learned to deal with every situation, and not always alone. No matter what the present state of your life, if you will be sure to do all God asks of you, you too, will learn contentment. And be sure not to be too proud to accept the help of others if you need it. Paul wasn't!

Launching Out

"You chart the path ahead of me, and tell me when to stop and rest. Every moment, You know where I am."
Psalm 139:3 (LB)

Lloyd Powlison
Missionary to Deaf

"You can't steer a boat that's standing still in the water." That's what a friend told me and my wife when we couldn't figure out what our next move would be towards getting support to go back to the mission field. We had been in Latin America for a dozen years already, but after we received the Baptism in the Holy Spirit, we lost the support of the organization that had been sponsoring us.

We knew that God was not finished using us in South America. But we didn't know where to go for help—or even to go looking for it. That's when our friend helped make this verse from Psalms real to us. He nudged us out to travel to seek support with reasoning like this: "You've stopped and rested for awhile, and God has been aware that you've needed it. But just as He knows where you are when you're at rest, He's also ready to chart your course ahead of you. God doesn't give any green lights. It's up to you to launch out and discover the course He has for you."

So we set a date to begin looking for support, and we began to travel, speaking wherever we could, and, sure enough, God brought us the help we needed. I believe that God blessed this willingness to trust Him. He put us right where He wanted us, in Bolivia, and later blessed our work with a generous grant from the PTL Club!

There's a time in your life to rest and a time to move out. Whichever position you're in, God knows your needs completely. You can trust God to be with you in each undertaking He calls you to, and in the lightening of each load He takes from your shoulders. Be sensitive to His voice: Let Him steer you out, and bring you safely to shore.

He Understands

"Hast thou not known . . . that the everlasting God . . . the Creator of the ends of the earth, fainteth not, neither is weary? there is no searching of His understanding."   Isaiah 40:28

Jan Dennis
Ministry to Singles

Forty men from our Church manually operated a respirator for 15 months so my husband could stay at home. He was slowly dying of the same degenerative disease that killed the famous baseball player Lou Gehrig. This horrible illness causes all the muscles in the victim's body to slowly slacken and atrophy, rendering him totally helpless. He died at home, not in a hospital, thanks to those faithful brethren.

The day my husband died, the Lord let me know that there could be victory even in this. During this time, I became involved in a small prayer group that helped me through the bitterness and pain I felt. My husband had left me with small children and no sure direction. I could not understand why this had happened.

I was asked not long after that to speak at a women's conference. Still embittered, I felt I couldn't. But though angry and not really wanting to, I spoke anyway. The Lord took me from that initial step to my present ministry to single and divorced people. As I moved on, I learned to lean on a God who *could* be leaned on, a God who never faints, who is never weary. I learned to know that whatever happens to a believer in Christ is within God's sovereign realm. We can know who He is without questioning everything, in a peace that trusts in His understanding.

Even in the midst of suffering and pain, we can still say, "Lord, I know I can't understand this. But I'll accept it anyway and rejoice in all You've done for me. I choose to trust You, and to lean on Your understanding." Can you trust Him with your whole life, good and bad times, today? You can, for He has perfect charge of it all!

Ever Faithful

"It is of the Lord's mercies that we are not consumed, because His compassions fail not. They are new every morning: great is Thy faithfulness."
Lamentations 3:22-23

Dean Dennis
Minister to Singles

When I found out that my wife was leaving me for another, younger man, I began to spiral down into a deep depression. I didn't know the Lord, though I'd been in ministry for twelve years. To all outward appearances, I was a success. People thought I "had it all together" spiritually, but a deep emptiness plagued me now and then.

My wife's leaving drove me to despair. I felt grief-stricken and guilty and wondered how I could continue in the ministry. But at that time, some friends asked me to attend a prayer group led by Pat Boone. There I was reborn and Spirit-filled. The Lord gave me a miraculous recovery from the depression, as He spoke these words from Lamentations to me when I thought all was lost. I knew then that God's compassion had upheld me and kept me from being consumed by depression and self-destruction. God told me that whatever I'd been through, He'd had a purpose in it which would help mold me into the image of Jesus Christ.

As I received of His compassion, He gave me a compassionate heart for others. Having suffered, I became more aware of others' sufferings and anguish. But most important, I learned that only God is truly faithful. I'm convinced that most marriages fail because people look to their mate or others as a source of happiness. Only God will never fail us. God showed me that there were many other divorced people and singles who needed His help and led me to form Single Purpose International.

"Single Purpose" means that there is only one goal in our lives: to serve Jesus Christ. His mercy alone can uphold you. His compassion will never fail you. This morning, every morning, He stands ready, to be served with a glad heart, and to be faithful, whatever your need.

Know What's Yours

*"The eyes of your under-
standing being enlightened;
that ye may know what is the
hope of His calling, and what
the riches of the glory of His
inheritance in the saints."
Ephesians 1:18*

Jimmy Smith
Music Evangelist

The Lord wants us to know all that we possibly can about Him. He wants us to know that we are truly His children and desires to impart His wisdom and knowledge to us. All of the hope of His calling and the riches of His inheritance is in us.

This takes away every inferiority, every fear. It's a constant reminder that He wants to continually enlighten us. He doesn't want us to walk without adequate light. He wants us to know who we are, what's ours, and what we're moving into.

I learned to appreciate this through my own struggles in ministry. I'd been baptized in the Holy Spirit as a boy, then drifted for a while from the Lord. When I decided to serve the Lord full time in singing, I felt as though the gifts of the Spirit ought to be operating in my ministry. But at first, I was working with people who didn't like this, not believing that these gifts were for today. This caused me after a while to question whether the experiences I'd had in the Holy Spirit were real. But though I had no encouragement, the Word of God began to come alive to me in my personal study. I realized through this scripture that it was possible if necessary, for me to grow in Him without teaching—just by revelation. God could open my eyes and show me the truth of His Word. He made me know that the walk in the Holy Spirit I'd had was true and vital for today.

I want you to know today, in the deepest part of your spirit, that all that God's given you is really your possession, now and forever. Salvation, fellowship in Christ, a personal relationship with Him, the fullness of the Holy Spirit—these are yours now. Ask the Lord to open your eyes and show you all that belongs to you.

Nothing's Too Hard For Him!

"Behold, I am the Lord, the God of all flesh: is there any thing too hard for me?"
Jeremiah 32:27

Frances Kelley
T.V. Talk Show Co-Host

I found my way to the little church. The evening service was already over; folks were just sitting around sharing in the back, I must have looked a sight: haggard, exhausted, my despondency hanging on my face. Kindness reached out to me there. Someone opened up a Bible and said, "Mrs. Kelley, look at this. Read this."

I took the Bible in my hands and read the scripture above. It meant little to me at first reading. But the second time, its meaning began to probe through my hopelessness and take form. God was saying to Israel through Jeremiah, "Behold, I am the Lord." My hair began to stand on end. I trembled from head to toe. I could feel the strength of that *"I,"* so much greater than my own. Then it was as if He spoke to me personally: *"Is there any thing too hard for me?"* And hope began to spring up within me. I left there that night, with the seeds in me of a great change which would last forever! From those moments on, I knew there would always be hope for me. That scripture has been the source of my determination to go on and my whole Christian walk. And as I grew in God, I found that indeed, Jesus was anything and everything I needed and will ever need.

There may be a lot of things in life that are too hard for you. You may have burdens today that you can scarcely bear. But I can tell you that when things get tough for you, Jesus gets ready to take over. Why go on trying to carry that load of heartache or worry or pain? Jesus can take it. He can manage it. Don't bear it a minute longer—give it all to Jesus right now!

Comforting Still!

"But when the Comforter is come, Whom I will send unto you from the Father, even the Spirit of truth . . . He shall testify of Me."
John 15:26

Frank Howard
Aerospace Engineer

Jesus before He died promised that when He left this earth He would send the Holy Spirit down to multiply His presence among His people. Well, He did send that Comforter. And He's still sending Him today. The Holy Spirit is having a great influence in churches of all denominations today!

There are many churches that haven't been for a long time open to the power and gifts of the Holy Spirit, to whom the Spirit is now making Himself known. He's causing people to get excited because He's demonstrating the power of the Lord. The Lord is doing the same kinds of things today that He did during the time of the apostles. He's coming in and breaking down the barriers that have separated Jesus' people for so long. He's getting around the Scribes and Pharisees of today, restoring fresh life to dry formalism.

I'm excited about the meeting in my house that's been going for about eight years now. It's a real joy to praise the Lord there with Baptists, Methodists, Episcopalians, Presbyterians, Catholics, old-line Pentecostals, and lots of others. It's so great to worship together and pray for one another, and share the love of Jesus. That's what the Spirit is doing today: bringing together the Body of Christ.

It could be that you've read this far in the book and are still bewildered about all this talk of the Holy Spirit. Well, I want to assure you that He's still around today! Have you ever received the Baptism in the Holy Spirit? The Bible says that the Father will give the Spirit to those who ask for Him. Why don't you, if you haven't done it already, ask the Lord to baptize you with the Holy Spirit right now?

Building Through Struggle

"Commit thy way unto the Lord; trust also in Him; and He shall bring it to pass."
Psalm 37:4

Kenneth R. Schmidt
Pastor/Evangelist/Author

Faith must be built in us through submission to God's will, not through struggle. Jesus said that "Many will say to me in that day, Lord, Lord . . . and then will I profess to them, I never knew you . . ." (Matthew 7:22-23a). Many people make public confessions of faith but never submit to God's will in their life.

Easy times don't build faith, trouble does. Where you stand in God becomes clear in your response to the problems you have. The time for this verse to become operative in my life has been when I've faced adverse circumstances, when I've been tense and frustrated. It's then that I've learned the blessing of a God to whom I can give the struggle.

When my first wife died of cancer a few years ago, I can't say I had an easy time accepting it. I had had a vision in which I saw my whole family taken up in the rapture, while I was left behind. This had moved my heart closer to God, but I had no idea that soon the "other half" as dear as myself would really be taken away. In my grief and questioning, in my thrashing it out with God, this verse is what sustained me. I couldn't change the situation. I couldn't alter what had happened. If I hadn't had the Lord, I don't know what I'd have done. The Lord blessed me with another mate, miraculously dear, once I had really commited my way to Him.

The world today is at an impasse, striving to bring something good out of sin and death. It can't be done. Your life may seem like a tangle of frustration right now. It's not in your hands to straighten it out. It's God who'll bring to pass the peaceful, eternally meaningful outcome. Is your life really committed to Him? Have you really trusted Him with your all? Will you let Him have His way from now on?

The Sixfold Gift Of Jesus

"Bless the Lord, O my soul: and all that is within me, bless His holy name."

Psalm 103:1

Virginia Lively
Healing Ministry

The Lord gifted me some time ago with a continual vision of Jesus for three months of my life that changed me completely. Whether I was awake or slept, His face was always before me. He appeared to me with shoulder-length, flowing brown hair, and a face of mid-Eastern cast, smooth and brown-skinned. His eyes were like pools of love, and He smiled constantly. I could feel love radiate from Him.

As I meditated on this vision day and night, I was led to Psalm 103, the opening five verses of which gave me a sixfold picture of a Lord who was Love itself, as the Jerusalem Bible puts it:

. . . in forgiving all your offenses,
   in curing all your diseases,
   in redeeming your life from the Pit,
   in crowning you with love and tenderness,
   in filling your years with prosperity,
   in renewing your youth like an eagle's.

If we would only commit these six things to memory and get them into our hearts, we would never again doubt the Lord. Whatever the problem, whatever the disease, whatever the financial need, or the effect of aging, Jesus is there with the answer and the supply.

Would you take time right now to consider this sixfold description of our loving Christ? Think of its meaning for you in your present need. Do you have need right now of forgiveness? Do you seek healing for your body? Have you assurance of your redemption? Do you need a touch of love in your heart? Are your pressing needs material? Have you need of strength and energy? Let your faith reach out for Jesus right now. Touch Him, and find your need met!

Creative Love

"Submitting yourselves one to another in the fear of God."   *Ephesians 5:21*

Dr. David Webb
Family Physician

The strength of family life lies right here. God has been giving me a concept that's really excited me and changed my life: Let me call it Creative Love. This is the love that a person demonstrates as they relate to another person and help that person to be recreated, to cause a new life to grow. Out of this new life comes a new life form, and the form is one of service to the Lord and to one another.

When Jesus loves us, something within us is caused to happen: new creation, new growth. Zaccheus becomes a new person, Simon becomes Peter, Saul becomes Paul. To love another person creatively, causing them to grow, is what submission is all about. This is what the Lord did for us on the cross: He loved us by submitting Himself to us.

A man must do this to his wife. A wife must do this to her husband. Both must do this to their children. When people complain that another person doesn't love them, what they're really saying is that that person is not doing the things that make them feel good. What we need to do is to ask about those close to us, "What kinds of things can I do to help these individuals grow, to fulfill themselves, to become people better than they were a year ago?" And then, we need to do those things and serve in a spirit of humility.

Does this seem difficult? Jesus did it for you. As a result of that submitting love, Jesus made you a new person. I pray that you'll really meditate on Jesus' love for you today. If He so loved His disciples as to wash their feet, to be the servant of all, with how willing hearts ought we to be concerned with ministering to others' needs, especially to those nearest and dearest to us?

Rule That Moment

". . . And who knoweth whether thou art come to the kingdom for such a time as this?" Esther 4:14b

Fred Frank
Singer

There's always a purpose in where we are, though we might not always understand it. We need to trust the Lord in all the circumstances of our lives—even when we're upset with the circumstances.

I went through a painful divorce over four and a half years ago. I didn't enjoy it. I wasn't a Christian at the time, and it was this experience that brought me to the Lord. So I learned from the start of my Christian life, and I am learning, that even when the chips are down, and things aren't going the way I'd like them to, to say, "Lord, thank you! I don't know why this is going on, and I don't like it. But I know that you're doing something good in my life, even in the middle of this, to help me to be a better person."

A lot of things that happen to us, we may not connect with being a part of kingdom living. They don't make sense. Wouldn't it be easier if we could be kings in an ideal world? It's not always easy to see yourself as a king in a world that will despise and reject you, just as it hated King Jesus when He was down here. But there are millions of people and moments in this hurting world that need the touch of a king. God says that's me. I don't always want to be king over the predicament I'm in. But God won't stop teaching me to rule.

You may have cause to wonder many times today, "What am I doing in the middle of this problem?" But God may be asking you this question: "How do you know that you weren't brought into My kingdom for a moment just like this?" God must have known that only you were fit to rule that moment. Thank God for that opportunity to be a king for Him. Try ruling. You'll start to like it!

A Glimpse Of Perfection

"Greater love hath no man than this, that a man lay down his life for his friends . . ." John 15:13

Dr. John R. Hornbrook
Author/Counselor

One day not long ago, an atheist, a woman who wouldn't believe in a God she couldn't see, snapped a photograph of an unusual cloud formation that was hovering in the sky. When the roll of film was developed, she became a Christian on the spot. For this picture, the last on the roll, was that of her loving Savior Jesus, who cared enough for her to leave heaven so that she could catch a glimpse of Him on film.

When this picture came into my hands, it didn't remain just a curiosity. Through it, Jesus became alive and personal to me also, transforming my life from one of outward success and inner defeat to one of a life laid down completely for God's service. I looked at the picture and felt His warm presence before me, face to face. I literally saw Him in all His glory, it seemed to me. He led me from there into an individual ministry in giving my life for others, and then into a worldwide ministry as larger doors opened before me.

If God was able to use a photograph so powerfully, imagine what Jesus' personal impact must have had upon those who had eyes to see who He was! "He that hath seen Me," Jesus said, "hath seen the Father" (John 14:9). Jesus Himself in the flesh was a "portrait" of the Father! Imagine what it must have been like for Him to come down in person to this earth, that His friends might see and walk with Him!

What will it be like to one day see Him as He is, King of Kings, and Lord of Lords? Scripture says that we will be like Him when we see Him as He is (I John 3:2). The glimpse of Him that He's given each of us who know Him ought to make us more like Him today: self-giving, loving, and strong in God. As He gave His life for us and to us, we ought to lay our lives down for one another more and more each day.

Learn To Lean

"Trust in the Lord with all thine heart; and lean not unto thine own understanding. In all thy ways acknowledge Him, and He shall direct thy paths."

Proverbs 3:5-6

Rev. Ernest Moen
Pastor

Jesus must be first. The priority of our life must be our Lord. If He is in the proper position, everything else falls in order. I've found this true in a lifetime of living and Christian ministry. When Jesus is first, everything in life will be supplied and taken care of.

It is often a temptation in life to lean on our own understanding. Trusting the Lord must be an act of the will, a position under His authority we must take. We must consider in every decision: Is this my own will or inclination, desire, or drive? In doing this thing, can I glorify Christ and extend His kingdom?

I honestly believe that the Lord wants us to use our common sense. He gave us a brain. When I get up in the morning, I have to synchronize my clothes in proper taste. I have to drive on the right side of the road. I have to choose the right food, and that's common sense.

But beyond that, there is the posture of leaning upon the Lord and trusting Him. I have learned to trust God in the little things. It's easy in the big things like marriage, career, occupation, relocation, and other major decisions. But it's delightful to have the Lord lead us in little things also. A good rule of thumb to follow is, whenever in doubt about anything, great or small, ask the Lord about it.

You may have large decisions to face today. There may be only little problems facing you. To God, the size of the experience isn't important. Putting Him and His interests first is what will please Him. Would you like Him to order this day successfully for you? Determine right now to glorify Him in all things and share your whole life with Him.

Soul-Prospering

"Beloved, I wish above all things that thou mayest prosper and be in health, even as thy soul prospereth."
3 John vs. 2

Pat Moehring
Pianist/Choral Director

When my husband and I started realizing that God's best for us meant having enough money to pay the bills, that He wanted us to be in good health, and have our material needs met, we didn't forget that this verse had a second part, too. Your soul has to prosper as well!

So many people want to get rich or just come to God when things are difficult. They have a lot of dreams that cave in because their souls haven't been prospering. You don't develop faith in a minute or a day. People find themselves with incurable diseases, but don't have the faith for healing because they've never trusted God with a head cold. If you've been taught that you can't expect God to always heal, faith won't be generated in you. Faith comes by hearing the Word of God. God is no respecter of persons. He *will* heal if His promise is met with faith. He *will* meet those needs. But faith has to cut its teeth on little things before it's ready for greater things.

"Death and life are in the power of the tongue" (Proverbs 18:21). We need to make our confession positive, like God's Word. We learned the tongue's creative power when we faced a debt of $250,000 from a business that failed. Someone told us of the power of faith, and we just kept confessing that the debt was paid. Bit by bit, that huge debt melted away within two years. All the money came in by faith. There was no bankruptcy. We made sure we gave God His portion of every penny He brought to us, and He multiplied it back.

We've made a list of the promises of God for every life situation. We suggest that you do the same, and read it aloud, as we do, every morning. Then, grow in believing and confessing the Word in little things and watch your soul prosper!

Healing For Now

". . . Bless the Lord, O my soul . . . and forget not all His benefits: Who forgiveth all thine iniquities; Who healeth all thy diseases."
Psalm 103:1-3

Rose Schmidt
Bible Teacher

If there's any disease the word "dreaded" *should* describe, it's diphtheria. When I was twelve years old, the effective vaccines we have now weren't as readily available. So, as far as the doctors were concerned, there wasn't too much hope of my living long after I caught it.

First, my whole throat and tonsil area became totally swelled and inflamed. Then I lapsed into a coma. About ten days later, I awoke from that, so weakened that my doctor said there was no way I could live for long. So they sent me home, and a few days after that, I collapsed on a short walk, totally paralyzed, unable to move a muscle. There was nothing for me but a slow, wasting death.

But my parents were part of a fellowship with a strong belief in the healing power of God. As I lay there one night, my Mom and Dad and a group of their friends gathered around me and sought God for my healing. A moment later, the power of God filled my body, and I instantly got up and walked! I walked from the bedroom to the living room, and have been walking ever since!

Friend in Christ, let me tell you something: even doctors admit that they don't heal anybody. All they can do is prepare the body to receive healing. The great Healer is truly Jesus Christ!

Do you believe God for the forgiveness of all your sins? This passage of scripture says you can. It also says that God heals all your diseases. Almighty God can touch your infirmity right now, if you will reach out in faith to Him. Yes, right now, Jesus can heal even you. Believe Him this moment, and receive His healing touch!

God Is For You!

"What shall we then say to these things? If God be for us, who can be against us?"
Romans 8:31

Richard Dortch
Dist. Supt.
Illinois Assembly of God

Jesus said on one occasion that in this world, "ye shall have tribulation" (John 16:33). I'm not claiming this by faith. There are some people who seem to claim persecution and problems by faith. We don't have to do that. Troubles are going to come along without our asking just because we're part of the human family. Not that we'll always have the devil buffeting us, either, though we know he will at times. Difficulties are our portion in an imperfect world.

How wonderful in the face of all "these things" to have the resolute knowledge that God is for us! We can be buffeted and hit and attacked, but nothing can stand against us if we keep the power of God in the forefront of our mind.

This is what holds me steady. You name the problem, I've had it. As a child, I had rheumatic fever and was unable to walk for three months. I was a missionary for seven years. My daughter had polio. Our house burned down. We've had heartbreak in our family over our children, though they're all now serving God. But that serenity of spirit, that peace that only He can bring, stems from that knowledge that *He will not fail!*

The last part of Isaiah 40:31 is precious to me: "they shall walk, and not faint." I will not faint. I may lose the battle, but I'm not going to lose the war! There haven't been many days when I've stayed down because the Lord has raised me up!

Yes, there are a lot of things in life that threaten our peace every day. But if we know in Whom we have believed, we can expect Him to keep us out of "the pits." Isn't it great to live out your days knowing that He's for you? Keep in that confidence all day today!

A Just God And You

"Give therefore thy servant an understanding heart to judge thy people, that I may discern between good and bad..."   *I Kings 3:9a*

Chuck Colson
Prison Evangelist

One of the most neglected areas of Christian understanding today is the justice of God. God *is* a God of love, and that's how most of us know Him. But He's also a God of justice. God was so pleased with the above prayer of Solomon for wisdom because it evidenced a concern for the kind of discernment that would bring justice to God's people.

Scripture speaks much of justice. This fact has been somewhat obscured by our familiarity with the King James Version of the Bible, in which the word for "justice" is most frequently translated "judgment." The Psalms are full of promises that God will some day administer perfect justice. Justice in ancient days was often sold at a premium to the highest bidder, a practice not altogether dead in our country today. Promises are made by God to free prisoners in the Old Testament, and Jesus echoed these promises as part of the Good News He preached personally. The depth of God's concern for justice has considerable bearing on my ministry with prisoners. If justice was a vital concern for God, it ought to be for me also, just as much as love and compassion.

We as Christians cannot reflect all of the Spirit of God and be unconcerned with human justice issues. We as Christians can't live life in a cocoon, merely satisfied with our own piety and spirituality, ignoring the demands of justice in society. That's why I'm trying to focus attention on the plight of prisoners. If our religion is strictly a private matter, we are not reflecting the Bible's strong emphasis on political and social issues. Like it or not, we are all involved in the system of law in our land. The question involved is, "Are we as involved in the cause of God's justice as we ought to be here and now?"

A Divine Destiny

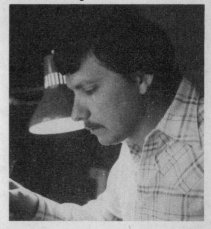

"Who hath saved us, and called us with a holy calling . . . according to His own purpose . . . Be ye therefore perfect . . ."

2 Timothy 1:9a
Matthew 5:48a

Robert Paul Lamb
Author/Bible Teacher

Many Christians don't understand that when God redeemed them, it was for a specific purpose that He had in mind. It wasn't just to take up space on a pew in some church in a particular location. God has planned a path of fulfillment for the life of every Christian.

God expects us to find that path. The scripture above from Matthew always puzzled me. The more I looked at it, the more I said to myself, "There's no way that I could ever be perfect, and if there's any way of blowing it in life, I'll find a way of doing it." But I began to study this verse and discovered that the word "perfect" comes from the Greek word, "teleos," which means a job or calling, or a plan. It's almost like having finished a race for a runner who's met his goal for that race. So, a perfect person is one who has fulfilled the purpose for which he was originally created.

Now I see that verse in an entirely different light. A perfect person isn't a model person, with no faults and the best manners. A perfect person is one fulfilling his divine destiny. Every born-again person has a destiny in God. We can fulfill that destiny by simply yielding our lives to Jesus Christ, receiving the infilling of the Holy Spirit, and fulfilling the thing God's called us to do, utilizing the gifts that are in us. Or we can thwart that destiny.

You have a destiny in you that began to be unleashed when you met God. He began shifting gears at that time, pointing you in that direction. There is nothing more fulfilling than being a part of that perfect path. Ask God to show you His perfect plan for today.

The Light

". . . I am the light of the world: he that followeth Me shall not walk in darkness, but shall have the light of life."
John 8:12

"Mama" Leo Rousseau
Pastor/Evangelist

It was long ago, in 1932. I was a young woman, from a proud heritage, bitter, enraged at God for having taken my father in the prime of his life. When I first heard the gospel from the lips of a Mexican evangelist who spoke near my home in Puerto Rico, I threw rocks at him. I shouted, "I don't want to hear from such a God! How could He be good and take my father?"

Two of my brothers had died from heart conditions, weakened by the life of grief and poverty following Father's death. Now I, too, was dying with heart disease, young, and more angry than ever at God. Some Spirit-filled Christians had heard of my plight and said they would pray for me. Nothing could have displeased me more.

I was in great anguish of soul, as great as was my pride. I waited for the night to come, to hide my face and cry. There was no one with whom to share this pain. One morning long before dawn, my heart began to jump rapidly, and I thought death had come. Just then I heard a voice telling me to kneel and pray.. At first I refused, but then the moonlight pierced through the blinds. As I went to close them, I fell on my knees and looked up to see a shining person. He spread His arms and said, "I am the light of the world!"

These words entered my heart with such authority, such kindness and love. I knew that here was help. I knew that there was no other light. It was Jesus. He healed me. He saved me. He gave me over the years, a vision for the souls of the discarded, the sick, the addicts, the prostitutes. He loves them. He wants them. He wants all of you. He would place His light within you, to drive away the darkness. Will you let Him today?

Help In Trouble

"Then they cry unto the Lord in their trouble, and He bringeth them out of their distresses."   Psalm 107:28

Gene Beaver
Missionary

We became very thankful for this verse while out on the mission field. We were stationed in Nicaragua for about one and a half years. The country was very troubled, wracked by civil war. As foreign ministers of the gospel, we were in worse danger. We were accosted by rebels and robbed. And as the political situation fermented and grew more violent, our lives were more and more threatened.

This scripture brought us assurance that He was still with us. It became evident before long that we would have to leave the country. At times we wondered whether we would suceed in getting out. The Lord confirmed to us that He would make a way through Psalm 121:8: "The Lord shall preserve thy going out and thy coming in from this time forth, and even for evermore." God had promised to keep us. And He did bring us out safely, protecting us from all harm during our journey.

God never promised to keep Christians from trouble or keep us from going through trouble. But He did promise us that we'd be able to go through it. And when we come to the place where our limitations are exhausted, God will open a door for us to escape. He will then bring us to our desired haven, stilling the storms and angry waves in our way.

Sometimes trouble is the only thing that will get us to cry out to the Lord. Today, you will probably confront your share of trouble. Danger may arise out of your being tempted. Your faith may be tried. God hasn't guaranteed that your path will be empty of obstacles. But as you seek Him in the midst of hard situations, He will undertake on your behalf to bring you to safety. Don't hesitate to call on Him!

Discipline Your Druthers

"Delight thyself also in the Lord; and He shall give thee the desires of thine heart."   *Psalm 37:4*

Suzy Hamblen
Composer/Singer/Speaker

The two surest facts of life for every born-again believer are that because God loves us He will never leave us and every promise we claim in the Bible He will fulfill.

When I discovered Psalm 37:4, it thrilled me to think God will give me the very desires of my heart. This phrase of the verse has always brought me encouragement when I felt down and out and sometimes doubted God's plan for me. Claiming this promise always renews my hope and gives me great expectancy of what God has in store.

But I have learned that in order to receive the blessings God promises, I must fulfill the condition stated in the first part of the verse—to delight myself in the Lord.

This is difficult when I act out of my old nature . . . like times when I would rather flip on the television than open my Bible and spend time with Jesus in obedience to God's instruction to "attend to my Word" (Psalm 4:21). Or I'd rather stay home than go see a friend the Holy Spirit is prompting me to visit.

I have learned that delighting in the Lord requires disciplining my "druthers" and choosing God's way at all times. Delighting in the Lord is praising Him in all things, obeying Him in my daily walk, and showing my love for Him by loving others.

It's true, self-discipline may hurt for a moment, but I have discovered it opens the floodgate of God's joy and peace. Delight yourself in the Lord by praising and obeying God and loving others. When you do, you will receive the desires of your heart.

It Is No Secret

"But they that wait upon the Lord shall renew their strength; they shall mount up with wings as eagles; they shall run and not be weary; and they shall walk, and not faint." Isaiah 40:31

Stuart Hamblen
Singer/Songwriter

It was just thirty years ago that I thought my life was a "goner." My career had risen and fallen. And because of my desire to drink and fight, it seemed like my life was heading downhill for the last time.

As the son of an itinerant Methodist preacher, maybe my life shouldn't have gone this way. But then, I couldn't figure out what God wanted with me. My folks wanted me to teach school, but I wanted to sing. Back in those days, however, we thought musical careers, at least in sacred music, were for women.

When God finally stopped me long enough to get me to wait on Him (through a Billy Graham meeting in 1949), He gave me a new inner strength that I never knew was available. God's creative strength is much greater than anything the world can offer.

For me, it was giving Him my natural talents and love for music and allowing Him to use it for good. The result was God giving me the first sacred song written for the pop market—"It Is No Secret." Not only did it become a hit, it started a whole new trend by which thousands have come to Christ through hearing Christian music.

Thirty years later, I am more active, having more fun, and have got more to live for than ever before. God has the same kind of creative energy and strength available for you, too. Just wait upon Him and give Him your all. He'll show you something great to do that'll help change our world for good.

Let God Pick You Up

"I can do all things through Christ which strengtheneth me."
Philippians 4:13

Sue Ellen Dodge
Singer

There have been times in my life when I've felt low, without a word from God, and unable to accomplish all I wanted to. In personal, spiritual, and family areas, nothing was "clicking." During one of these phases, my husband preached a sermon based on the verse above.

"Never say, 'I can't,'" he cried, "With Christ, all things are possible. No matter how low you feel, always know that your self-worth in God's eyes is much greater than your own. I feel that with God's help, anything that I want to accomplish that's in His will, I can do."

Well, it's possible to hear from God even when your husband's the preacher! He really got through to me that day. But though this scripture did sink into my heart, it wasn't long before it was put to the test. This past June, we went through an extremely difficult time in our ministry, feeling like there really wasn't a place for it. I'm one of those people whose health starts to break down when I'm tense and nervous. I kept saying, "I just can't make it," I was ready to chuck the ministry, not to sing anymore, because I felt I wasn't needed. But all of a sudden that verse kept coming to me over and over again: "I can! I can!" With that, I picked it all up, and now I feel better spiritually, emotionally, and physically than I've felt in years and years! I wake up in the morning feeling something good's going to happen, rather than looking for the bad. I know I can make it!

You can, too, you know! You may not feel sometimes like you can get through, but God's Word says you can. So you've got to start agreeing with Him. You're worth a lot to Him. And He cares enough to make you able. Don't say you can't. Yes, really, you can! Give it a try!

Trying Your Faith

"My brethren, count it all joy when ye fall into divers temptations; Knowing this, that the trying of your faith worketh patience."

James 1:2-3

Tim Foli
Major League Shortstop

Playing major league baseball is not an easy life for a Christian. There are a lot of temptations and ups and downs every day. I can be playing really well and be the hero of the crowds. Then I can get into a slump and have the fans needling me. I can start thinking that my career is coming to an end. Baseball is a young man's sport, and it can all be over just like that.

My wife packs up our whole house three times a year. That's how often the family, kids and all, relocates. At these different homes, my daughter has to change schools. The hours on my job constantly change. I go to bed at three o'clock one morning, get up and go the the ballpark for an afternoon game. The food's not regular, and just the traveling gets to you after a while. It's not hard to get envious towards other players; your pride can take over; you can get embarrassed over mistakes; so many things happen, like a whirlwind around you all the time.

So the Lord brings the trials, and Satan brings the temptations. But Jesus said that these would come. And for a purpose: I learn patience for living. That's why I can meet the difficult things with joy. There's something good tucked into everything that seems bad. So I don't run away from the trials God gives me. They have a work to do in me, and I try to work hard and stand on God's Word. That's my strength.

You'll always come out on top if you keep God on top. If you can keep in mind that He's using trials to improve you, you can let them channel you right into His perfect will. Thank God for the trials you're going to experience today. And ask Him to make clear what He's trying to teach you through them. Be patient with Him—and yourself!

Move Towards Your Goal

"I press toward the mark for the prize of the high calling of God in Christ Jesus." *Philippians 3:14*

Neil Eskelin
Author/Motivator

Today, you need to do something specific to help you reach your highest goal. You have one: how are you going to reach it?

What is that objective? Can you describe it? Do you see it clearly?

Most people waste a large portion of the 86,400 seconds they are granted each day. We usually don't think in terms of seconds or even minutes. Instead, we waste hours of time with activities seldom related to that goal tucked away in our mind.

It reminds me of the three boys who were playing in the snow. A man walked up and said, "Would you like to try a new kind of race? I'll give the winner a prize."

The boys quickly agreed, and the man told them that the race would be one that required skill. "I will go to the other side of the field," he explained, "and when I give you the signal, you will start to run. The one whose footsteps are the straightest in the snow will be declared the winner."

The race began, and the first boy kept looking at his feet to see if his steps were straight. The second fellow kept looking at his friends to see what they were doing. But the third boy just ran on with his eyes fixed on the man at the other side of the field.

The third boy won the race because his steps were straight in the snow. He kept his eyes firmly on the objective.

There is a powerful lesson we can learn from the boys. Why not put it into practice?

Today, make your minutes count. The highest goal is to fulfill your calling in Christ. Make His will your goal. Keep moving straight towards Him.

God Never Backs Down On His Word

"This is my comfort in my affliction: for Thy Word hath quickened me."
Psalm 119:50

Walt Mills
Singer/Evangelist

The Bible says that "Whoso despiseth the Word shall be destroyed" (Proverbs 13:13). Jesus said, "You do err, not knowing the scriptures" (Matthew 22:29). He quoted scripture to Satan: "Man shall not live by bread alone, but by every word that proceedeth out of the mouth of God" (Matthew 4:4). The Word of God is utterly important to keeping our lives in balance.

Whenever people have laid aside the Word of God, they have become law unto themselves. Always, man by himself has never attained enough knowledge to maintain his balance. The result of sin and lawlessness has been, and always will be, death and decay, sickness and misery.

The Psalmist wasn't immune to all this. Neither are we, in those times when we forget God's Word and try to live by our own rules. We are always eventually going to find ourselves afflicted in some way, out of touch with God and our brethren, dry spiritually, and listless physically.

This is where this scripture becomes really important. If God just let us continue to suffer the full consequences of our straying from Him, we'd be in a really bad way. When we're in trouble, we need a Word from the Lord to comfort us and impart life to us. God has given us His Holy Spirit also, to build our spirits up and give wings to His Word in our daily walk.

Perhaps you have drifted away from that close fellowship with the Lord that you once held so dear. There is comfort for you today. His Word can quicken you, bring you refreshment, and restore that lost joy. Set aside time today to prayerfully, diligently seek Him in His Word. He will meet you, and move you back into victory.

Wait For The Fulfillment

"For the vision is yet for an appointed time . . . though it tarry, wait for it; because it will surely come, it will not tarry." Habakkuk 2:3

Dick Mills
Evangelist/Author

You have looked back, remembering the vision I gave you. With this vision came also an assurance of a work I would do in your life.

You have waited for fulfillment. You have waited for the prophecy to come to pass. You have waited long, wondering when . . .

The enemy of your soul has tried to flood your mind with doubts. He has even suggested that you repudiate the promise I made you. He has suggested that you reject the dream I gave you—that you refuse the vision, casting it off as something spurious and unreal.

But—the vision is for an *appointed time*. Even as My Word was given to Mary regarding those things I would do for her at an appointed time, so you must wait for the appointed time of your vision.

You shall have your performance. You shall have your fulfillment. I, the Lord, am the Author and Finisher of your faith. I authored the vision. I began it. And I will finish it.

In the mean time, I am preparing you, conditioning you, training you, disciplining you, that you might be ready for the hour of My visitation.

In this time of waiting, I have shown you many things. I have developed longsuffering and patience within you.

Soon, the time will come for fulfillment.

I, who have spoken to you, will shortly bring My Word to pass. My promise will not be delayed without purpose. That which I have spoken to you *shall be done*.

"My covenant will I not break, nor alter the thing that is gone out of my lips" (Psalm 89:34).

Excerpted with permission from *He Spoke, and I was Strengthened,* Cop. 1973, Whitaker House, Springdale, PA.

Ages of Grace

"That in the ages to come He might show the exceeding riches of His grace in His kindness toward us through Christ Jesus." Ephesians 2:7

Dr. Nelson B. Melvin
Editor, VOICE magazine

We are certainly richly blessed by God's grace here and now. We are forgiven, gifted with eternal life, sealed with the Holy Spirit, quickened unto new life from the death of trespasses and sin, and raised up to sit with Christ in heavenly places. Hallelujah! What a heritage!

And yet this verse opens our eyes to an even deeper purpose in the mind of God that we can only begin to imagine. Here we get a glimmer of an amazing prospect: that God has riches upon riches of grace to unveil to us, not only during this present age, but during ages upon ages to come! What we are enjoying in this life is only a beginning!

What more can possibly be in store for us? What will life be like when this old heaven and earth have passed away and the new has come. There God Himself will be the light, all things will be under the feet of the King of Kings. There will be no regrets, no tears to dim the eye. There will be no more division within Christ's Body, nor will there even be any remembrance of wickedness or sin. There will be no obstacles to our becoming all that God has planned us eternally to be. We will be unable to imagine any more than the complete fullness of seeing God all in all!

Just think: no matter how you have been blessed in this life, you have ages of joy to look forward to! The whole purpose of God's bringing you into new life was to begin to pour out His love and goodness upon you. How much this should inspire gratitude and faithful service in us all. O let this bright hope illumine all our days and make us generous in spreading our blessings to others.

Living Out Christ

"I am crucified with Christ: nevertheless I live; yet not I, but Christ liveth in me: and the life I now live in the flesh I live by the faith of the Son of God, Who loved me and gave Himself for me."

Galatians 2:20

John Perkins
Pastor/Author

This was the verse that caused me to really think about where I stood with God. The Holy Spirit began to use it to convict me of sin. At that time back in 1957, I realized that I was without Christ and that Christianity was not just the religion that I was used to seeing. Christianity was the outliving of the inliving Christ.

I had been an elementary school dropout. But when He saved me, God gave me a vision for a ministry among the black community. It started with a grassroots discipleship work in rural Mississippi. I had a burning desire to see young black people equipped not only to preach the gospel, but to meet some of the basic needs of poor people in the name of Jesus, just as He did here on earth.

Saved souls are not just to be salvation statistics. I wanted to train people to get down to earth with one another. A living involvement with people turns poor people from statistics into friends. I'm not willing to lay down my life for a statistic. But I am more willing to lay down my life for my friends. As Christians, we have to minister to the whole man, as Jesus did. Out of this concern has grown a variety of community services: health center, educational programs, libraries, a cooperative farm and housing project, a gymnasium, Bible studies, youth ministries, a print shop, a bookstore, and much more.

The possibilities for doing good in our world are almost limitless. But to do this kind of good requires a commitment in the natural realm not just the spiritual. God may speak to you to have a part, great or small, in being an extension of His loving hands on this earth. Be open, to lending your hands, as well as your heart.

Real Satisfaction

"Yea doubtless, and I count all things but loss for the excellency of the knowledge of Christ Jesus my Lord . . ." Philippians 3:8a

Tom Netherton
Singer

In the world's terms, the apostle Paul had lost a lot by the time he wrote this verse from prison. Some might even say that he had wasted his entire education, health, reputation, freedom, and livelihood by following Jesus Christ. Yet he was bold enough to say that without a single doubt, Jesus meant more than all these things.

People tend to think that the things of this life are more important than they really are. A lot of people who've seen me on television have come and told me, "Tom, I wish I were you. You have everything that a man would need to be happy." But I tell them that the outward things don't bring happiness and contentment. If all of that were thrown away, I could still have happiness because of knowing Jesus, because He's the center of my life.

You see, the love of God can't be taken away from you if you belong to Jesus. Fame, wealth, and the admiration of people can be very short-lived. I'm truly grateful to God for my ability to sing, and for the success I've enjoyed. But these were all gifts from His hand, at His disposal. They don't belong to me. But God's love is available to everyone in Jesus Christ, from housewives and plumbers to queens and kings.

We should never envy another person for the things that they have or the limelight they're in. The tangible things in life don't really count, and they can never bring us fellowship with one another. In Christ, I can enjoy being a "regular" person, and being with "regular" people. For we have in common friendship and love for the greatest person the world has ever known, Jesus Christ. Now that's what I call really satisfying!

Taking The Land

> *"Every place that the sole of your foot shall tread upon, that have I given unto you, as I said unto Moses."*
> Joshua 1:3

Larry Titus
Pastor

Israel's possession of the land of Canaan is in many ways a type, or illustration of the personal walk of each Christian believer.

Possession of the land itself was the fulfillment of God's promise to Israel made in Egypt. But whereas in the wilderness, God did everything for these people, feeding them, defending them, supplying their every need, once they got into the land, *they* had to begin to do everything for themselves. Their possession meant that they had to tread across that land and claim it, meeting giants and walled cities all the way.

Just so, many Christians think that when they come into spiritual maturity, they will arrive at a state in which they can sit down and take it easy. The problem is that when you enter the "land" of maturity, that's when the "giants" and "enemies" and "walled cities" start meeting you in earnest! Yes, in the land of the abundant life, everywhere you tread, Satan will be under your feet. But every time you step on his head, he's going to inflict a wound on your feet!

It's when you're on the verge of accomplishing something in God that the enemy opposes most strongly. God gave us a vision for a church, schools, radio stations, publishing enterprises, and a promise that He would give us the territory we lived in on a wave of His glory. The price we had to pay to bring this to reality ranged from persecution to giving up our own home to constant spiritual battles. But we won!

The more you mature in the things of God, the more battles you'll face. You'll confront difficulties and active opposition, and you'll pay a price: Jesus always promised His followers they would. But His victory will be your victory if you'll press on and never give up trusting in Him and His promise that the good land is yours.

The Virtuous Woman

"Favor is deceitful, and beauty is vain: but a woman who feareth the Lord, she shall be praised. Give her of the fruit of her hands; and let her own works praise her in the gates."   Proverbs 31:31

Devi Titus
Wife/Magazine Editor

Women in today's world are crying out for fulfillment, many of them never realizing the great concern that God's Word shows for their happiness and the high value God places upon women in His kingdom.

This scripture is the culmination of a remarkable chapter extolling the many virtues and accomplishments of the sort of woman who is truly fulfilling God's purpose for her life. Consider for a moment all that this woman's talents have encompassed. She has earned the trust of her husband, and what she does is always best for him as well as herself (vs. 11-12). She makes fine clothing, is involved in merchandising, supervises others in her household (vs. 13-15). She deals in real estate and plants a vineyard (vs 16). She keeps herself in good physical condition (vs. 17). She is a talented craftswoman (vs. 18-19), she is generous to the needy (vs. 20). She is fearless (vs.21), her husband holds a position of authority (vs. 23), she is known as skillful, strong, honorable, wise, kind, and diligent (vs. 24-27). Her children and her husband praise her highly. And no wonder! If this is what God thinks a woman ought to be, I'm all for it!

What a shame it is that women of such accomplishment have neglected to undertake the teaching of younger women "to love their husbands, love their children, to be discreet, chaste, keepers at home" (Titus 2:4-5). Such women have no need to seek for praise; their own works, as this scripture says, will cry out for praise, among men, as well as other women.

Have you accepted Satan's myth that God-fearing women must be doormats or second-rate human beings? Has your life been lacking in fulfillment? Emulate this terrific woman. Do all that you can to the glory of God, and let your works praise you, too!

His Perfect Path

"Thou wilt show me the path of life; in Thy presence is fullness of joy; at Thy right hand there are pleasures for evermore." Psalm 16:11

Vern McLellan
Senior Vice President
PTL Div. of World Missions

This is a strong, personalized declaration from the Psalmist, something that I have been able to rely upon as an individual. God has a keen interest in me; He has a distinctive concern about my life's direction and my fulfilling His purpose for me in this world. And if I will follow clearly that master plan, God has promised His abiding presence, fullness of joy in this life, and continued pleasures for all eternity.

In each of our lives, God has a good, better, or best arrangement of its elements. I've had to make some critically important decisions at various junctions of my life. Before Jim Bakker invited me to become Director of World Missions for PTL, I had three other opportunities at the same time, one with another Christian television network, another with a well-known literature ministry overseas, and third, an offer of the pastorate of a fine church in California. All of these were good opportunities; I could have been content in any one of them. But I had a responsibility to determine where I could best serve the Lord. I said to the Lord, *"You* show me the path I should take." As soon as I made the decision to come to PTL, confirmations came to indicate that I had moved in the right direction, and that the Lord was pleased with the steps I had taken.

You need to ask yourself, especially as you make decisions between the good things God may send your way, "How can I find the way that God would find most fulfilling for my life? Each of these possibilities may be interesting and satisfying. But where can I do most for His honor and glory?" If you will seek God's best, and obey the direction He gives you, He will prove this scripture and reveal to you the joy of walking in His perfect path.

Understanding Why

"For whom He did fore-know, He also did predesti-nate to be conformed to the image of His Son, that He might be the firstborn among many brethren." Romans 8:29

Dr. Robert Frost
Biologist/Author

The whole intent of this passage is that within the very heart of God our Father, He has a plan and purpose for each of His children. It is His desire to have a family of sons and daughters through whom He can bring forth the life of His Son to be extended and manifested to others.

By realizing the full significance of Romans 8:29, we can better understand the preceding and very familiar verse, Romans 8:28: "And we know that all things work together for good to them that love God, to them that are the called according to His purpose."

We often quote verse 28 when facing seemingly needless circum-stances that award us only suffering and heartbreak. The phrases "all things work together for good" and "according to His purpose," offer us a light at the end of the tunnel. By claiming this verse we trust that there is a good purpose being accomplished behind the present miserable-ness of our circumstances.

Romans 8:29 explains that good purpose: the Father conforming us to the image of His Son. God is continually working in us, changing us from glory to glory (2 Corinthians 3:18) that we might individually and corporately become as a family. Every difficulty as well as every joy we encounter, God allows for the ultimate purpose of bringing us into a greater likeness of Jesus.

As we understand this truth, and respond to God, then we can appreciate the hardships we experience. God is the Clearance Official by whom all circumstances, trials, and temptations must pass before they can come our way. And He is the Basic Foundation upon which everything will arrive. Ask yourself how much you desire to be like Jesus. Then take a few minutes to thank God for how He is using your present circumstances to make you more like Him.

He Can Hear And Save

"Behold, the Lord's hand is not shortened, that it cannot save; neither His ear heavy, that it cannot hear."
Isaiah 59:1-2

Sister Francis Clare
Teacher/Author

The Lord spoke this scripture to me and a Christian sister after a very hair-raising experience that nearly took our lives.

A few years ago while enroute home after speaking at a service in a nearby town, we hit an ice slick and went into a spin. There were only the two of us in the car as it whirled out of control. With every spin we cried out the name of "Jesus." On the last one we were headed straight towards a mailbox with a steel bar embedded in concrete. On impact our car pivoted around and landed in a ditch with all four wheels in the air.

Once the world quit spinning we found ourselves lying in the car with our hands up, our glasses still on our faces—not a bump, not a bruise, not a scratch, and praising God. It was enough that we weren't killed, but not to receive even a bruise—Praise God!

As we lay there praising God the verse Isaiah 59:1-2 came to our minds: "Behold the Lord's hand is not shortened, that it cannot save; neither his ear heavy, that he cannot hear."

I could just see God rushing His angels to pack themselves around us like air cushions to protect us from every blow and jolt. He even sent special ones to hold our glasses on our noses.

The words of the song "He's Got the Whole World in His Hands" took on special meaning to me. I knew if God could have His hand on our ear, He has His hand on the world.

God hears our cries and He is able to save those who otherwise would perish. Whatever situation you now find yourself in, take comfort in the promise of Isaiah 59:1-2. Call on the name of Jesus and He will bring you through.

Our Need For Wisdom

"Wisdom is the principal thing: therefore get wisdom: and with all thy getting get understanding." Proverbs 4:7

Naomi Bacon
Bible Teacher

If there's anything we sorely need in the anxious and confusing days we live in, it's wisdom and understanding. "Winds of doctrine" (Ephesians 4:14) are blowing all around us. Cults are on the rise. Eastern philosophies and the occult are seducing the minds of many Americans. Even in the move of God, teachings and spiritual "fads" springing from inadequate understanding of God's Word have misled unwary believers and divided fellowships.

Wisdom and understanding are the balance weights of the Christian life. Let me define *wisdom* as "supernatural revelation for daily living imparted by God upon request through the whole of His Word." James 1:5 tells us how to get wisdom if we lack it: ask God for it in faith, expecting to receive. Then, weigh what you have received against the teaching of God's Word. If scripture doesn't disagree with what you've received, you can act upon it. If scripture disagrees, wait upon the Lord for a surer answer.

Understanding I'd define as "sanctified common sense." The best place to learn it is through a close examination of the life of Jesus. Take note of what He did during His life here on earth. We've been instructed to "walk even as He walked" (1 John 2:6). So get familiar with the way He acted.

If you balance all of the advice you get and the teaching you receive against these "weights," you'll avoid a lot of pitfalls in your walk with God. The true Wisdom of God, who is Jesus Christ, is dwelling within you to help you every step of the way. Have you sought His direction yet for the day ahead of you? If not, take time to do so right now.

The Glory All Flesh Shall See

"And the glory of the Lord shall be revealed, and all flesh shall see it together; for the mouth of the Lord hath spoken it."   Isaiah 40:5

Paul Kauffman
Missionary/Author

Promises like Isaiah 40:5 are what keep me going as a missionary. Serving in Asia for 20 years, I live among 60% of the world's people, who for countless centuries have lived in spiritual darkness, bound by superstition and fear.

It often perplexes me why they live in such oppression while we here in the United States have such access to the gospel. It did not seem fair that such a small percent of the world's population could hear about Jesus Christ by simply turning on a radio or television, picking up a Bible off a bookrack, or choosing which of several churches to attend in any town.

As a missionary it would be too much for me to bear to believe there will never be an end to the misery, disease, and death among which these people live. I could not be a missionary if I thought they always would be bound by false religions that rob them of all hope, comfort, and love.

The reason I have been able to continue serving God as a missionary is because of God's promise in Isaiah 40:5. God assures us His glory will be revealed, "and all flesh shall see it together." Joel 2:28 says "And it shall come to pass afterward, that I will pour out my spirit upon all flesh."

All means everyone! What an encouragement!

Perhaps without realizing it, you are a missionary where God has placed you. Your mission field may be your family, job, church or neighborhood. There may be times you feel overwhelmed by the impossibility of reaching certain people with the love of Christ. Don't lose hope. Continue to serve God in faith, knowing He will reveal Himself to every person.

Glorify The Temple

"What? know ye not that your body is the temple of the Holy Ghost which is in you . . . therefore glorify God in your body, and in your spirit, which are God's."
1 Corinthians 6:19-20

O. Quentin Hyder, M.D.
Psychiatrist/Author

Since giving my life to Christ, I have found the Bible to be the greatest source of answers in both my personal life and professional work. The discovery of one answer I found in the Bible has greatly influenced my life and many of the people I counsel as a psychiatrist.

Several years ago I found myself in a constant battle with fatigue and an overall feeling of ill-being. I began to search the scriptures and found 1 Corinthians 6:19 and 20. As I read the part "therefore glorify God in your body," I took stock of my eating and exercise habits.

I realized my diet mainly consisted of foods high in sugar, starch, and additives. I rarely exercised and when I did I never exerted myself. It became clear to me why God had not answered my prayers to feel better, because I was blatantly ignoring the prescription in His Word for good health.

After a thorough check-up and talk with my doctor, I began to eat a healthy diet of fresh vegetables, less beef, more fish and chicken and whole grains. I also began to jog every day. Immediately, I began to feel better. My fatigue left and I felt a renewing in body, mind, and spirit.

In my work I see a lot of Christian people struggling with mental and emotional problems created by anxiety, depression, and a low self-esteem. I found over the years, when I recommended that they get into good physical shape they find a lot of their emotional problems disappear automatically.

1 Corinthians 6:19 and 20 stresses the importance of honoring God in your body. If you are struggling with mental or emotional problems, I urge you to take stock of how you are treating your "temple." Eating right and getting proper exercise are as important in the Christian life as daily Bible study. Get into the good habit of taking care of your health.

How To Make Right Choices

"What man is he that feareth the Lord? Him shall He teach in the way that He shall choose." Psalm 25:12

Kevin Hofer
PTL Singer

As long as we fear, honor, respect, and obey the Lord, we don't have to worry about making wrong choices. He will direct our paths.

"Fear" the Lord, did I say? Well, if He is almighty, all-powerful, all-knowing, and all-sufficient, He has a right to be feared and reverenced! We ought at least to really desire to make sure we are doing His will as completely as possible.

I went through a time when I was confronted with three possible directions in my life, each of which seemed like it could be the Lord's will. I just didn't know which one to pick. This verse came to me then, and I grabbed onto it.

As I considered the verse, I started to relax, saying to myself, "I'm fearing the Lord, and He's going to tell me which way to choose." I had peace in my spirit about the matter and believed that God would eliminate the possibilities that weren't best for me.

This was a very serious decision, the kind it was easy to worry about and insist on making myself. But it was so complex that I just had to let it rest in God. I'm glad I did. He worked it out just beautifully, leaving no doubts or loose ends.

There are decisions you're going to have to make, big or small, today. How they are going to turn out is directly related to the place God has in your life. Are you striving to be in complete obedience to Him? Are you trusting Him so as to really rest in His Word to you that He has your future in His hands? Consider these questions carefully right now. What's at stake is your own peace of mind and the correctness of the decisions that confront you. Prayerfully place yourself totally in His hands, at this moment.

The Better Battle Plan

"When Jesus then lifted up His eyes, and saw a great company come unto Him, He saith unto Philip, Whence shall we buy bread, that these may eat?"   John 6:5

Ernie Frierson
PTL Singers

Jesus lifted up His eyes because He had been praying. He had just received the sad news that John the Baptist had been executed. He must have wanted to be alone with His Father at this time. But a whole host of people followed Him. What He did then tells us a lot about His character and gives us an example of how we ought to react to unfortunate events in our lives.

A natural reaction to this tragedy might have been to get angry and arouse a crowd to go after Herod and get revenge. But Jesus was not one to react to individuals or situations. He knew who the real enemy was, and how best to "fight back."

The response of Jesus was to have compassion on this multitude of people. He might have been tempted to say, "Please, send these people away; I'm just not up to ministering right now." But He didn't become a victim of discouragement. He glorified God by reaching out to meet the people's needs. He taught them and miraculously fed the whole group. He immediately directed His attention away from Herod and from John's death to the greater honor that His Father would get as He met the needs of the people.

You can never wage war effectively against Satan as long as you spend a lot of time nursing grievances against other people. People are not your real enemies. You can't win a fight against an enemy if you're not doing battle with him. You've got to direct your blows towards the target you intend. By concentrating on loving others and meeting their needs, and seeking the Lord's face in all situations, you will do far more to defeat Satan and further the kingdom of God. Pray that God will give you the kind of discernment that Jesus had right now.

The Light Of This World

"Then spake Jesus again unto them, saying, I am the light of the world: he that followeth Me shall not walk in darkness, but shall have the light of life."   John 8:12

Jon Mohr
PTL Singers

There are many portions of the Bible that we often gloss over that contain remarkable evidence, even scientific, of Its truth. The verse above holds a startling revelation about God and the nature of the universe as scientists have discovered it to be.

The great physicist Albert Einstein put forth the theory that the closer the speed of a moving object comes to the speed of light (and that's 186,000 miles a second!) the more slowly time will pass in relationship to that object. Here's an illustration of this: Suppose you took off in a rocket ship at almost the speed of light and went out into the universe for three years, according to the clock and calendar aboard ship. If you turned around and came back to your point of departure, many generations would have passed at your starting point, and yet you would not have aged a moment! Einstein goes on to say that at the speed of light itself, time would stand absolutely still. Experiments have shown that this theory is almost undoubtedly true.

The Bible says that God is light. Jesus is called the light of the world. The Bible says that to God, a day is as a thousand years, and a thousand years is as a day. In other words, God is not subject to time, for He dwells in eternity. Time for Him stands still. This is why His prophecies all come true, for He can see all of time, from beginning to end. What wisdom is compressed in this one portion of God's Word!

Doesn't it make you feel secure to know that God holds the whole of your life, all in an eternal moment? He has said that He will never leave you, forsake you, or let you go. You can trust Him today. You can trust Him every day. Let His wisdom light your way!

A Tip On Submission

"Wives, submit your-selves unto your own hus-bands, as unto the Lord."
Ephesians 5:22

Luanne Mohr
PTL Singer

My husband and I have been married for a little over three years, and the Lord's been working especially on me and our marriage lately. The other day I was looking in Ephesians, and this verse stood out before me. Those last four words, *"as unto the Lord,"* almost shouted from the page!

I had seen verses about giving a cup of cold water to a thirsty person, and that being done "unto the Lord," and giving money to the church, and that being "as unto the Lord." But I'd never thought of treating my *husband* as I'd treat the Lord *Himself*! This verse was saying that when I loved my husband and tried my best to do good to him, that was pleasing to the Lord, because He saw it as done to Him! I began to see that to love and respect my husband was almost a form of worship to the Lord. And I had to trust him, just like the Lord, too.

Sometimes John comes home late. He always has a good reason. But one time, he was not only late, he brought a friend home with him, without letting me know. This friend thought I would be really mad. But I had told myself, "Trust him, it's all right." So I was calm, much to the friend's astonishment. John told me that he had noticed that I had changed and was trusting him more. In return, because I expected the best from him, John has made certain not to abuse my trust. Now he always lets me know if and why he's going to be late!

If you're a married woman, you might just try loving, respecting, and trusting your husband as you would the Lord. God will honor that and work through your husband to meet your needs. Even if you're not married, or a man, perhaps there's a lesson for you in learning to give the Lord the benefit of the doubt when you think He's "late!"

He's Not Finished Yet!

"Being confident of this very thing, that He which hath begun a good work in you will perform it until the day of Jesus Christ."

Philippians 1:6

Karen Kelley
PTL Singer

Lately, as I look back on the last couple of years of my life, I can see how the Lord has been putting me through trials and testings to teach me more about myself. He wants me to be more on guard about things that are wrong in my life and need changing.

It just makes me feel better whenever I'm down to know that Jesus has not stopped working to make me all I ought to be. In the PTL Singers, we keep a very demanding schedule. We're constantly having to learn and rehearse new music and keep familiar music fresh. We know that we have a tremendous responsibility to minister in a fresh spirit. But sometimes when we're really busy, the pressure has a way of getting to me. Though I'm so often "on stage" professionally, I'm really a kind of private person. I like things around me to be peaceful and quiet and in calm order. But being involved in a live television production every day, I'm thrust into the middle of a whirl of tense activity. Musicians are tuning up, directors and lighting men and prop people rush by. Equipment rolls all around me, people take sound levels, makeup checks my face—it can make me pretty uptight and grouchy!

So the Lord has taught me to quiet down and hold myself in check a little better. He assures me that the time will come when I'll learn to stay in even better touch with Him, no matter how busy life gets.

I imagine your life gets hectic at times too! If you're a mother with a family scurrying around you, calling and singing and pounding toy drums, you know just what I mean. Perhaps on your job, the pressure of your schedule can be trying. But always keep in mind that even in the middle of all this, God is at work perfecting you, even when you forget about Him. That's really good to know, isn't it?

Let's Be One

"And the Lord said, Behold, the people is one, and they have all one language . . . and now nothing will be restrained from them, which they have imagined to do."
Genesis 11:6

Bob Bailey
PTL Singer

This was God's comment when He came down and saw the incredible progress made towards building the Tower of Babel. He was so struck with this feat because of the unity of purpose and speech that had brought it about. He realized that if men could accomplish this, nothing that they could imagine would be impossible to them.

God had to confuse their language in order to divide their purpose, for the wickedness of their imaginings would have done terrible harm to the world. Notice that He didn't take away their bricks or cause the death of the bricklayers or cut off their finances. He had to destroy their unity.

This makes me know that the unity *we* have as the Body of Christ is so vital that we need to work at developing it daily. If we can draw our purpose together consistently in Christ, nothing can possibly stand against us. The most important things for the prospering of the Church are not finances, buildings, and programs. These are all of secondary importance. The most important thing is the unity of the Spirit.

This means that our lips are uttering as one the same language of praise and worship to the Lord Jesus. This means that together we are reaching out in love toward the lost and in fellowship towards all who are part of God's great "household of faith."

Are you building up a spirit of unity in your church fellowship? Are you a part of lifting up and encouraging others of like faith with whom you come into daily contact? Is your life set upon the one purpose of lifting up the name of Jesus Christ? Are you letting others know of His saving power? Be a builder of the City of God today!

Never Destroyed

"Persecuted, but not forsaken; cast down, but not destroyed."   *2 Corinthians 4:9*

Lyn Robbins
Actress/Assoc. T.V. Producer

Sometimes the devil can make you feel like you're barely worth throwing away, can't he? When I suffered a broken marriage, my confidence was stripped away. I asked myself, "Who are you? You're really nothing!" I felt discarded, like an old, ripped up piece of clothing tossed on a pile of rags.

In the world, I had had it all: career success, money and glamour. It had taken sickness, almost death, to make me realize that I needed Jesus in my life. He miraculously healed me, but as my commitment to Him became stronger, my husband began to drift far away from me. He wanted no part of Jesus. Almost as if from inner compulsion, he turned from me to a life of restless infidelity. For four years, I tried to stay by him, but finally the breach became too great. We were separated and finally divorced. I had not sought for this, but he could not turn to God or remain with me.

Cast down and tossed aside, I went to a little house up in the mountains, with just my two poodles, to seek God's face. Somehow I knew that as long as I was in the center of God's will, just like a little child in His hands, nothing could destroy me. In some of the darkest times, if I hadn't had this scripture, I couldn't have stood.

While there, I received a call to appear on the PTL Club. Months later, I began the new future God had for me working at PTL. There I met my future husband when he came to sing as a guest.

God has not guaranteed that your heart will never be broken, or that you'll never be cast down or forsaken, even by those you love. But if you'll place your trust firmly in Him, not looking to men, He will never allow you to be destroyed. You will stand, He'll restore you, and give you a new hope to walk in. He loves you that much, now, and always.

To Know Him

"*That I may know Him,
and the power of His resurrection, and the fellowship of His
sufferings; being made conformable to His death.*"
Philippians 3:10

Peter Marshall
Author/Bible Teacher

One of the deepest problems of the charismatic movement today is that a lot of us are very happy to know Jesus in the power of His resurrection, but we don't want to know Him in the fellowship of His sufferings. There is a tremendous emphasis on the victory and the goodies, and on how to get them without paying a price.

Now, Paul states in this verse that his "determined purpose in life," as the Amplified Bible puts it, was not first and foremost winning souls, but knowing Jesus more and more. The big question is not, "How can I serve the Lord?" but, "How can I know the Lord?" Real service flows out of knowing Christ. It's a matter of first things first. And if we are to know Him, are we willing to know Jesus in the fellowship of His sufferings? Jesus suffered while doing the will of God, putting His Father's desires first, especially above the desires of self. He owned and craved nothing material. Jesus said that if we are to follow Him at all, we would have to be bearers of the cross.

God wants to bless us, but materialism is not even a consideration in the abundant life as I understand it. There is an emphasis in certain circles of teaching on what we're going to *get* out of God. This emphasis is self-centered. God says that what's in it for us is that we learn to worship Him. To get to know Him is to give up all this self-centered striving to get God to do what we want Him to.

Let's not masquerade our selfishness under scripture verses. Let's confront what we are, the sin in ourselves, repent, and put Him first. An old Puritan pastor said, "You won't ride to heaven on a feather bed; if you pick up the cross of Christ, carrying it will make you sweat!"

The Chief Corner Stone

". . . Behold I lay in Zion a chief corner stone, elect, precious: and he that believeth on Him shall not be confounded."   1 Peter 2:6

Riley Kaufman
Pastor/Missionary

At a crisis time in our lives, my wife Flossie and I asked the Lord for a verse of scripture on which we could stand in faith for the guidance we urgently needed. God gave us the passage above.

It was immediately encouraging to us to realize who that "corner stone" was: Christ Jesus the "Rock," upon whom the Church is founded so firmly that "the gates of hell shall not prevail against it" (Matthew 16:18).

We next discovered that there are many different shades of meaning in the phrase "shall not be confounded." It is translated, "shall never waver" in the New English Bible. The Revised Standard Version says, "will not be put in shame." Weymouth has it as, "shall never be disappointed." The Twentieth Century New Testament renders it, "shall have no cause for shame," and yet another translation says, "never need run away."

Further research brought to light an impressive and encouraging list of synonyms for the word "confounded"—things that will not happen to the one who stands firmly in faith upon the Rock Foundation that is Jesus Christ: He will not be *confused, embarrassed, deranged, dislocated, disturbed, muddled, unhinged, unbalanced, upset, agitated, perturbed, flustered, disoriented, ruffled, crushed, bedeviled, or perplexed.* You can see why this brought us such rest!

The enemy is stepping up his offensives against many today, including Christians. He may try to overwhelm you with depression, discouragement, and despair. Let it be a source of special comfort to you to know that you can stand firmly in the faith, knowing that victory is assured in the One who will never leave you nor forsake you!

Forget, And Reach Out

" . . . Forgetting those things which are behind, and reaching forth unto those things which are before . . . whatsoever things are honest . . . just . . . pure . . . lovely . . . of good report . . . think on these things."
Philippians 3:13b, 4:8

Mary Alice Bourgeois
Organist/Lyricist

When I was sobbing there before the altar, not knowing how my life could go on, my pastor came to my side and leaned down to me. He had no idea of the torment I was going through. My personal life had turned into a horror, through no fault of my own. I felt that no one cared, even God.

I heard the pastor speak quietly the words from these verses above, and as he spoke, the Holy Spirit touched me. For in them I sensed the key to my release. I knew that I had to forget, to put aside what had happened and begin to move forward again.

But even that wouldn't have been enough in itself. I had to reach out for the things that God had before me. I couldn't let my soul remain a vacuum; it had to be filled with things that would build me up and restore me.

And what were those things? They were those that Paul spoke of as honest, just, pure, lovely, of good report, worthy of virtue and praise. I knew that if I could look steadfastly forward to these becoming a part of my life, that God would make them realities.

Oh, how much Jesus loves us! He took me and filled my heart with good, lifted my spirits, put my emotions back together, and restored me to fresh joy, on the solid foundation of His truth.

At this very moment, you may be suffering from unexplainable heartache. Discouragement may have brought you so low that you don't know how your spirits can be restored. Listen: the people or events that caused the hurt need no longer control you. Set your mind on Jesus, and the good things that He is waiting to bring into your life. Let Him love and restore you as you seek Him right now.

God's Unmerited Favor Toward Us

"Thou therefore, my son, be strong in the grace that is in Christ Jesus." 2 Timothy 2:1

Bob Vetter
President/Co-Founder
Christian Singles Foundation

This verse has been used by God to drive me deep into Christ's love by freeing me to give Him my total being. For God's grace in Christ Jesus is the only source of strength that can be relied upon when natural inner resources fail.

This was Christ's message to me the first night after my wife's death. My background was Christian, but legalistic: don't do this, don't do that, don't hang around with people who do. When grief struck, however, there was no strength in this framework of fear and guilt. Paul says in Roman 8:3 that the Law is "weak through the flesh," meaning that though the Law of God is good, filtered through the fallible nature of weak men, it cannot produce the strength of Christian character. Only grace, God's unmerited favor in us, can do that.

The law, you see, can only point out to us what we ought to do. It cannot supply the ability necessary to accomplish what it demands. But grace gives strength because what the Law cannot do, God Himself has done in the finished work of Jesus Christ, and given to us as a gift of life.

So after many years of striving to be good in myself, not recognizing the Holy Spirit's working in my life, I discovered the grace of God setting me free from myself. That grace enabled me to see myself as a very valuable new creation of the God of heaven whom Jesus Christ came to redeem.

I hope this makes you, as it did me, realize the value of your life. Think of the price that was paid for your salvation. To grow and mature in Christ, learn to live in understanding and appreciation for all that God's done for you. Bow your head and just thank Him right now.

The Single Need

"The Spirit of the Lord is upon me . . . to set at liberty them that are bruised . . ."
Luke 4:18

June Vetter
Co-Founder, Christian Singles Foundation

When Jesus had successfully resisted the temptations of the devil, He returned to the town of Nazareth and read these words in the synagogue. Jesus cared for the emotionally bruised and the broken-hearted. His concern for people went beyond just physical healing. He cared about people with inner bruises and hurts that no one knew about but them—and He, Himself.

He cared about people who had been divorced, like the woman of Samaria. He loved people whose background was unsavory, like Mary Magdalene. Both were single or divorced people with deep problems.

I don't know how I could have coped with life had I not accepted Christ at 17. I didn't enjoy the "normal" road of finishing up school, finding a husband right away, and settling down to raise a lot of kids. I lived a single, often lonely life until I was 33, when God brought Bob into my life.

Bob endured the tragedy of losing his first wife suddenly, tragically, finding himself immediately single again, and the father of three children to boot. He had to face all over again the matchmakers, dating, threatened couples, the loneliness and discouragement.

Our ministry began out of concern for the problems of single people. We learned how much Jesus cares, for young people without mates, widows, and those who have experienced the heartache of divorce. Have you considered how you might be a help to some of these whom life seems to have "passed by?" Are you a single who dislikes being put into that category? If you seek Him, Jesus will come into your life where you need Him most. He knows the point of your need right now.

Healing Stripes

"But He was wounded for our transgressions, He was bruised for our iniquities: the chastisement of our peace was upon Him; and with His stripes we are healed."

Isaiah 53:5

Eva Mae LeFevre
Singer/Evangelist

Today, I wear fancy evening gowns when I sing. I perform before large audiences in big towns. Now I get around the country in a custom-built bus. They call me "The First Lady of Gospel Music." It wasn't always that way.

In this life, if we're moving with God, we're going to get our share of stripes. The Lord's given me my share. My family formed the first traveling gospel singing group in this country over 55 years ago. But the glamour part of it came a lot later. Most of my life I lived in poverty. As a girl, I never had a dress of my own, always hand-me-downs. Later on, I became the first lady gospel singer to wear evening clothes. That was kind of fun, after the hard years.

I used to walk with my daddy as far as 85 miles to services where he was speaking. Sometimes it took us three days, including short rides. Then we started going places faster, if not too much more comfortably. We drove in a series of old cars with no heaters.

My dear husband died just recently. When I was on the PTL Club, he was laying in a hospital with cancer. He insisted I go. He'd seemed in perfect health. Then they found a tumor on his brain. We'd been married 45 years. We had a retarded son we finally had to put in a home. It broke my heart. Another son left gospel music, got on drugs, and played rock. Jesus has got him back now, praise God.

I thank God for the stripes of Jesus. The ones He took were a whole lot worse than any you or I have ever had. I thank God He bore my sorrows, and yours, too. Jesus has taken the pain out of those wounds for me. He's even going to take the sting out of death for you and me some day. Let Him bring peace to your hurts today.

How To Get A Crown

"Blessed is the man that endureth temptation: for when he is tried, he shall receive the crown of life, which the Lord hath promised to them that love Him."
James 1:12

Sue Bourdeau
PTL Prison Ministry

Even though we may go through a lot of trials and hard times in our lives, the Lord is there, and if we stand faithful, continuing to rely on His Word, He will keep His promises. He never leaves us or forsakes us. If we can't depend on Him, who can we depend on? We can't turn to the world again; we know that it has nothing to offer us.

For every temptation we endure, the Lord sees to it that we get a crown of life. And even greater blessings await us when we get to heaven to be with our Father. Though we may fail Him, His unconditional love is still there for us.

Five years ago, I was constantly tempted to put down the talents God had given me. I wanted to be like this person or that person whom I admired. But in my heart, I never wanted to build my life around a career. For a while I didn't realize that I could be really creative, like I thought I was in drug-taking days of my old life. But during the last year or so, God has opened my eyes to many fulfilling ways in which to express myself. I have started making many beautiful things through crafts. Satan sometimes tries to tell me, "You can't do it." But the Lord is rewarding me with creative life, so I just stand in Him and don't listen to the old devil.

That's the joy of knowing Jesus, even in the midst of trials. Even though we wonder sometimes why the Lord doesn't seem close, we can know that He will keep all His Word to us, and He will give us the desires of our hearts, when He sees that we're ready to handle them. So there's a way in which even though a trial or temptation might seem like a horrible thing, God is holding even more life out to us, if we'll just cling to His Word and endure!

Mercy And Judgment

"I will sing of mercy and judgment: unto Thee, O Lord, will I sing."   Psalm 101:1

Willa Dorsey
Gospel and Concert Artist

This explains why I sing, what I'm singing about, and Who I'm singing for. It's the total summation of what I'm doing for the Lord in these last days. The signs of the times are pointing very clearly to our Lord's coming again. For us who know Him, we're eagerly looking forward to this event. It's going to be pure mercy for the people of God, to be taken out of a world of sin and death and translated into eternity, where we'll "sing of the mercies of the Lord for ever" (Psalm 89:1).

But for those who don't know Jesus, there remains the prospect of judgment. It would be a lot more pleasant for me just to sing about God's mercy and love. But I would not be loving if I also didn't let people know that a day of reckoning is at hand. People need to know that before God's throne, no secrets will remain. Every deed of wickedness will be exposed, and every motive of the heart will be laid bare. I have to tell people, before it's too late, of the account they will have to give.

I sing, too, of a mighty and loving, but just God who has the wisdom, power, and authority to be the perfect judge. He who made every living thing, every last particle of the immense universe, is ready to sum it all up, to bring time to fulfillment. He stands ready to judge the saved unto righteousness and unbelievers in "weeping and wailing and gnashing of teeth." I have sung sacred music and opera, but Who more majestic and worthy of praise exists to sing for?

God also stands ready to give mercy to all who will call upon Him, no matter what their sin, asking for salvation. If you have never met Him, seek His face right now. Then you, too will be able to sing songs of praise and victory to Him.

Which Victory?

"But thanks be to God, which giveth us the victory through our Lord Jesus Christ." 1 Corinthians 15:57

David Flagg
"The Singing Judge"

Which victory does Jesus give us? Well, which victory do we need? That dawned on me one day as I was reading this verse: that I could name the victory and claim the victory specifically on the basis of this verse. Whatever area of my life needs victory, I just hold that up: "Thanks be to God which giveth me the victory—as a husband . . . as a father . . . as a gospel singer." I name the victory I need.

We found out that we needed a new roof on our house. Experts told us that the roof on our house was so worn that it couldn't last another winter. We had a modest income, two toddlers, and an elderly mom to care for, and the bids for the roof were staggering. How could we pay for a roof? But we believed God because we had our own written contract in the Word of God. "My God shall supply every need of yours according to His riches in glory in Christ Jesus" (Philippians 4:19). On that basis, we could claim that roof as a victory through Christ.

Every day, we prayed about our roof. Every day we thanked God that he would supply that roof. Then one day, a man came to the door from an aluminum company and told us that we'd been chosen to receive a free roof, no strings attached. It turned out that it had taken them months of searching to find just the right kind of house to demonstrate this new kind of roof. And to top that (how do you top a roof?), we were also given a sun deck and masses of flowers to improve the appearance of our house for advertising!

Athletic coaches claim victories, politicians claim them, why shouldn't we? We've got the Victor over sin and death, the Lord of the universe on our side. Claim, and keep claiming that victory that's yours in Christ Jesus today!

Sons And Heirs

"Wherefore thou art no more a servant, but a son; and if a son, then an heir of God through Christ."

Galatians 4:7

Leo Price
Author/Teacher

To be a son and heir of God through Christ means that right now we reflect the humanity of God (because Jesus was a man) and also His deity. So we have the inheritance of God's best in the now, as well as all the spiritual blessings of the forever realm.

If we desire God's best, we can't put any limitations or boundaries on God's Word. We must depend upon Jesus Christ for our constant supply of energy or faith so that when we pray, we're not saying just words, but we have a knowing and an understanding that God has already begun to move in our behalf to bring our requests into reality.

Even before we open our mouths, God knows what we will say. But He wants us to really feel our relationship to Him as sons and heirs. He wants us to ask so that we will know that He has moved *at our word*.

We are God's children and the sheep of His pasture. We have been made members of His family; God is our Father, and Jesus is our Elder Brother. And we are no longer alone, but have His Spirit and power to guide and lead, and protect. Our unlimited faith power tells us that He can do all things.

How do we come into the reality of this great inheritance here and now? Isaiah 45:11 says, "As concerning the works of My hands, command ye Me." That's what God said: "Command it." Of course, you can't command God without the Word. And you can't command God without *saying* something. Turning your faith loose is saying, "That need that I have, I know God, that it's mine already. I thank You for it. I believe You, that I have it now." And praise Him for it. Do it right now. Through the Word, through faith, through the Spirit, through divine revelation, it's yours, because you're God's son and heir!

God Can Handle It

"And we know that all things work together for good to them that love God, to them who are the called according to His purpose." Romans 8:28

Doug Oldham
Gospel Singer

I wasted thirty-two years of my life, at least it looked like it. I'd been doing radio, television, and a lot of other things. But after I met the Lord, He took all of that experience, and now He puts it to use every day as I minister. That's how I started to understand this verse: even my "waste" was useful to Him when He picked it up. It didn't take me long in the Lord to begin thinking that this Word from God was true.

Now I've spent the last eighteen years trying to make myself realize how true it is! Every day it seems I get "hit in the head" with something: Four weeks ago, my bus engine died. I sat around thinking, "Yeah, how is this part of 'all things?' I guess I've got to start thanking and praising Him for all this!" Whew!

This is an interesting verse to live with. I mean, it's so easy to quote, and especially to other people when they're having troubles: "Hey now, listen, this is just a part of the 'all things.'" I've been guilty of doing that, haven't you? It's different when you're in the middle of a mess yourself! Then you've just got to praise the Lord and hang in there.

I haven't always understood what's happened to me. There have been times when it's taken quite awhile to piece together the threads of past events and see all the good God's done.

But one thing I know: I don't care what you're going through, God is going to work it into something good. "All things" just doesn't leave much out, does it? Even the things that are out of your control are still in His hands. Why don't you just give God the credit for all the sense His Word says He's got and take some relief from working it all out yourself? He can handle the job!

Four Links Of Joy

"Trust in the Lord, and do good . . . delight thyself also in the Lord . . . Commit thy way unto the Lord . . . Rest in the Lord . . ."
Psalm 37:3-5, 7a

Don Argue
Bible College President

I believe this is a Biblical pattern for joy. You might say that joy is composed of pieces of all four of these things: trusting, delighting, committing, and resting.

All of these "components" build upon one another. You cannot feel delighted with someone you don't trust. Delight and uncertainty can't coexist together. When you have put your trust in someone, and have really found him trustworthy, you will surely feel delight towards that person.

Then, when you are pleased with the reliability of a person, you will be glad to place more trust in them, and lean on them in more situations. The Hebrew word translated "commit" here implies *rolling* objects onto a surface that can hold them. Real commitment necessitates a separation of one thing from another, in this case, a separation of you from your problems, as you "roll" them into the Lord's hands.

Finally, when you have trusted, delighted, and committed, you can have perfect peace and rest, because you are certain that God will bring the matter to pass. About four years ago, I went through a major time of testing in my ministry, in which I went through some severe relational problems within the Body of Christ. But after I had fulfilled this fourfold pattern, God directed, brought beautiful healing and restoration of fellowship.

If your life is lacking in joy, perhaps it's because one of the links in this chain is missing. Have you really entrusted the problem to God? Are you really happy because you know He's going to do well by you? Have you "rolled" the problem from your shoulders onto His? And have you rested in His promise to bring it to pass? If you haven't done one or more of these things, "link up" right now.

The Victory Of Faith

"For whatsoever is born of God overcometh the world: and this is the victory that overcometh the world, even our faith."   1 John 5:4

Ken Woolridge
Pastor/Evangelist

God did not save us for defeat. When faith in Jesus came into our hearts, we immediately began to taste victory. The world need not intimidate us, circumstances need not discourage us. With faith in our hearts, we have the overcoming power of God.

I wish we could all truly see this. How John emphasizes it in his letters! *"Greater* is He that is in me than He that is in the world" (1 John 4:4)! Why do we let things get us down so much if this is true? Friends, if we trust God's Word, nothing can get the better of us for long.

You might feel a little worried if you had to walk down the streets of a dangerous neighborhood at night all alone. But if you had beside you a good friend who happened also to be about six and a half feet tall and weighed 250 pounds, your mind would be considerably more at rest. And yet you may claim to trust God and still be fearful of events and people around you, fearful you're going to be snatched away by the devil. Are you really trusting Him or are those just words (I trust Jesus) that one day you thought would give you a free pass to heaven?

"He that overcometh shall inherit all things; and I will be his God, and he shall be My son" (Revelation 21:7). A freeborn child of God is an overcomer. How? By exercising the faith that's in him.

I can't make this too clear: if you have faith in your heart towards Jesus Christ, you can overcome the world. When disillusionment comes your way, you can fight back—and win! When temptation faces you, you can resist the tempter and watch him run! Do you dare today to start battling and overcoming? Don't just lie down and let life walk all over you. You take on the first thing that tries you today—and win!

God Makes Perfect Sense

"Trust in the Lord with all thine heart; and lean not unto thine own understanding. In all thy ways acknowledge Him, and He shall direct thy paths."

Proverbs 3:5-6

"Buffalo" Bill Carson
Actor/Ventriloquist

When I'm performing anywhere for children, I get them to repeat this verse over and over, till they learn it and lock it in their memory. Often, many years later, an adult has come up to me and said, "Thank God I learned that verse and wrote it on the wall of my memory." That has always been such a blessing for me.

I gave my heart to the Lord when I was 18 years old. The Lord spoke to me out under the open sky, while I was riding a horse. Since I didn't meet Him at an altar, maybe it became a little easier for me to start trusting Him rather than my own understanding—and to keep doing so.

I've learned that the Lord always knows best, even when a situation doesn't always make perfect sense. I was once performing before an audience of both English and Spanish speaking people. Now, I don't know any Spanish, and there was no interpreter. So I just started to give a simple devotional *in English* on how to be born again. Then I gave an invitation, again in English, to everyone to accept Jesus Christ as their Savior. Many Spanish speaking people responded. I was amazed, and just to be sure that what was happening was real, I asked a lady who knew Spanish to ask those at the altar if they knew what they were doing. She asked and told me that they knew and had somehow understood everything I'd been saying!

Now, I felt silly for a while as I was speaking, but look what the Lord did with it! Now, if the Lord can use the "foolishness" of an insignificant cowboy's preaching to win souls, He can do anything. You may be called upon by God to do something amazing someday. Today might be the day. But amazing or not, you can always stay available for God to use you however He wills!

Don't Be An Adult—Be A Wise Child

"My son, attend to my words; incline thine ear unto my sayings. Let them not depart from thine eyes; keep them in the midst of thine heart. For they are life unto those that find them, and health to all their flesh."
Proverbs 4:20-22

Hope Hunter Lippard
Interpretive Dancer

The greatest disappointment I have discovered since accepting Jesus Christ is my failure to totally trust Him and His Word. Jesus has never disappointed me, but I have let myself down by ignoring His words of advice, instruction and promise.

I can never forget the reality of meeting Him that September night in 1976. The clarity of realizing Someone . . . Jesus had actually stepped into my heart and picked up all the sorrow and misery, guilt and sense of futility that I had carried for my twenty-three years. He picked it up and threw it into God's Sea of Forgetfulness, never to be remembered.

For those first eight months as a baby Christian, I fed on His Word and promises every day, spending every spare moment reading and memorizing scripture verses. I could not seem to get my fill. Like a child I believed every word my Father said, and I acted and lived in total confidence of what I learned from His Word. You know what? It always worked. Always!

Gradually, I became busy with activities, friends, and personal druthers, until I was only glancing at the Bible and tossing my prayers over my shoulder as I ran out the door. I became a Christian who was too busy doing for Jesus to have any time for Him. As scripture verses faded in my memory because I no longer took time to recall or meditate on them, my faith became diluted and ineffective. I began to lose confidence in God's promises and doubt the purpose of my salvation.

Where was the joy I first knew and the love I had for God and the new life He had given me? In a very gentle way God showed me that growing up in Christ does not mean becoming a spiritual adult, but rather a child who is wise for knowing, loving, and doing His Word. As I began to daily read and memorize God's Word again, my faith returned

with that fresh childlike energy and confidence I once had. I rediscov-
ered that God's advice and promises still always work. Always! If you
long to have the faith and trust in God you once had, return to His Word.
"For they are life unto those that find them, and health to all their flesh."